Pastors & Parishioners
in Württemberg
During the Late Reformation
1581–1621

Pastors & Parishioners
in Württemberg
During the Late Reformation
1581–1621

List of Tables

Contents

Sabean, and James Vann for reading the whole manuscript and offering me their detailed criticisms. None of these scholars, of course, bears any responsibility for the inadequacies that remain.

My colleagues and the staff of Stanford's Department of Humanities Special Programs were a source of support and encouragement. The program director, Paul Robinson, provided the financial support that enabled me to read preliminary results at various conferences.

I am deeply thankful to Lewis Spitz, whose steadfast encouragement, cogent suggestions, and eternal optimism sustained me in both the research and writing of this book. My thanks also to Ron Davies for his help and constant encouragement.

Above all, I am grateful to my wife, Kimberley, for her interest, support, and unflagging confidence in my endeavors and for the sacrifices she has made so that this book could come to fruition.

B.T.

Acknowledgments

I wish to express my thanks to the scholars who have nurtured my growth as a historian: Jonathan Beecher of the University of California, Santa Cruz; Basil Hall, formerly of Cambridge University; Robert Kingdon of the University of Wisconsin, Madison; and all of my colleagues at Stanford University.

In the various stages of my research I have received help and kindness from many people and institutions. I am grateful to the Stanford Center for Research in International Studies (CRIS) and the Deutscher Akademische Austauschdienst (DAAD) for the exchange fellowship that made my research in Germany possible. I am indebted to my host in Tübingen, Heiko Oberman, former director of the Institut für Spätmittelalter und Reformation, for first suggesting that I work on visitation protocols and for the hospitality that he, his wife, and family extended to me. I am also very grateful to the Tigges family for adopting a homeless scholar during his sojourn in Tübingen.

The reference and interlibrary loan staffs of Green Library at Stanford University have always been professional and prompt in their services. Moreover, this project would not have been possible without the able, knowledgeable, and courteous assistance of the staffs of the University Library, Tübingen, and the Stuttgart State Archive, and especially of Hermann Ott, archivist of the Archive of the Evangelical Church in Württemberg, Stuttgart.

I am also grateful to Carolyn Lougee and Lawrence V. Ryan, who read a very early version of this manuscript, and I thank Kenneth Gouwens, Robert Shoemaker, Edna Spitz, and Bruce Thompson for their helpful comments on various preliminary versions of the book. I am especially indebted to Robert Kingdon, James Kittelson, David

To Kimberley, Emma, and Nathan

The Frank S. and
Elizabeth D. Brewer
Prize Essay
of the
American Society
of
Church History

Stanford University Press
Stanford, California

Printed in the United States of America

CIP data are at the end of the book

Stanford University Press publications are
distributed exclusively by Stanford University Press
within the United States, Canada, and Mexico; they
are distributed exclusively by Cambridge University Press
throughout the rest of the world.

Pastors & Parishioners
in Württemberg
During the Late Reformation
1581–1621

Bruce Tolley

STANFORD UNIVERSITY PRESS
STANFORD, CALIFORNIA
1995

Introduction

During the late 1970's and early 1980's, research into the impact of the Reformation on popular religious life in Germany sparked a small controversy challenging the traditional assumption that Protestantism had a deep and lasting effect on all levels of sixteenth-century life.[1] Although the exchange itself might have created more heat than light, it reflected the growing research interest in the German Reformation as a social phenomenon and the increasing need to base research on local and regional archival sources. This study uses previously neglected archival sources, the records of the Württemberg church visitations, to investigate various areas of church life touched on by the debate and of significant interest to social and church historians of the sixteenth and seventeenth centuries. We will examine the social and cultural nature of the pastorate as a professional group, areas of conflict and agreement between representatives of the official church and the parishioners, the nature of the church visitations, and the standards and expectations of the visitors concerning lay religious life and discipline.

Church visitation records enable us to describe the establishment of the Lutheran territorial churches and the nature of lay religious life. Following the example set by French Catholic studies of post-Tridentine episcopal *procès-verbaux*, visitation protocols have become the subject of detailed investigation.[2] They are now recognized as one of the most important sources for the study of parish life, since they offer information about almost every aspect from the condition of widows and orphans to the quality of the pastors' sermons.[3] Despite the richness of these documents, the protocols remain largely untouched.[4]

The Württemberg records furnish a singular opportunity. They are especially detailed, since the superintendent visited each parish in his administrative district (*Amt*) rather than summoning the ministers to a central town.* They are also amazingly well preserved; reports are complete for practically every parish in the duchy for fourteen of the visitations conducted from 1581 to 1621. While earlier visits did take place sporadically from 1534 on, the early records survive only from 1536 to 1540. These records concern primarily the inventories of parish and monastic revenues and do not offer much information about parish life.[5] Records of the later visitations before, during, and after the Augsburg Interim (1555) have been lost. They may have been destroyed or carried off by the Austrians during their occupation of Stuttgart following Württemberg's defeat at the battle of Nördlingen in 1634.[6]

The reports are digests or summaries of the answers collected by the visitor during his interviews of the pastor, schoolmaster, *Schultheiss* (village mayor), and other selected laymen concerning the performance of each in office and the general ecclesiastical life of the parish. The Tübingen district visitor was usually the pastor of Lustnau, who held the position of church district superintendent (*Spezial Superintendent*), while the Tuttlingen district visitor was the city pastor of Tuttlingen and the superintendent of his district. Their reports were forwarded to Stuttgart, where the consistory (*Konsistorium*, or *Synodus*) reviewed the conditions in the parishes, acted on specific complaints, and recorded its decisions in the margins of the protocols. The consistory was the ecclesiastical arm of the ducal church council (*Kirchenrat*), whose secular arm was called *politischer Kirchenrat*.

As defined in the Church Ordinance (*Kirchenordnung*) of 1559, the political church council was responsible for administering church property, regulating medical doctors, and distributing poor relief, while the consistory supervised doctrinal matters, adminis-

---

*Apart from the spelling of proper names and certain commonly used words, no attempt has been made to standardize the orthography of contemporary German words. Because even the standard reference, the *Schwäbishes Wörterbuch* edited by Hermann Fischer (Tübingen: H. Lauppschen Buchhandlung, 1904–24, 1936), recognizes several variants for many Swabian words, the text follows the spellings found in the printed and manuscript sources.

tered pastoral appointments, and supervised the visitations. In practice, however, there was a great deal of overlap in functions, since the duke's ranking councillor (*Landhofmeister*) sat on both agencies and the visitation reported on both secular and church matters.

This study is based on visitation reports and other archival sources drawn from a geographic sample consisting of two administrative districts (*Ämter*, or *Superintendenzen*) in the duchy of Württemberg: Tübingen and Tuttlingen. Tübingen was the seat of the ducal university and the territorial court (*Hofgericht*) and lay only a short distance from the capital, Stuttgart. In contrast, Tuttlingen was basically an enclave far from the centers of administrative control and political power and was completely encircled by Catholic territories belonging to other sovereignties. It was hoped that a comparison of these two districts would determine the effectiveness of the sanctions imposed by the central power in support of the establishment of the Protestant religion. But as the following discussion will show, no consistent pattern is evident.

We begin this study at 1581 because this date marks the first post-Interim visitation whose records are complete and extant.[7] Because the Thirty Years War, which had begun in 1618, reached Württemberg in 1634, 1621 was chosen as the ending date in order to include information from the last visitation conducted before the disruptions caused by the war. This period will be referred to generally as the late Reformation period or simply the late sixteenth century.

This period was a time of rapid social change. During the sixteenth century, a rural elite was emerging whose power was built on a long-term growth in grain prices together with rapid population growth. Economic pressure to break up large farms was resisted, and a class of poor peasants grew up alongside their neighbors who were doing relatively well. Crises began to hit in the 1580's. The next four decades were marked by a series of harvest failures and epidemics that undercut the real wages of the rural poor, resulting in increased social differentiation within Württemberg villages. The visitation protocols provide brief glimpses of the social tensions caused by such rapid change. The complaints about bad householders that we discuss in Chapter 5 are affected by these stresses. More overtly, the protocols from the mid-1580's contain numerous complaints about foreign beggars and vagabonds invading parishes and stealing food and property. The increasing number of local poor strained village poor relief and forced parish officials to petition the visitors for subventions from the capital.[8] These social tensions also provide an important context for the church's intense interest in discipline and order throughout the late sixteenth and early seventeenth centuries.[9]

Although our investigation is limited to a period of 40 years, the discussion proceeds analytically rather than chronologically; with the visitation protocols offering such detailed information about so many topics, the discussion is necessarily selective. The subjects chosen represent the twofold focus of the visitations on the state of the clergy and the condition of lay religious life; they also have a direct bearing on the controversy concerning the relationship between the official Protestantism, represented by the visitation and the local clergy, and parish life. Since it was the parish clergy who carried the Reformation to the parishioners, we examine the clergy's social and geographic origins in Chapter 1, their education and culture in Chapter 2, and their economic conditions in Chapter 3. These chapters will lay the groundwork for our investigation of the religious life of the parish in the final two chapters. Chapter 4 analyzes the attitudes and behavior surrounding popular religious practices, and Chapter 5 evaluates the church's attempts to reform and discipline family life and social mores. In this way, our investigation will unveil the social and cultural origins of the clergy as a professional group and the relationship between parishioners and the discipline of the state church.

CHAPTER I

The Social and Geographic Recruitment of Pastors

Although the Reformation would have had no lasting effect without the support of the ordinary layperson, it was, from its inception with Martin Luther, the creation of the clergy. Thus our understanding of both the social nature of the evangelical movement and its relationship to particular social and professional groups can be greatly enhanced by investigating the pastorate as a social entity. While work has been done on the recruitment of the first generation of Protestant clergy in Saxony, Prussia, Nuremberg, and Württemberg, little attention has been paid to the recruitment of Protestant clergy in the late Reformation period.[1] Since any analysis of the long-term effects of the Protestant Reformation must consider the nature of the churches established during this period of confessional consolidation, the omission is somewhat striking.[2]

This chapter will show that in general there was continuous recruitment from a variety of social and professional groups with particular ties to the urban magistracy and well-to-do artisans. Overall, the clerical estate recruited primarily from among Württemberg officials and clergy, and by the end of the second quarter of the seventeenth century, the clergy tended toward self-recruitment.[3]

What was the social and political role of the rural Württemberg clergyman in the sixteenth century? Though not affluent, and perhaps hurt by inflation, pastors in Württemberg enjoyed a respectable standard of living, equivalent to that of the better-off rural parishioners. Notwithstanding the Württemberg proverb "Pastors bequeath only books and children,"[4] they were able to send many of their sons to college and to marry their daughters to men of comparable social standing. As the Church Ordinance of 1559 makes clear, in Württemberg the state represented Christian authority; therefore the local pastor was a minister or servant of both church and state. The pastor could at times stand on the side of the peasant community. He could even develop a network of godparent relationships with his parishioners. But he remained, nonetheless, an outsider. He came from outside the village, as did his wife, and he married his children outside. Though many pastors had lifelong tenure in one village, others left after a few years. They never owned land in the village. As the only officials appointed by the state to serve in the villages who came from outside, pastors represented the duke's ruling authority there.[5]

In Württemberg, confessional history and geography determined the makeup of the first generation of clergy.[6] Württemberg found itself situated amid the orthodox Lutherans of Saxony, the Upper German reformers of Strasbourg and the other South German cities, and the Zwinglians in the Swiss cantons. Duke Ulrich, on his restoration with the help of Philip of Hesse, introduced the Reformation by fiat in 1534. Ulrich did not have many native-born university-educated men to call on, so he recruited Lutheran, Upper German, and Swiss pastors to staff his pulpits. Some Catholic clergy joined the Reformation in 1534, but few clergy were either converted or attracted from other occupations.[7] The orthodox Lutherans eventually gained the upper hand and forced the Upper Germans out. After the Schmalkaldic Wars, Württemberg gained the services of such distinguished refugees as Johann Brenz from Schwäbisch Hall and Mattaeus Alber from Reutlingen. With the establishment of a system of clerical education—the cloister schools in the appropriated monastic establishments and the *Stift*, the seminary and college for the training and residence of theological students that was established in the university town of Tübingen—recruitment centered on natives of Württemberg. After 1550, most clergy were former students of the Stift.[8]

I

The Württemberg Reformation church and school ordinances provide evidence of the attempt by the dukes to recruit pastors from the entire populace without regard for social origin. For example, Duke Christoph of Württemberg, with a genuine concern for the spiritual and physical welfare of his subjects, took great pains to implement a comprehensive plan for the life of the church in the Church Ordinance of 1559. This ordinance was reissued in 1582 and remained in effect until well into the seventeenth century. Inspired by humanism and nurtured by his evangelical faith, Christoph sought talent and learning and promoted discipline and godliness in his clergy. He provided scholarships for the poor students to the Latin elementary schools (*Particularschulen*) and decreed that all subsequent promotion be based on merit. If the student showed sufficient ability, he would be promoted to a secondary school, either a secular Latin *pedagogium* or a cloister school (*Konventschule*), the special humanistic gymnasium for prospective ordinands.[9] Either school would prepare a student for university. To support the university studies of theology students, Christoph increased from 70 to 100 the number of scholarships at the Tübingen Stift, all of which were intended for "the poor children of the land who are without means," in effect the children of poor pastors.[10]

During the sixteenth and seventeenth centuries, the ducal church council, Stift teaching faculty (*Superattendenten*), and the head of the Stift (*Magister Domus*) were instructed to exercise impartiality and objectivity in their examination and promotion of candidates, so that promotion "will be treated not according to favors, disposition, or gifts, but only according to [the candidate's] erudition and financial need."[11] Of course, the existence of such a regulation suggests that precisely the opposite practice was actually taking place. A survey of the Stuttgart examination and promotion records for ministerial candidates reveals that some candidates who received poor marks in their examination, which consisted of presenting a sermon and answering questions on points of doctrine, were sent back to Tübingen until they were able to demonstrate an acceptable degree of competence. In some cases where there was a pressing need for a deacon or junior pastor, a probationary posting could be obtained despite poor or mediocre marks. Candidates were exhorted to improve before reexamination and evidently did so, for some subsequently received superior marks. In 1617–18, Johann Jakob Erbin had to be examined three times before he finally passed with a good report and was appointed to a position.[12] Candidates were motivated to improve because all future promotion rested in the hands of the consistory's vetters.

Even a well-connected name was no guarantee of easy advancement, as Lucas Osiander found out. Osiander's father, Lucas senior, was a court preacher and former chancellor of Tübingen University. Lucas's older brother Andreas had been a professor since 1619 and became chancellor in 1620.[13] In November 1617, Lucas junior was judged mediocre in both his preaching and his answers to the set questions. When he was retested the following February, the examiner found him deficient once again. Only in December 1619, two years after his initial examination, did he receive passing marks and obtain his first appointment.[14] Despite his early failure to live up to clerical academic standards, Lucas junior became a noted theologian and polemicist, and emulated his father and brother by also serving as chancellor.[15]

II

Württemberg sources indicate that some of the evangelical clergy had close ties to the urban magistracy. And while the clergy continued to recruit a minority of its members from artisan families in the spirit of Duke Christoph's meritocratic principles, the trend toward enlisting the sons of pastors grew more marked.

The following analysis of the clergy's social and geographic origins focuses on the late sixteenth and early seventeenth centuries.[16] The 140 pastors who served in the districts of Tübingen and Tuttlingen from 1581 to 1621 represented only a minority (about 5 percent) of the total number of Württemberg pastors.[17] An examination of the matriculation records, the visitation protocols, and other sources has established the geographic provenance of all but three of these pastors.[18] In contrast, the social origins of only about half of the pastors have been recovered.

The Württemberg pastors who served in Tübingen and Tuttlingen districts from 1581 to 1621 were, with few exceptions, members of the second and third generations of evangelical clergy. (See Appendix A for a list of parishes in these two districts.) Most of them were born after the 1534 Reformation in Württemberg and entered the ministry when opportunities increased with the end of the Augsburg Interim in 1555. There were, however, some direct familial and intellectual connections with the first generation of German Reformers. Two of the pastors were sons of friends or close colleagues of Luther, two were converted Catholic monks or clerics, and several were offspring of two of the first Württemberg reformers, Erhard Schnepf and Jakob Andreae (or Andreä).[19]

That there were only two converted Catholics in the group is understandable considering that the age of reformatory ferment lay over half a century in the past. One convert, Primus Truber, the eldest of our pastors, was born in 1508 in Rascia, near Auersperg, in the Austrian province of Lower Carniola, in what is now Yugoslavia.[20] After studies in Fiume, Salzburg, and Vienna, Truber was ordained as a priest in 1527 and subsequently served in Trieste. His activity as a reformer in 1531 in Celli-Kanonikas prompted opposition from the Catholic hierarchy, and despite support from the Protestant estates, he lost the favor of his patron, the bishop of Trieste, and left Carniola under excommunication in the 1540's. After he had done reforming work in Nuremberg, Veit Dietrich recommended him to positions in Rotenburg an der Taube (1548–52) and Kempten. While in the latter, he won the Italian Piero Vergerio to the cause of the evangelization of the Slovakian people. An active publicist for the mission to his native country, after serving as an evangelical pastor in the town of Laibach in his homeland from 1562–65, he was driven out, and returned to Württemberg.[21]

The other convert among the Tübingen district clergy, Johann Kölner, had been a monk in the Widenbach convent in Cologne.[22] After coming over to the Lutherans, he was recommended to the Württemberg consistory, and took up his first post in 1558 as an instructor in a Latin school in Calw. By 1566, he was a pastor in the village of Gönningen in the district of Tübingen, and after a half-century of service to the Württemberg church, he died in 1607.

As Table 1 shows, clergy serving in Tübingen district from 1581 to 1621 were recruited predominantly from the city of Tübingen itself (20 percent), the capital, Stuttgart (8 percent), and other cities and towns (47 percent). The recruitment was thus largely urban, with only 15 percent of the Tübingen pastors and 26 percent of their Tuttlingen colleagues deriving from villages; half of these were the sons of pastors serving in rural parishes. Since university officials did not record peasant backgrounds in the matriculation rolls, the social origins of the remainder of the pastors, some of whom might have come from rural villages, is unknown.

Although pastors from outside the Württemberg territories con-

TABLE 1

Geographic Recruitment of the Clergy in
Tübingen and Tuttlingen Districts, 1581–1621

	Tübingen district		Tuttlingen district	
Place of recruitment	No.	Pct.	No.	Pct.
Unknown	2	2%	1	3%
In Württemberg				
Stuttgart	8	8	1	3
Tübingen	20	20	3	8
Tuttlingen	0	0	2	5
Tübingen district villages	9	9	0	0
Towns	25	25	16	41
Small towns	10	10	4	10
Villages	12	12	9	23
Outside Württemberg				
Cities and towns	12	12	2	5
Villages	3	3	1	3
TOTAL	101	100%	39	100%[a]

SOURCES: Binder, *Kirchen- und Lehrämter*; Hermelink, *Die Matrikeln*; HStA Bü. 1282 (1601), 1283 (1602), 1284 (1603), 1285 (1605), 1325 (1601, 1602, 1603, 1605), 1327 (1601), 1328 (1602), 1329 (1603), 1330 (1605); LKA Stuttgart A1 1581, 1582, 1583I, 1583II, 1584I, 1584II, 1585I, 1585II, 1586I, 1586II, 1587I, 1587II, 1588I, 1588II, 1589, 1590, 1621; Sigel, "Das evangelische Württemberg"; Stoll, *Sammlung*.

NOTE: Data represent recovered aggregates for all parish pastors in office in the years 1581–1621. To avoid double-counting, those who shifted from parish to parish or district to district are counted only once.

[a] Percentages in all tables may not add to 100 because of rounding.

stituted a significant minority, for example, 15 percent in the district of Tübingen, most of these came from the Imperial Cities of the Swabian Circle. While they were not born subjects of the dukes of Württemberg, as fellow Swabians they had much in common culturally, linguistically, and historically. The Imperial Cities, such as Reutlingen, had received the Reformation earlier than Württemberg and had fostered Protestantism during the 1530's, when the duchy was under the rule of the Catholic Habsburgs.[23] By 1621, the number of pastors recruited from outside Württemberg dropped because of the rapid confessionalization of the evangelical states (see Table 2).

Although some graduates of universities other than Tübingen, the ducal university, held positions in 1581, the Württemberg dukes ensured social and, more importantly, doctrinal homogeneity throughout the land by promoting to the ministry only their own scholarship holders (*Stipendiaten*) who had studied at the cloister schools and the Tübingen Stift. Only four of the non-Württemberg pastors had not graduated from Tübingen, and all but one of these had entered the service of Württemberg in the years immediately following the lifting of the Interim. This trend toward increasingly territorial recruitment of the pastorate ran counter to the recruitment pattern of the territorial university. The proportion of non-Württembergers attending the university remained relatively constant throughout the sixteenth century. In 1477, students from outside the duchy composed 51 percent of the matriculated students. At midcentury (1545–50), foreigners made up 63 percent of the students. At the end of the century (1595–1600), nearly two-thirds (59 percent) of the students were from outside the duchy.[24]

While the shortage of qualified evangelical clergy at the beginning of Ulrich's reformation had resulted in substantial recruitment from outside Württemberg, by 1550 Württemberg was providing its own recruits for the pastorate.[25] More than 75 percent of the clergy were former stipend holders of the Tübingen Stift.[26] Table 1 shows that from 1581 to 1621 the Tübingen clergy were predominantly, and the Tuttlingen clergy almost exclusively, of Württemberg origin. In 1621, although two pastors, one in each district, were recruited from outside Württemberg (see Tables 2 and 3), both of them were graduates of Tübingen. This tendency to enlist only natives of Württemberg as pastors is one facet of the trend of the clerical corps toward replenishing its ranks by recruiting the sons of its members.

III

Despite the incompleteness of the evidence, the social and professional origins of about half of the Tübingen district clergy have been recovered (see Table 4). The sparse data for Tuttlingen are more difficult to evaluate (see Table 5), although since 26 percent of the Tuttlingen clergy came from villages, many of them probably had social backgrounds of less status than their Tübingen colleagues. Since genealogists have been most zealous in tracing clerical origins, the figures are more reliable for the clergy than for other professions, especially the less prestigious ones, which are likely to be most underestimated. In Württemberg, as elsewhere in Germany, ministers were recruited preferentially from certain groups in numbers dispropor-

TABLE 2

Evolution of Geographic Recruitment of the Clergy
in Tübingen District, Selected Years, 1581–1621

	1581		1590		1601		1621	
Place of origin	No.	Pct.	No.	Pct.	No.	Pct.	No.	Pct.
Unknown	2	7%	2	7%	0	0%	0	0%
In Württemberg								
Stuttgart	3	11	1	4	0	0	5	17
Tübingen	5	19	3	11	7	27	7	23
Tübingen district villages	5	19	5	19	3	12	4	13
Towns	5	19	5	19	5	19	6	20
Small towns	1	4	2	7	5	19	3	10
Villages outside Tübingen district	1	4	2	7	1	4	4	13
Outside Württemberg								
Cities and towns	4	15	7	26	5	19	1	3
Villages	1	4	0	0	0	0	0	0
TOTAL	27	100%	27	100%	26	100%	30	100%

SOURCES: Binder, *Kirchen- und Lehrämter*; Hermelink, *Die Matrikeln*; HStA Bü. 1282 (1601), 1283 (1602), 1284 (1603), 1285 (1605); LKA Stuttgart A1 1581, 1582, 1583I, 1583II, 1584I, 1584II, 1585I, 1585II, 1586I, 1586II, 1587I, 1587II, 1588I, 1588II, 1589, 1590, 1621; Sigel, "Das evangelische Württemberg"; Stoll, *Sammlung*.
NOTE: Data are for those parish pastors in office in the years 1581, 1590, 1601, and 1621.

tionate to their representation in society as a whole.[27] Representatives of both ends of the social spectrum—the nobility and small farmers and peasants—were totally absent, whereas members of the lower echelons of the powerful domestic elite, known as the *Ehrbarkeit*, contributed candidates. High functionaries and merchants contributed only a few candidates to the ministry.

The Ehrbarkeit was an elite whose membership consisted of officeholders in the district and towns. Represented in the territorial parliament (*Landtag*), the Ehrbarkeit served as a "political counterweight" to ducal authority throughout the early modern period. Moreover, the urban guilds often served the Ehrbarkeit as a source of economic and political power.[28]

For Tübingen district, recruitment reflects the pattern obtained by Martin Brecht for the whole duchy in the mid-sixteenth century.[29] Among the laity, two groups predominated: artisans and magistrates. Eleven percent of the pastors of known origin had artisans for fathers, which is about the same as the 9 percent found by Brecht for Württemberg as a whole. Since less-distinguished forebears were underrepresented in the matriculation records, the actual proportion of pastors of artisan origin was probably much higher, but how much higher is uncertain. Nevertheless, the artisan class in the district of Tübingen does not appear to have been the "veritable reservoir of pastors" that Vogler reports for the Rhinelands.[30] The strong connection of various livings in the district to special social groups probably accounts for this difference. The Tübingen city pastorate and its two diaconates had close ties with the Tübingen Stift, the university theological faculty, and the clerical elite in Stuttgart, and at least three livings were intimately bound to the urban magistracy.[31]

Only one pastor has been identified as coming from an ordinary artisan family. Johann Steeb's father was a cartwright. Steeb (d. 1615) achieved a master's degree and served in the comparatively modest living of Bodelshausen.[32] His son Elias (b. 1578) was the Schultheiss, the village mayor or chief administrative officer, in Bo-

TABLE 3

Evolution of Geographic Recruitment of the Clergy in Tuttlingen District, Selected Years, 1581–1621

Place of origin	1581		1590		1601		1621	
	No.	Pct.	No.	Pct.	No.	Pct.	No.	Pct.
Unknown	1	11%	1	11%	0	0%	0	0%
In Württemberg								
Tübingen	0	0	0	0	1	11	1	10
Tuttlingen	1	11	1	11	2	22	0	0
Towns	5	56	5	56	5	56	6	60
Small towns	1	11	1	11	0	0	0	0
Villages	1	11	1	11	1	11	2	20
Outside Württemberg								
Cities and towns	0	0	0	0	0	0	1	10
TOTAL	9	100%	9	100%	9	100%	10	100%

SOURCES: Binder, *Kirchen- und Lehrämter*; Hermelink, *Die Matrikeln*; HStA Bü. 1282 (1601), 1325 (1601), 1327 (1601); LKA Stuttgart A1 1581, 1590, 1621; Sigel, "Das evangelische Württemberg"; Stoll, *Sammlung*.

NOTE: Data are for those parish pastors in office in the years 1581, 1590, 1601, and 1621. No pastors were identified as originating from the city of Stuttgart or from villages outside Württemberg.

TABLE 4

Social Recruitment of the Clergy in Tübingen District, 1581–1621

Profession of father	No.	Pct. of pastors of known social origin (N = 52)	Pct. of all pastors (N = 101)
Unknown	49		49%
Clergy			
Higher	12	23%	12%
Lower (pastor, deacon, or preceptor)	28	54	28
Laity			
Treasurer	1	2	1
Commandant	1	2	1
University professor	1	2	1
Ducal bailiff (Vogt)	2	4	2
Subtotal, high official	5	10%	5%
Town councillor	1	2	1
Town councillor and artisan	2	4	2
Artisan	4	8	4
Subtotal, other laity	7	13%	7%
TOTAL	101	100%	100%

SOURCES: Same as for Table 2.

NOTE: Data represent recovered aggregates for all parish pastors in office in the years 1581–1621. To avoid double-counting, those who shifted from parish to parish or district to district are counted only once.

delshausen. Whereas Elias's son Johann became a sheepfold administrator in Tübingen, Johann's son Elias (b. 1631) followed the profession of his great-grandfather and obtained a living in his hometown of Bodelshausen, possibly through the action of the patron, the duke of Württemberg.[33] Two of the other artisan fathers practiced the relatively prestigious trades of silk tailor and painter. The remaining pastors of artisan origin derived from families with connections to the magistracy. For example, Ludwig Gebhardt, a tailor, was elected town councillor (*Ratsverwandter*) in 1596 and again in 1606. Two of his sons, Ludwig and Nicolaus, married the daughters of pastors, and Ludwig became a pastor.

Recruitment from artisan families seems to have decreased among the pastors serving in Tübingen district after 1600. Subsequently, all pastors of artisan origin came from families with officeholders, which underlines the close ties between the urban artisans and the town elites.[34]

The Tübingen artisan families that were contributing sons to the ministry appear to have already been quite comfortable, with close links to local officeholding families. The incomplete but nonetheless persuasive evidence listed in Appendix B suggests that the sons of prosperous Tübingen artisans entered the ministry as a means of exceeding or maintaining the status that their fathers or uncles had achieved within the lower and middling ranks of the local elite.[35]

The second group of pastors' fathers who were laymen consisted of members of the urban magistracy. In Tübingen, some of the fathers were identified in the matriculation records both by their office and by their trade.[36] Three were town council members (see Table 4), an office held by members of the leading local families.[37]

Few pastors came from the highest rank of the urban magistracy. One son of a Tübingen *Vogt*, the duke's bailiff and chief administrative officer for the town and district of Tübingen, became a pastor. A son of the *Burgvogt* of Göppingen, a much smaller and hence less prestigious town, also joined the ministry. Since there were only some 50 Vögte (chief district officers) at any one time, the small number of their sons who were recruited comes as no surprise. Absent entirely were sons of *Bürgermeister* (chief financial officers of villages or towns) and justices (*Gerichtsverwandten* or *Richter*), officers at the apex of the local elite. This absence can be easily explained, in that there were relatively fewer members of the local

TABLE 5

Social Recruitment of the Clergy in Tuttlingen District, 1581–1621

Profession of father	No.	Pct. pastors of known social origin (N = 9)	Pct. of all pastors (N = 39)
Unknown	30		77%
Clergy			
Higher	1	11%	3
Lower	8	89	21
Laity	0	0	0
TOTAL	39	100%	100%

SOURCES: Same as for Table 1.

NOTE: Data represent recovered aggregates for all parish pastors in office in the years 1581–1621. To avoid double-counting, those who shifted from parish to parish or district to district are counted only once.

court (*Gericht*) than of the local council (*Rat*). The closest connection of any pastor to this group is that of Stefan Kienlin, the pastor at Lustnau. While the profession of his father is unknown, his uncle, grandfather, and son all served as Bürgermeister—the other chief official in the village next to the Schultheiss. The Bürgermeister was usually a member of the council or court.

In the city of Tübingen, the close relationship between the urban elite and the church manifested itself in the entrance of the sons of the leading Tübingen families into the ministry and their promotion to some of the better, though not the richest, livings in the district.[38] Through intermarriage with the magistrate and notable class, the pastoral class consolidated its relationship to the Ehrbarkeit and achieved entry for some of its members and scions. The middle and upper levels of the pastorate, who numerically represented only a minority of the parish clergy, appear to have been closely connected with the urban government. For the post-Reformation Ehrbarkeit, as for its predecessor, it was to the benefit of the family reputation to stand in a good relationship with the church.[39]

Four of the Tübingen clergy serving in our period were sons of magistrates, and conversely, some of the magistrates were sons of pastors.[40] Patronage relationships also undoubtedly played a role in solidifying relationships between the Tübingen pastorate and magistracy. The patronage of the parishes of Derendingen, Kusterdingen, and Weilheim belonged to the Tübingen city hospice that the city court administered.[41] Consequently, sons or close relatives of Tübingen magistrates often held these livings.[42] For example, Ludwig Gebhardt served as pastor of Kusterdingen from 1597 to 1615; his father had been elected town councillor twice. Jakob Haag served in Kusterdingen in 1615 and in Weilheim am Neckar from 1624 to 1635; Haag's grandfather, Jakob, had served as town councillor between 1564 and 1571, and his uncle Jakob had also been a town councillor.[43]

The richest livings in the two districts were located in Tübingen with the city church pastorate and its two diaconates. These two deacon positions seem to have been reserved for clergy whom the hierarchy had earmarked for preferment in the church or university, for no clergy with family connections to the urban magistracy were appointed to these posts.

Three fathers represented early modern Württemberg's growing bureaucracy of ministers and officials: a Tübingen Vogt, a *Rentkammerrat*, and a *Hauptmann*.[44] The Vogt stood at the top of the hierarchy of local government in Tübingen, representing the city's sovereign lord, the duke of Württemberg. The Rentkammerrat, in effect the ducal finance and tax minister, was an office of the highest rank of the Ehrbarkeit. The Tübingen Vogt was named Martin Vogt (1564–1627). While his first marriage was to Judith, daughter of the Württemberg reformer Johannes Brenz, his second marriage was to Katherina, a daughter of the nobility, the Beer family in Wildberg, and the mother of the pastor Johann Martin. The Hauptmann of Hohen-Neffen was both commandant of the largest and strongest of the Jura fortresses and jailer of the duke's most eminent enemies, such as the Tübingen Vogt Konrad Brenning in 1517 and the ducal chancellor Matthäus Enzlin in 1609.[45]

As mentioned earlier, no pastors were sons of the peasantry, the most numerous social group, at the bottom of the social scale. Some may have been overlooked, since not all the pastors of village origin have been identified. Elsewhere in Germany, this lack of pastors of peasant origin has been explained by the absence of parish schools.[46]

This explanation cannot apply to Württemberg, for by the mid-sixteenth century, the duchy had established one of the most elaborate school systems in all of Germany.[47] In 1581, 76 percent of the rural districts in the Tübingen district had their own resident schoolmaster or a school taught by the pastor.[48] Conditions were somewhat poorer in Tuttlingen district, where in 1581 only 43 percent of the parishes had resident schoolmasters.[49] But circumstances rapidly improved, for by 1590, 57 percent of the parishes had schools, and by 1621 each parish had its own schoolmaster.[50] Furthermore, the analysis of the protocols reveals an amazingly high rate of school attendance (see Appendix C). In Tübingen district, for example, in April 1601, 19 percent of the catechumens were reported to be attending school at the time of the visitation.[51] Since the catechumens constitute a larger age group than school-age children, this percentage is remarkable.

Although we know little about the success of village school instruction, the village schools did not teach Latin. Latinity was the first hurdle on the path leading to a future pastoral career.[52] All the examinations and most instruction at every level of the educational path leading to church office were conducted in Latin. Such knowledge could only be obtained in the usually separate Latin schools. Although the Reformation had sponsored the use of German in worship, prayer, and the cure of souls, Latin remained generally the language of common intellectual discourse in the European republic of letters and specifically the language of theological education and examination. In practice, chiefly the children of townspeople had the opportunity to learn the language, since the Latin schools were located in the towns. Furthermore, the Latin schools served as the training ground for sons intended to be functionaries in the local or territorial government.

The financial burden of prolonged studies might have contributed to the lack of recruitment from the peasantry. Although since 1534 a system of ducal scholarships enabled worthy candidates to study free at a cloister school as preparation for entering the university, in practice these scholarships seem to have been reserved for the sons of clergy.

Apart from finances, educational opportunity for a peasant boy would then depend on the availability of Latin instruction at the elementary level from a tutor, a nearby Latin school, or a city school where the schoolmaster taught both the German and the Latin curriculum, as was the case in Tuttlingen. More intangible but nonetheless important factors affecting educational opportunity probably included the peasant father's reluctance to dispense with a son's labor even in the winter months, a perception that even schooling in Latin would not gain the son entrance into a cloister school or a profession, and perhaps even a lingering anticlericalism. It is also possible that the officials administering the scholarships actively discriminated against peasants, although this would be difficult to prove. Such discrimination, which preserved the scholarships for the sons of clerics and notables, has been reported for the eighteenth century, and it directly contradicts the intent of the original ordinance to reserve them for "the poor."[53] In sum, intangible but nonetheless real barriers prevented recruitment of peasant sons into the pastoral estate. Sons from even comfortable peasant families must have tacitly perceived these barriers and decided not to consider pastoral careers.

Despite Luther's claims concerning the affinity between the vocations of schoolmaster and pastor, the sons of schoolmasters made up only a very small proportion of the pastors.[54] The fathers of some of the pastors had served brief terms as preceptors of Latin or cloister schools before advancing to a parish position, but none of the fathers had been regular Latin schoolmasters and none had been a master of a village German school. This was in marked contrast to the Rhinelands, where teachers made a significant contribution to the clerical order.[55] Tübingen district differs from the Rhinelands because of the centralized nature of the educational track that led to the pastorate.

Turning to the highest social order, we find no pastors from noble families among the Tübingen or Tuttlingen district clergy and only a few in the whole duchy.[56] The nobility were by no means excluded from educational opportunity, constituting on the average 7 percent of the 4,967 matriculations at Tübingen University between the years 1575 and 1600.[57] The Reformation accomplished the abolition of the large prebends that had attracted the younger sons of the nobility to the church. Moreover, with the restoration of Duke Ulrich in 1534, the Reformation marked the beginning of the development of ducal power in Württemberg.[58]

The Tübingen clergy recruited appreciably and with increasing frequency from their own ranks. Sons of pastors constituted 77 percent of the pastors of known origin in Tübingen district (Table 4) and 63 percent in the whole duchy.[59] This process of self-recruitment was common throughout Germany, and some princes actively encouraged it. For example, Duke Johannes of Zwei Brücken decreed such a preference on January 4, 1599, "so that before others the children of ministers might be able to serve the church again."[60] Including pastors of unknown origin, the sons of pastors constituted 40 percent of the total clergy serving in Tübingen district (see Table 4), a percentage much greater than the range of 10 percent to 20 percent found by Bernard Vogler in the Rhinelands and greater than the 11.8 percent determined by Brecht for the whole duchy.[61] These percentages are most likely very reliable since, as noted earlier, genealogists have taken great care to recover clerical ancestors. The contrast with the Rhinelands can be attributed to Württemberg's well-developed system of clerical education, the generous scholarships for boys studying for the ministry, and the tendency to favor the sons of clergy in awarding scholarships.[62]

An analysis of the evolution of the recruitment of the Tübingen pastors from 1581 to 1621 is presented in Table 6. In 1581, in the Tübingen district, 22 percent of all pastors were sons of both higher

TABLE 6
Evolution of Social Recruitment of the Clergy in Tübingen District, Selected Years, 1581–1621

Profession of father	1581			1590			1601			1621		
	No.	Pct. of pastors of known social origin (N=8)	Pct. of all pastors (N=27)	No.	Pct. of pastors of known social origin (N=8)	Pct. of all pastors (N=27)	No.	Pct. of pastors of known social origin (N=13)	Pct. of all pastors (N=26)	No.	Pct. of pastors of known social origin (N=17)	Pct. of all pastors (N=30)
Unknown	19		70%	19		70%	13		50%	13		43%
Clergy												
Higher[a]	4	50	15	1	13	4	4	31	15	4	24	13
Lower[b]	2	25	7	4	50	15	5	38	19	8	47	27
Laity												
Ducal officer	0	0	0	1	13	4	0	0	0	1	6	3
Urban magistrate	0	0	0	0	0	0	3	23	12	3	18	10
Artisan	2	25	7	2	25	7	1	8	4	1	6	3
TOTAL	27	100%	100%	27	100%	100%	26	100%	100%	30	100%	100%

SOURCES: Binder, *Kirchen- und Lehrämter*; Hermelink, *Die Matrikeln*; HStA Bü. 1282 (1601); LKA Stuttgart A1 1581, 1590, 1621; Sigel, "Das evangelische Württemberg"; Stoll, *Sammlung*.

NOTE: Data are for those parish pastors in office in the years 1581, 1590, 1601, and 1621.

[a] Includes university professors.

[b] Pastors, preachers, deacons, and preceptors.

and lower clergy, while by 1621 the proportion had increased to 40 percent. The proportion of pastors' sons among those of known origin remained relatively constant, 75 percent in 1581 and 71 percent in 1621. The formation of pastoral dynasties was not uncommon, with members of three or more generations in one family entering the ministry, a practice that in Württemberg, unlike in the Rhinelands, does not seem to have been interrupted by the Thirty Years War.[63] Very often a son would succeed his father in a position and one family would hold the same living for three generations in succession.[64] The three sons of Jakob Andreae occupied the living of Hagelloch in succession, and at one time they all held benefices in Tübingen district. Although well connected to the church hierarchy, these brothers did not obtain a fat living in Hagelloch, for even after its reorganization and the improvement of its revenues in 1580, it possessed 56 florins in specie income, below the district average of 64 florins. (See Appendix D, on money in Württemberg.) Even so, the income of an average living still gave the pastor an economic position superior to that of most of his parishioners.[65]

The pastorate's trend toward the enlistment of its sons to replenish its ranks reflects in part the growth of the clergy as a newly self-conscious professional elite. In the sixteenth century at least, this practice was also a matter of economic self-interest. The establishment of dynasties reflects a strategy by pastors and the consistory to deal with the clergy's tenuous financial position at retirement and the clergy's apparent lack of heritable wealth.[66] One pastor, Sebastian Scholl, retired at age 63 to hand his benefice over to his son-in-law, presumably in order to be able to continue living in the manse in his declining years.[67] Many of these dynasties seem in fact to have been the result of the inability of the clergy to own land in their parishes that they could bequeath. Because most clergymen served until their death, and pensions, if paid, were insufficient and without provision for the support of widows and orphans, an aging incumbent pastor could encourage his son's promotion as successor to ensure that someone would take care of his widow and dependents.

The consistory seems to have encouraged such a practice. When the pastor of Kusterdingen, Johann Erhad Küpferlin, died in 1653, the Württemberg consistory worked quickly to transfer his son Alexander to Kusterdingen. The officers in Stuttgart first recorded the death on January 14. Four days later they wrote Alexander, informing him officially of the vacancy, and on January 28 they appointed him to his father's former parish. Since he was not to take up the post until St. George's Day, April 23, the consistory instructed the widow and orphans, who were receiving the salary, to employ a vicar to conduct services through Lent and Easter.[68]

Pastors seem to have married toward the end of their diaconate and before taking up their first pastorate.[69] Some of the more prominent Tübingen clerical families tend to intermarry among themselves and with Tübingen magistrate families, as the genealogy of the Haag family illustrates. The patriarch of the family, Jakob (d. 1564?–71), a councillor, married the daughter of a Schultheiss from Hausen an der Zaber. Their son, Martin, became pastor of Nehren, near Tübingen, and married a clergyman's daughter from Geradstellen. Martin's first son followed his father into the ministry, while the second son, Ludwig Friedrich, took up a less prestigious trade as a surgeon and barber. Ludwig Friedrich, however, gained social prominence through his election as a councillor like his grandfather before him, and in 1647 he ascended into the Ehrbarkeit with his appointment to the city court. Ludwig's sister, the third child of the pastor Martin, married Nicolaus Gebhardt, who was also the son of a councillor and the brother of a pastor. (See Appendix B.)

IV

By the eighteenth century the principle of family connection had become so entrenched in Württemberg that the following proverb was current: "In other countries the giving of gifts rules, but in Württemberg it is family connection."[70] The 700 or more church positions in Württemberg represented an avenue of opportunity for the sons of clergy, the urban magistrates, and, to a lesser degree, the urban artisans.[71] But the only avenue to these positions lay through the selective sieve of the educational structure, particularly the limited number of places in the Latin pedagogia, the cloister schools and the Tübingen Stift. Competition therefore was very keen.

The pattern of recruitment of the Tübingen district clergy was neither one of co-optation of the petite bourgeoisie nor one of social mobility; in contrast, most clergy were recruited from the urban magistracy and the pastorate. It is not yet certain whether this connection can also be found in the recruitment pattern of the first generation of pastors or whether it developed only subsequent to the early decades of the Reformation. The most prominent lay social group was the artisans who were connected with the magistracy. Where most of these artisans stood precisely in the socioeconomic hierarchy, however, is not yet clear. The few who are identified seem to have been at the top of their profession and were by no means small burghers. In fact, from the data in Table 4 for the clergy of known origin, we see that 87 percent of the clergy in our sample came from either the pastorate or official families, two of the professional groups that ruled the duchy of Württemberg. This percentage becomes even higher if we include the two sons of artisans whose fathers were officeholders.

In summary, despite the official princely intent to establish the clerical estate upon meritocratic principles, the prerequisite of a Latin education and the close association of the urban magistracy with the church in the localities resulted in a substantial proportion of the clergy originating either from the middling-level families of the urban elite or from the clergy's own ranks. This tendency toward the formation of a self-perpetuating group ran counter to Duke Christoph's original intent to recruit sons from families unable to finance a Latin education. A clerical career might have served into the mid-eighteenth century as an avenue of social mobility for a small number of the sons of artisans. But many of these candidates appear to have already been connected to the local urban officeholding groups.

CHAPTER 2

The Education of Pastors

Our young people are buried in forests and desolate places during the most important period of their intellectual and moral development. They know how to express themselves in the most beautiful Latin phrases, but when they meet someone who is not their everyday acquaintance, they are embarrassed because of those few German words.... This bashfulness, which is a natural consequence of cloistral discipline, seldom disappears.[1]

During the eighteenth century, the Württemberg estates voiced this criticism of the cloister schools, the rural preparatory schools attended by young boys pursuing theological careers. The institutions and practices that the critic condemns as causes of the clergy's embarrassment, anxiety, or standoffishness in the face of the everyday German-speaking world were established in the sixteenth century. The basis of the Württemberg clergy's educational and cultural formation was a secluded, quasi-monastic environment, an emphasis on the Latin language and literature, and a commitment to theology and doctrine.

Graduates of the urban Latin schools were granted ducal scholarships to attend the rural cloister schools. They studied there until they reached the age of seventeen or eighteen, when they matriculated at the university in Tübingen and subsequently began their residence in the ducal foundation for prospective clergy, the Stift. While most received a master's degree within four or five years, almost all continued residence in the seminary in order to study theology for two years or more. They were not appointed to their first parish until they were in their mid-twenties.

While the first chapter showed that the clergy were mostly townsmen, this chapter demonstrates that they were townsmen who were molded in a unique way by the Württemberg educational system. Knowledge of the clergy's education and the process by which they were socialized as a group will increase our understanding of the development of the Württemberg state church in the late sixteenth and early seventeenth centuries.[2] By drawing on the Württemberg educational legislation, archival sources, and local studies of schools and colleges, this chapter describes the clerical educational system and its curriculum, the students' lifestyle, and the disciplinary regime under which they lived.

Excluding the time spent in Latin school, prospective pastors received nine to ten years of a very special education that promoted the socialization of theological candidates as a professional class. From their early teen years they lived together in boarding schools and were separated from the rest of the population, even from other university students. They advanced through various levels of the system in small groups. They learned the ancient scholarly languages revived by the Renaissance pedagogues and practiced academic rhetorical exercises based on models from Roman antiquity. They lived a common life that was theoretically modeled on a quasi-monastic ideal of discipline. Even cases of violations of Stift discipline indicate that the clerical candidates were conscious of themselves as a group set apart from ordinary Württembergers.

I

The education of the prospective pastor began with attendance at one of the many local Latin schools, the *schola particularis*, the first step on the ladder of the *studium generale* leading to the university. The Latin schools were intended to recruit gifted boys who might be prepared to serve their church, state, and local community.[3] In contrast, the German village schools were intended for the working children of "common peasant subjects."[4] Though sometimes the Latin and German schools were physically combined in one building, as in Tuttlingen, where the Latin school consisted of those boys desiring to learn Latin, the instruction was supposed to be entirely separate.[5]

What was the nature of the curriculum studied by the prospective theology student at a Latin school? Following standard humanist ideals, the authors of the 1559 school ordinance prescribed that the Latin schools teach "useful" languages, since they believed that the study of the languages themselves might promote correct theology, learning, government, and household management.[6] The Reformation pedagogues considered the humanistic curriculum to be eminently practical. Although they recognized that a school system could serve the needs of the state, foremost in their minds was the training of theologians and pastors for the post-Interim era. According to the plan of the ordinance, the Latin schools were to consist of five grades, or forms, the lower grades teaching reading, writing, and grammer, while the fifth and final grade concentrated on rhetoric and dialectic. The number of grades in each school was to depend on local need. The Tübingen Pedagogium and its Stuttgart counterpart tended to assume the place of the fifth form, so that many of the Latin schools, such as the one at Tübingen, consisted of only four grades.

The textbooks of Philip Melanchthon formed the heart of the Latin school curriculum. The first grade began with the time-honored fourth-century grammarian Donatus and then moved on to the *Quaestiones Grammaticae Philippi*, which the three subsequent grades used as well. In the fifth grade, grammar and style were polished with the larger *Grammaticum Philippi* and the *Syntaxim Philippi*, while the *Erotemata Dialecticae* and the *Rhetorica* were used to teach rhetoric. The reading of proverbs and aphorisms played an important role in the curriculum. Starting in the second class, the Proverbs of Solomon, the *Dialogues* of Selbaldi Heiden, Aesop's *Fables*, and the *Fables* of Camerarius were set as lessons. The works of Terence, Livy, and, most frequently, Cicero provided models for the upper grades' exercises in rhetoric. The preceptors were, however, charged to point out to the young pupils "how the blind heathen knew nothing of God and his word. . . . Moreover, [they should] indicate an example and testimony of sacred Scripture [that demonstrates] how the Lord God severely punishes this blasphemy."[7]

Despite the ordinance's allusion to the Old Testament, there was no Hebrew instruction in the Latin schools. Greek grammar and reading began in the fifth form with texts from Aesop's *Fables*, Isocrates' letter to Demonicus, or the *Paedia* of Xenophon.[8] Although German was forbidden in conversation, it was used in rhetorical exercises throughout the Latin schools.[9]

Since in theory the Latin schools were open to all applicants, did the educational system serve as a means of social mobility? Poor students were freed from the obligation of paying the school fees. In the city of Tübingen an institution called the *Pauperat* provided choir scholarships for the sons of poor townspeople.[10] The scholars received daily instruction in singing and were to accompany the teacher of the third form, who acted as cantor, in church services and at funerals, weddings, and processions. Further promotion and advancement of any student, regardless of social origin, depended on a central examination, the *Landexamen*. This was conducted before the church authorities in Stuttgart, who decided the worthiness of the pupil for future study, a decision supposedly guided by the parents' lack of income and the boy's "good and fruitful talents."[11] By law boys were accepted for the exam from the ages of twelve to fourteen;[12] specifically, the 1559 church ordinance stated that the examination was to be taken in about the fifth form "or [the students] were to be promoted to our Pedagogium in Stuttgart." In practice the candidates were anywhere between eleven and fifteen years of age.[13] The examination became obligatory in 1582.

The emphasis on Latin presented a cultural barrier against recruitment of the sons of peasants and artisans of meager means. Latinity was perhaps a two-edged sword, hindering those from the lowest end of the social spectrum from acquiring social mobility through education but enabling those from the middling and comfortable classes to rise by acquiring first education and then office.[14] Without a doubt, the urban Latin schools contributed to the influence of the urban classes on the development of the pastoral estate. In Württemberg, although the sources are silent about which Latin schools our pastors attended, evidently the urban location of the Latin schools, attending which was the first step in the future pastors' education, largely determined the urban origin of the pastorate.[15]

The Latin schools also served to sift out those who would enter professions immediately from those who would go on for further education in one of the preparatory schools for future clergy, the cloister schools or one of the two Pedagogia. Though either path could lead to the territorial university in Tübingen, one key distinction existed between the two paths. Those students who went on to the cloister schools were supported financially by stipendia from the prince, and in return, they vowed to devote their lives to clerical careers.

II

After the appropriate tenure at a Latin school, a future pastor attended one of the cloister schools, whose purpose was to introduce the university curriculum and to prepare the young boy for the pastorate. There were originally thirteen cloister schools established on former monastic lands, often with a small number of pupils. Their maintenance must have appeared too costly to the dukes. By 1599, there were a total of five cloister schools: two higher schools, Bebenhausen and Maulbronn, and three lower schools, Adelberg, Blaubeuren, and Hirsau.[16]

These schools were supported by the income from sequestered monastic lands. In Württemberg, in contrast to other Protestant territories, the appropriated property and incomes of the many prereform monastic lands were dedicated primarily to the education of future pastors and the maintenance of pastors in office. Although the ecclesiastical treasury was administered separately from the ducal treasury, both funds were managed by government officials. Only after the expenses of the church had been paid could the surplus be devoted to the expenditures of the duchy. Thus the duchy had both the money and the buildings to allocate for establishing a comprehensive system of clerical education. At the same time, the education of the future pastors was completely in the hands of the ducal church consistory, which was under the direct authority of the sovereign.[17]

Such appropriation of rural cloisters for the purposes of humanistic education, as was the case in Württemberg, had been criticized by Luther early in the Reformation. He had argued that monastic property should be used to establish high schools in the towns rather than in rural areas, because urban social life would provide examples of practical, active life to complement book learning. Luther evidently envisioned a great deal of face-to-face contact between students and townspeople on the streets and in the marketplaces. For Luther, isolated studies could accomplish nothing.[18] But isolated studies were the practice in Württemberg.

Not only was the cloister student isolated in the rural countryside, but his social sphere was limited to a few teachers and a dozen or so fellow students. These small schools were very suitable for the initial stages of the socialization of the pastorate as a professional group because they provided a homogeneous and consistent background and education for the clerical corps and an opportunity for the prospective clergy to know each other. Toward the end of Duke Christoph's reign (1550–70), Maulbronn, with 24 pupils, was the largest cloister school in the land. According to the estates law (*Landtagsabschied*) of 1565, 200 pupils were to be maintained in the existing four higher schools, with an additional 50 scholarship holders at the Tübingen Stift.[19]

The cloister schools were intended specifically to prepare boys for a future church position. Their curriculum mandated a full program of lessons in the liberal arts and theology.[20] Accordingly, the schools were headed by two preceptors, one for theology and one for the arts, teaching a curriculum of biblical exposition, dialectic, and rhetoric. The lower cloister schools (*Grammatistenschulen*) taught the arts curriculum of the fourth form in order to compensate for the diverse background of the students and the lack of higher forms at many of the Latin schools, while the arts curriculum of the upper schools corresponded to that of the fifth form.[21]

For the upper schools, the ordinance outlined a curriculum in grammar, dialectic, and rhetoric based on exercises from Melanchthon's textbooks and the reading of Cicero and Virgil. With the 1559 ordinance, instruction in Greek became obligatory, the lower schools teaching the fundamentals of grammar and pronunciation and the upper schools reading such texts as the *Paedia* of Xenophon.[22]

Although more hours were devoted to arts instruction, theology held a prominent place in the curriculum.[23] The upper school students studied the Latin texts of the Old Testament and the Pauline epistles, while the lower school students studied the easier Evangelists and Acts of the Apostles. The preceptors were to explicate the texts in such a manner that the pupils "be instructed in both grammar and theology, according to their intellectual ability."[24] The 1582 revision of the Church Ordinance presented a detailed plan of readings that reflected an increased emphasis on dogmatics by setting Jakob Heerbrand's *Compendium Theologiae*, the standard Württemberg dogmatics, as the theology text.[25] History was important within the intellectual horizon of the school. During both breakfast and supper, one chapter of Eusebius and another historian were to be read aloud.[26]

Valentin Vannius, abbot of the cloister school in Maulbronn, published a theological compendium, presumably as a text for his own students, that emphasized humanist rhetoric and the defense of doctrine. On the basis of Erasmus's *De Copia Verborum*, Vannius explained that reading is profitable only if its results are set down in distinct loci, that is, specific individual themes, so that the student is always prepared to give a speech. He referred to Melanchthon for the structure and use of loci. Following the precedent of the Strasbourg gymnasium, he recommended that the pupil form his own copybook. Vannius intended for the pupil to prepare for his future vocation as a preacher by compiling, through the use of the copybook, his own theological compendium supported by prooftexts. He thereby recommended a humanist pedagogical procedure for a scholastic end, the defense of doctrine through the citation of prooftexts.[27]

With a strictly regulated common life, the spirit of the medieval cloister lived on in the Württemberg cloister schools. The head of the school retained the title of abbot, the new students were called novices,[28] and school life was regulated according to monastic hours. According to the prescriptions of the first Cloister Ordinance (*Klosterordnung*),[29] following their waking at five o'clock (or six in the winter), the scholars dressed in their black cowls and proceeded to the morning worship service, a combination of the medieval lauds and prime, which consisted of two or three German or Latin psalms, a sermon consisting of a *lectio continua* from the Old Testament, German psalms, and prayer. At eight o'clock, in place of terce, biblical lessons were held with the exposition of Scripture, especially the psalms. At midday, in place of sext, teachers were available for instruction of the pupils in literature and other liberal arts. From one to three o'clock either the normal daily work or the heavily emphasized private studies were to take place. At three o'clock, another worship service occurred, none, consisting of one to three psalms, New Testament readings, a German psalm, and prayer. At vespers, hymns and the Magnificat could be sung.

Discipline was rigorous, and the youngsters were surrounded by lists of commandments and restrictions. Speaking in German, making unauthorized excursions, visiting public houses, laughing during prayer, and speaking with girls were forbidden and severely punished, at the very least with loss of the day's wine ration. The ordinances made no specific provisions regarding corporal punishment in the cloister schools, possibly because such discipline was implicitly understood.[30]

This conservative, almost monastic spirit was repeated in the subsequent Cloister Ordinances. The 1556 Cloister Ordinance mandated the continuation of the existing monasteries insofar as they were "in accordance with Scripture" and "meaningful." The ordinance also emphasized the singing of psalms according to the traditional divine offices. Sunday communion was termed the *christliche Messe* and was to be conducted in Latin. This ordinance was succeeded by the educational provisions of the Church Ordinance of 1559, drafted by Vannius with Johannes Brenz, Sebastian Hormald, and Kasper Wald, which reduced the worship services and increased the hours of instruction.[31]

When a young boy accepted a position as a cloister school scholar, he vowed to prepare for the ministry by devoting himself "to theology alone, that I might with time be used as a minister in the church of God, according to his divine call."[32] In return, he was provided with food, lodging, a Latin Bible, shoes, and a bed complete with linen. The precincts of the cloister school became the student's home for most of the year, and his social contacts were limited to his fellow students and his teachers. Although with promotion to the Stift the adolescent moved into an urban setting, the ideals and practices of the Stift continued to foster the separation of the clerical candidates from the town and its encumbering temptations.

III

The next step in the educational career ladder was residence in the ducal Stift at Tübingen. Like the cloister schools, the ducal Stift was in many ways a continuation of a medieval predecessor called the *Bursa*. Many of the Bursa's former customs were taken over: the regulated common life and the reading aloud of biblical texts and preaching during meals, when silence was otherwise required.[33] Although within the city, the Stift, like a monastery, was a self-contained building where entrance and egress were regulated and whose gates were closed at night.

The students arrived in Tübingen from the cloister schools with a respectable knowledge of Latin and Latin authors, elements of the trivium and rhetoric, and some Greek. This philological education was developed further in the first semesters leading to the master's degree. The 1559 ordinance recommended that those admitted to the Tübingen Stift be "of a considerable age, about sixteen or seventeen."[34] During the late sixteenth and early seventeenth centuries, the pastors from Tübingen and Tuttlingen districts matriculated between the ages of seventeen and nineteen, advanced to the baccalaureate usually within a year, and received their master's degree within four or five years.[35]

During the same period, the total number of residents in the Stift (*Stiftler*) fluctuated but was usually less than 160.[36] In addition to the students' common social and educational background as townsmen, sons of clergymen, and graduates of the cloister school, the small population of the Stift, and especially the small promotion classes, further contributed to the socialization occurring among classmates, and to the formation of intraclass bonds and friendships. For a typical example, in February 1581, 21 students were awarded a master's degree, and in August of the same year 25 more were promoted.[37]

The spirit of Protestant humanism pervaded the curriculum of the Stift. The studies emphasized written and spoken latinity, the reading of classics, and the trilingual ideal of Greek, Latin, and Hebrew. The students were obligated to study theology and to prepare for the ministry under the penalty of losing their scholarships.[38] Like the scholarship students in the cloister schools, the residents of the Stift were often called Stipendiaten. Luther's own ideal curriculum for the training of pastors emphasized intense biblical studies through the study of the text itself, with the help of Melanchthon's *Loci*. He recommended the study of the *Loci* as a means of obtaining "eloquence" and a "wealth of words."[39] This method of biblical study was generally followed at Tübingen, although Melanchthon's *Loci* was only a popular, not a required, textbook.

The Stift was headed by one of the professors of the philosophy faculty, the Magister Domus. The actual theological instruction, however, was carried out by the two professors of theology who served as superintendents. Lectures in the faculties were to be attended by all members of the Stift, according to their ability and in consideration of their age, with the young students attending arts lectures and older students attending theology lectures. Initially, the teaching staff members were responsible for the review (*Repetition*) of the theology lectures, while the six Magisters "of ability" who had been selected to pursue a doctoral degree in theology, were responsible for the review of the arts subjects: physics, rhetoric, dialectic, catechism, music, and ethics.[40] But by the end of the sixteenth century, these teaching assistants (*Repetenten*) were holding weekly reviews and discussions of the lectures in all subjects, including theology, in order to assess how well the students learned and applied the material.[41]

Besides the six teaching assistants, four other Magister of a total of 120 or so were also designated for future doctoral degrees in theology.[42] For the scholarship holders of the Stift, achieving a doctoral degree was a certain means of social advancement. To enable them to complete their academic studies, they were appointed to the two Tübingen diaconates and the pastorates of Lustnau, Derendingen, Weilheim, Kilchberg (formerly Kirchberg or Kilberg), Jesingen, and Hagelloch.[43] Thus the high proportion of doctoral degrees among the pastors serving in Tübingen district comes as no surprise. In addition to their parish and academic duties, these Magister were also appointed to preach in the outlying areas and to serve communion in the Tübingen *Stiftskirche* (collegiate church) "in order that they might be much better informed of and experienced in the rituals of the church."[44] Serving as a teaching assistant was, as a rule, the precondition for all future higher preferment in the church. Candidates were chosen from among the best and the brightest of the scholarship holders by the headmaster and the teaching staff.[45]

In addition to attendance at the lectures, the 1559 Church Ordinance required participation in disputations and other exercises, both in the arts faculty and in the Stift, where the more advanced Magister also had to be present. The scholarship holders were allowed to study theology formally only after attaining the master's degree.[46] So while the nonscholarship students (the *Brotstudenten* of the other faculties) were compelled to complete their studies as quickly as possible, the Stift students only began their special theological education after promotion to master of arts. Thus while his professional contemporaries, lawyers and medical doctors, had already begun to practice their profession, the prospective pastor was only beginning the formal study of theology, which consisted of sermon exercises in the Stift and disputations and declamations in the arts faculty along with Greek and Hebrew studies. Meanwhile, those chosen for service as preceptors in the schools were not able to advance to the master's degree and were thus excluded from the sermon exercises, participating only briefly in the theological studies.[47]

A complaint made in 1568 about a student's delay in returning borrowed books reflects the humanistic and philological content of the Stift's curriculum. The lender named the several titles by Erasmus and books by Valla, Terence, and Cicero.[48] The significant place of Erasmus's works in the list manifests his continuing influence on the German intellectual world—an influence that lasted well into the eighteenth century.[49]

Melanchthon was also a significant influence. The large number of his works in the holdings of the Stift's library before the end of the seventeenth century reveals his significant influence on the theological enterprise and the arts disciplines.[50] If the holdings of the Stift library are representative, Luther was known only secondhand and the collection of his writings was incomplete, the library holding neither his exegetical nor his systematic works.[51] Not surprisingly, Brenz, the father of Württemberg theology, was strongly represented.[52] Works by other Lutheran theologians, such as Andreas Osiander, Georg Maier, and the elder Schnepf, were either absent or only poorly represented, which indicates that the Württemberg church leadership achieved a certain uniformity of mind and theological peace.[53] Remarkably, Reformed works were strongly represented.[54] Apparently the Calvinist systematic works were read for the sake of polemic, while the Reformed exegetical works were valued in themselves.

The visitations also give some indication of the private studies of the pastors after they left the university. Pastors were reported to read mostly Lucas Osiander (19 pastors) and Brenz (13), while only a few (3) read Luther. Some were interested in Reformed theology, with one pastor reading Bucer and another Zanchius.[55]

There was a very substantial rhetorical component to the Stift's educational system. The students did more than attend lectures. In addition to their advanced Greek and Hebrew studies, theology students conducted sermon exercises in the Stift and disputations and declamations in the arts faculty. The sermon exercises took place in the common room at midday, at the beginning of the major meal, and in the evening.[56] After the sermon, the candidate went to the high table where the headmaster and teaching staff discussed his sermon and criticized its deficiencies in pronunciation, rendering, and method.[57] With the daily practice sermons the approximately 120 Magister had the opportunity to preach perhaps three times a year, assuming that everyone took his turn and the schedule lasted the whole calendar year, or six times in the course of the Magister's residence in the Stift.[58] This limited opportunity to practice perhaps accounts for the poor evaluations that some of the candidates for the pastorate received from the consistory.

Life in the Stift was not altogether different from life in the cloister schools, except that university study allowed more freedom to the individual. There was a weekly schedule of prayer, worship, and study. Lectures and exercises in the arts faculty were required, and occasionally instruction was received in classes of the Tübingen Pedagogium.

During the semester, the workday began early in the Stift, at quarter to five in the summer and at five in the winter. Within fifteen minutes each student had to be at his table in the common room for morning prayer; absentees lost their daily wine ration. Academic lectures followed. Those who had no lectures to attend were not permitted to enter the town in the morning, but had to pursue their private studies in their rooms, a regulation supervised by the porter. The first meal, during which the gates to the Stift were locked, was served at nine o'clock. After breakfast there was an hour of free time, for recreation, which the students were to use "with appropriate discretion" (*mit rechter Bescheidenheit*).[59] At one o'clock the student servants went from room to room and noted those absent. On Thursdays the teaching staff taught lessons in the common room, and on other days the teaching assistants held exercises. At five o'clock in the evening the second meal took place. In summer, the evening meal was followed by another free period for recreation and walks. Staying out overnight, however, was punished by internment in the Stift's jail.

The eating arrangement in the common room reflected the Stift's hierarchy, which in turn was a microcosm of the Württemberg ecclesiastical hierarchy. The students and faculty all arrived dressed in black cowls. The superintendents and the headmaster sat at the high table (*Herrentrippel*) together with their guests: the preacher of the day, other *doctores*, some of the teaching assistants, and others. Other frequent guests sat at the oval table of the teaching assistants, beneath the high table. The tables of the students were arranged according to academic status: masters of arts, graduates, and novices all sat with their respective groups.[60] During meals a sermon was held, in which the foreign scholars, mostly from Montbeliard, practiced in their native tongue, giving rise to countless complaints concerning the rattling of spoons and knives among the bored Swabian students, who could not understand French. The Bible and confessions were also read aloud.[61] Talking during these activities resulted in deprivation of the wine ration or time in the lockup.[62]

The education of the Stift students culminated with their examination and placement by the consistory in Stuttgart.[63] Members of the consistory already had some knowledge of the candidates from the quarterly reports submitted by the Stift and the regular visitations to the Stift and the cloister schools. The examination consisted of a short sermon and an oral examination conducted in Latin.[64] As we saw in Chapter 1, the examiners expected a good performance and could send back to Tübingen those whom they deemed lacking. Next to indebtedness, nothing was more contemptible among the Württemberg pastorate than ignorance.

The Stift exercised strict discipline. It was enforced through a network of covert and overt supervision, coupled with a threefold system of sanctions: fines, deprivation of the wine ration, and confinement in the lockup.[65] Although no explicit provision for corporal punishment appears in the ordinances governing the Stift,[66] this does not mean that such punishments did not occur. The teaching staff did not hesitate to confine students to the lockup or even to expel reprobates. According to the church ordinance, the headmaster

shall also establish secretly in the week among the scholarship holders several inspectors to report to the Magister on oath each lapse in and transgression of the statutes; and to determine each Sunday after dinner what has been reported or otherwise discovered and what should be punished according to the statutes, to determine immediately [the fines] to be paid and penances done, [or] to arrange no punishment.[67]

For example, the statutes decreed that when a student entertained a prostitute or was found under suspicious circumstances with a single woman, on the first offense he would be punished with fourteen days in the lockup on bread and water rations. After this penance, the guilty party would be rebuked before the whole community and admonished to improve. On the second offense, the punishment was increased to one month. The third offense resulted in the loss of the scholarship and imprisonment for as long as the prince deemed appropriate.[68]

Although, like all Reformation pedagogues, the authors of the Stift ordinances were intimately concerned with order and discipline, some flexibility was allowed in the implementation of that order. In enforcing the godly life, the officers of the Stift were to adjust the level of the punishment to fit the severity of the crime. For example, when a student swore, used God's name in vain, or said something unseemly about the humanity of Christ out of a contentious disposition and a bad habit, he would be deprived of two days' wine ration for each instance of swearing or cursing. But when a student swore violently and extensively out of anger or willful boldness, he would receive several days in the lockup on bread and water.[69]

Gerald Strauss has rightly observed that modern critics of early-modern pedagogy have exaggerated the excessiveness of corporal punishment in the school systems. While in Württemberg the Latin school ordinances were very careful to lay down strict guidelines for school punishment and to limit the physical abuse of students, the cloister school and Stift ordinances made no specific provision for physical punishment. While little or no bodily punishment was mandated, there was, nonetheless, a great deal of discipline.[70]

The Stift students were under the authority of a small number of masters, who were aided by a network of informants, chief among whom were the student servants. The church ordinance stipulated that besides the ordinary scholarship students, three (and later four) "children . . . who want very much to study but cannot support themselves on account of poverty" be appointed by the headmaster and the steward (*Hausverwalter*).[71] These student servants were to accompany the steward to the market, carry purchases back to the Stift, wait on tables, and fetch wood for the Magister. Otherwise they were to be "in all the statutes equal to the other scholarship holders."[72] However, since they were also responsible for watching over the lecture attendance and the lifestyle of their fellow students, they were in a somewhat awkward position, having a certain coercive power over their fellows by virtue of their responsibility for reporting infringements of the Stift's discipline while remaining inferior to them in social status.

All the scholarship holders, from the youngest student of fifteen to the oldest Magister (including retired pastors and those between positions), were subject to the same system of discipline, which was fundamentally equivalent to that in force in the cloister schools. The lack of emphasis on the rod and the fact that all, even the adult Magister, were subject to a uniform discipline indicate, however, that though little distinction was made between young boys and adolescents in terms of disciplinary sanctions, the cloister and Stift students were not disciplined like children. Rather they were considered to be members of a corporation with certain obligations and privileges, which is what they in fact were.

Even the cases of student violations of Stift discipline indicate the special status of the scholarship holders and their consciousness of themselves as a group set apart from the average Württemberger. They acted like an elite group in training. They had the leisure to wander around. They got drunk, gambled, chased women, frequented prostitutes, bore arms (and presumably dueled), and wore sumptuous clothing. We have already seen the sanctions against visiting prostitutes. A 1594 visitation of the Stift reported that several Magister liked to wander about. One in particular, named Senkinger, was haughty and proud and studied nothing. Magister Schitzer came across as too morose in his sermon. Magister Weiland was impudent. Magister Elenheinz had recently caused a scandal by his drunkenness on a public street after sunset. One such complaint had a sad ending: "Magister Schaubel has incurred debts everywhere, and on account of the same, he desired to go home at Shrove Tuesday, which was allowed. When he was unable to raise any money (as we have been informed), he went to Ulm, and afterward he soon died, having fallen out of a window."[73] During the seventeenth century, Stift authorities carried on an apparently unsuccessful battle against sumptuous dress and the bearing of arms.[74] The complaints indicate that the students were attempting to emulate the fashions of Catholic, Baroque Europe and style themselves a cut above other Württembergers.[75]

The effect of the curriculum on the students is difficult to assess, for we know little about the studies of particular individuals. The church ordinances decreed Latin as the obligatory conversational language in the cloister schools and the Stift. This rule, however, required strict and ever vigilant enforcement. The reports from visitations of the Stift recorded numerous instances of poor latinity and the speaking of German.[76] The majority of students were able to master Latin, and the standard seems to have become even stricter as the system of education developed subsequent to the Reformation. A story exists, perhaps apocryphal, concerning the chancellor of the university, Jakob Andreae. Reportedly, when he arrived at the Stift in 1541 at the tender age of twelve, he had to translate into Latin the sentence "I have twelve animals at home." The examiner led him through word by word and finally the boy accomplished, "Ego habes domus duodecim animal."[77] By the first decade of the seventeenth century, the students had mastered the language sufficiently to pass the examination for ordinands that was conducted in Latin before the consistory vetters in Stuttgart. When they did fail, it was because of their inadequate theological knowledge or their inability to preach well.

In the late sixteenth century, emphasis shifted from biblical studies to dogmatics. The 1559 Church Ordinance prescribed that one of the teaching staff read aloud and explicate every Thursday afternoon the *Margarita Theologiae*, which centered on biblical texts. In contrast, the 1582 Church Ordinance prescribed in its place extracts from the systematic and dogmatic *Compendium Theologiae* by Heerbrand.[78]

There are distinct indications of the cultural and social effect of life and education in the Stift. For certain, the clerical candidates liked to use academic and polemical jargon and techniques that would set them apart from other people, especially their future parishioners. Polemical subtleties enjoyed great popularity among the professors, teaching assistants, and students. The consistory condemned such practices and pressed for the cultivation of biblical knowledge and exegetical skill.[79] Toward the end of the seventeenth century, the consistory expressed its reservations as part of a detailed *Instruction* that particularly noted the alarming interest in scholasticism among the students.[80] The students had been trained to be erudite in Latin, Greek, Hebrew, and orthodox theology. They had practiced rhetoric and sermonizing for years—so much so that they were always ready to make a speech or prove an argument.

In 1619 Johann Valentin Andreae published a scathing verse criticism of the education of clergy. His account consisted of a narrative dialogue between a freshly graduated master of arts, eager to take up his position as deacon, and a wise, old country pastor under whom the deacon is to work. In their encounter, the new Magister is very proud of his education and hopes to impress his new boss and his peasant flock with his erudition:

I was well prepared, for I had the benefit of all the arts and sciences. I had thoroughly learned the course of logic and the thick little book of rhetoric. I had memorized the celestial sphere and what ethics says about proper behavior and what story Homer told. I could do all of this. It was as easy as pie. No peasant would believe me capable of it.[81]

The old pastor rejects the usefulness of the deacon's theoretical book learning. To him, the universities have made masters of arts out of the skins of asses.[82] He also thinks little of the Magister's rhetorical skill and his desire to depose, defend, and prove himself.

Mocking the deacon's academic long-windedness, the pastor facetiously invites him to prove his case: "Until the building vanishes into thin air, until this pappy mush is digested, until your brain evaporates, until this storm of wit blows over, only then will the practical come home, which drives out everything theoretical."[83] Andreae's satire condemns the Württemberg teaching program with its emphasis on erudition because it produced pastors who were separated from their parishioners by the long years of training in rhetoric, ancient languages, and theology. The older pastor recommends to the astonished and frightened young deacon that he be willing to learn his job from the peasants in his flock. The Magister's response is telling, for he asks what good is the university if it does not enable him to restrain the unlearned.[84] It is not certain how many Tübingen graduates were willing to learn the art of practical theology on the job in their parishes. But it is clear that little in their scholarly education would have predisposed them to take Andreae's advice.

Even Andreae's cocky Magister had to wait for a position to become available. The students' long sojourn in school must have contributed to their sense of being apart, especially since as long as they remained in the Stift, the church regulated their sexual lives. As noted above, the Stift students were allowed to proceed to the formal study of theology only after having received their master's degrees. As shown by the data in Table 7, the Tübingen district deacon was, on the average, in his mid-twenties when he left the Stift and took up his first position. This delayed entry into adult professional life after a long period of residential education in the boarding schools can in part be attributed to the pedagogical need to postpone adulthood, especially adult sexuality, in order to have the time to mold students'

TABLE 7

Demographics of the Clergy at Times of Visitation
in Tübingen District, Selected Years, 1581–1653

Category (average)	1581 (N=27)	1586 (N=27)	1605 (N=26)	1621 (N=30)	1641 (N=24)	1653 (N=16)
Age at first ministry	24.6	24.7	23.8	23.0	26.7	26.4
Years of post-M.A. study	2.3	2.5[a]	3.0	3.4	3.8	4.0
Age at visitation	40.1	45.0	51.5	42.0	44.8	45.3
No. of children	4.8[b]	5.3	4.8	4.7	3.9	4.4

SOURCES: HStA Bü. 1285 (1605); LKA Stuttgart A1 1581, 1584II, 1586I, 1587I, 1621, 1641, 1653.
NOTE: Data are for all parish pastors in place at the time of the visitations.
[a] Datum for 1587.
[b] Datum for 1584.

minds and habits.[85] The presence of disciplinary sanctions against fornication and licentious behavior shows how difficult it was to realize a complete moratorium on the students' illicit sexuality. Since the Tübingen pastors were quick to establish moderately large families of about five children on the average (see Table 7), this attempt to regulate sexuality did not seem to have substantially hindered their eventual expression of licit adult sexuality in marriage.

The long period of education and the extensive residence of the Magister in the Stift after receiving their degrees can be explained in terms of the law of supply and demand. Since in the sixteenth and seventeenth centuries, the total number of clerical positions in the duchy remained relatively stable, there would have been only a limited number of openings at any one time for the most advanced Magister. The supply of new clergy could adjust itself most easily to meet demand by the lengthening of students' tenure in the Stift. In fact, the length of time students spent in the Stift studying theology after advancing to the master's degree increased by about two years between 1581 and 1653, probably because of a relative scarcity of openings (see Table 7). Such a lack of openings might also account for the apparently high standards the consistory could expect in its examinations for promotion.

IV

The pastors' education and the consequent orientation toward the Latin-speaking, European republic of letters tended to separate them from the particular, German-speaking culture of their parishioners. Many discussions of the boundaries between elite and popular culture, with the notable exception of Strauss's work, either assume that the peasant world was largely and relatively illiterate or are based on cases involving the linguistic and political colonization of peripheral areas by a growing centralized state.[86] Neither of these conditions existed in Württemberg. In Württemberg both the pastors and the parishioners spoke Swabian, and the school attendance rates, discussed earlier, indicate that the Württemberg peasantry was becoming increasingly literate.[87] The social distance that existed between the pastors and their parishioners was caused, first, by the pastors' predominantly urban origin and, second, by their socialization over a ten-year period as a group of learned, Latin-speaking theology students.

The elaborate educational system and the appropriation of resources to support it indicate that the Württemberg dukes conferred a definite rank and status on the pastorate in the duchy. Duke Christoph had bound the towns and districts to the financial obligations that established the system of scholarships. He had also established the Stift completely on the income of appropriated church property and had limited scholarships to education for ecclesiastical service. This preeminent role of the prince in the foundation of the educational system, along with the constant activity of the visitations—21 took place over 40 years—contributed to the strong centralized character and polity of the Württemberg church. Pastors were under the lifelong watch of the consistory, from their entry into the cloister school through their education in the Stift and during each successive promotion and transfer. Because the consistory could supervise the whole path of education, the unified and integrated system of schools guaranteed the theological and social homogeneity of the clerical order.[88] Furthermore, the urban location of the Latin schools reinforced the predominantly urban character of the Württemberg pastorate.

It is particularly interesting to surmise about the consequences of the students' long tenure in school. After spending several years of preparation in Latin schools and convent schools, the ordinands would normally matriculate at Tübingen between the ages of seventeen and eighteen. Before taking up their first post, they had from six to seven years of study in the Stift and university to complete. Although the archival sources are silent on this issue, one cannot help but wonder what motivated these young boys to bear the personal and social costs of more than fifteen years of education in preparation for the pastorate: the daily regime of the Latin school, the quasi-monastic discipline of the cloister school, the lengthy semisecluded life of the Stift, and the delay in establishing a family and household.

In addition, there existed certain economic costs: the foregone opportunities of secular careers in trade, law, and state service. Such careers might have been more financially remunerative and would not have required the extended postbaccalaureate and postmagisterial residence in the Stift. What motivated these pastoral candidates? What did they hope to gain in return for their years of educational investment? Possibly they looked forward to the intellectual status that they would obtain by being parish pastors. Maybe they understood their psychological commitment in terms of the evangelical doctrine of the calling. Andreae's fictional young Magister anticipated a comfortable material life as a respected official of the state church.

CHAPTER 3

The Material Conditions of Pastors

"In my young days I heard people say of good benefices how there were no fatter soups than those given to the gentlemen of the church."[1] Thus begins Andreae's satirical poem depicting the departure of the young, "freshly baked" theology student from Tübingen and his journey to the hinterlands, where he is to take up his first post as deacon. Expecting to find a land of wine and grain, the sixteenth-century Württemberg equivalent of the biblical land of milk and honey, the young man is shocked by the ramshackle poverty of the village and the parsonage. He asks the villagers: "Where are the wine, fruit, wood, and meadows? I never hear a good report. Sometimes I get stuck in the holes in the village street. The church tower does not please me. The clocks aren't set correctly and soon I won't be able to endure the manse. Everything was supposed to be completely different for me!"[2] When the deacon then encounters the old pastor, the old man explains the virtues of practical theology, and like Dante's Beatrice, prompts our hero to turn toward the spiritual good, in this case ministering the word of God to the needy souls of the parish. Andreae considered it uncommon for a young deacon to find a parish that would provide him with "fat soups." In fact, Andreae's poem reflects the disparity between a new deacon's expectations of material abundance and the impoverished reality of the life of a rural Württemberg pastor.[3]

An examination of the economic conditions in Tübingen and Tuttlingen districts reveals that the pastors in Württemberg in the 1560's and 1570's were not so well off as their Saxon counterparts of a few decades earlier, but apparently experienced material conditions equivalent to those of their Rhineland colleagues. Detailed income inventories survive that enable us to create a detailed picture of these conditions.[4] Between 1559 and 1580, pastoral incomes decreased markedly in Tuttlingen, and in Tübingen incomes probably only managed to keep up with the rapid inflation of the sixteenth century. Although the impact of the sixteenth-century price revolution is not easily evaluated over a twenty-year period, it has been calculated that the cumulative effect of inflation on, for example, grain prices in the sixteenth century averaged about 1.4 percent a year.[5] Given such inflation, while Württemberg pastors might have been recruited from middle-class backgrounds and, like the young Magister, might have expected benefices that would provide a comfortable living, many were disappointed by what they found.[6] Nonetheless, as noted earlier, in terms of income they were probably better off than most of their parishioners.

I

Although the Württemberg parish revenues consisted of various elements and derived from diverse sources, they generally fell into two categories: specie incomes and in-kind grain and wine revenues. The specie incomes held probably the prominent place in the aggregate revenues of the livings.[7] They came from several sources: a salary contribution from the patron, called the *corpus*; tithes; and proceeds from the sale of produce from the parish gardens, pastures, and fields or from the leasing of the same. Usually the patron would collect the large tithes, both in kind and in specie, and supplement the incumbent's income with a salary, also consisting of payments in kind and in specie.

As Table 8 shows, the specie portion of the salary was the major component of the cash revenues. While the Tuttlingen livings experienced a gross decline in their specie income, practically all the Tübingen livings received a substantial portion of their income as a salary, in kind and in specie, from their patron, who was most often either the duke of Württemberg or the prelate of Bebenhausen. The patron, or rather his agents, in turn collected the revenues or leased out the lands of the parish as they saw fit. In 1559, the salary paid by the patron provided 75 percent of the Tübingen cash revenues but only about 40 percent of the Tuttlingen specie incomes. Although the relative poverty of the Tuttlingen area plays a role here, this disparity can also in part be ascribed to the large number of Catholic

TABLE 8

Sources of Specie Income for the Clergy
in Tübingen and Tuttlingen Districts, 1559 and 1580

Income source	Tübingen district[a]				Tuttlingen district			
	1559 (N = 22)		1580 (N = 24)		1559 (N = 8)		1580 (N = 9)	
	Florins	Pct. of income	Florins	Pct. of income	Florins	Pct. of income	Florins	Pct. of income
Salary[b]	869	74.7%	776	50.3%	121	39.2%	89	34.9%
Small tithes	121	10.4	352	22.8	13	4.2	10	3.9
Hay tithes	29	2.5	157	10.2	75	24.3	84	32.9
Gardens	32	1.0	0	0.0	7	2.3	0	0.0
Fields	5	0.6	5	0.3	0	0.0	10	3.9
Pastures	138	10.5	134	8.7	64	20.7	24	9.4
Rents	4	0.3	120	7.8	12	3.9	38	14.9
Other income	0	0.0	0	0.0	17	5.5	0	0.0
TOTAL	1,198	100.0%	1,544	100.0%	309	100.0%	255	100.0%
Avg. total income	53		64		39		36	
Avg. salary	40		32		15		13	

SOURCES: LKA Stuttgart A12, no. 41, 1559 Kompetenzen and 1580 Kompetenzen.
[a] Excludes city of Tübingen clergy.
[b] The *corpus*, or contribution from the parish patron.

patrons in Tuttlingen district, who were paying very little or no salary at all. This was the case in the parishes of Tuttlingen—Neuhausen, Trossingen, and Talheim—whose patrons were respectively the bishop of Constance (on behalf of the monastery of Reichenau), the monastery of Allerheiligen, and the Constance Stift.[8] Consequently, in these parishes, as a result of the Religious Peace of Augsburg, the temporal lord, the duke of Württemberg, exercised the right to appoint evangelical clergy, and he provided for their financial maintenance.[9] In one case, the town of Villingen, the Catholic patron of the living of Tuningen, did continue to pay a salary and hence was entitled to collect the grain tithe and certain other incomes.[10] Because of their minimal salaries, the Tuttlingen pastors evidently had to rely heavily on local sources of revenue: their tithes and the land belonging to the parish living, the exploitation of which will be discussed more fully below.

The salary, paid both in specie and in kind by the ducal church administrator, derived almost exclusively from the ecclesiastical revenues and properties appropriated and secularized at the time of the Reformation and destined in principle for pious use. In Württemberg, the sequestered revenues and properties, although maintained in a church treasury separate and apart from the ducal treasury, were administered by ducal officials.[11]

Considerable disparity existed in the amount of cash revenue allotted to different parishes. In 1559 the richest benefice in Tuttlingen district, the city pastorate, took in over 65 florins in specie income. Almost half of its specie revenue came in salary from the ducal church administrator, nearly one-third from cash rents of parish lands and over one-fifth from tithes. The poorest parish in the district, Neuhausen, received less than one florin from its Catholic patron, the monastery of Allerheiligen. The incumbent earned the rest of his cash through the sale of produce from his garden, which brought in a meager three pounds ten shillings (about two and a third florins) yearly.[12] (For an explanation of Württemberg money and measures, see Appendix D.)

In contrast, the specie income of the Tübingen city pastor consisted wholly of a cash installment from the patron, the prelate of Bebenhausen, and no part of his income derived from parish glebe lands.[13] Similarly, one of the poorer livings in the district, Altdorf, received all of its income, in specie and in kind, from the patron, the same prelate of Bebenhausen.

In Tübingen district the contribution of the salary to the total specie income decreased from 75 percent in 1559 to 50 percent in 1580 (see Table 8). At the same time, as Table 8 shows, the average salary in the district decreased from 40 florins to 32 florins, although the total specie income increased from 53 florins to 64 florins. Although the 1580 income records included two new parishes, Kirchentellinsfurt and Kilchberg, these additions did not lower the average, since both had fairly substantial incomes.[14] In Tuttlingen district between 1559 and 1580, both the average total specie revenue and the average salary declined slightly. If the Württemberg clergy preferred to have their salaries increased by cash installments, as did their colleagues elsewhere in Germany, the duke and his church administrators must have been either unwilling or unable to accommodate them.[15]

Because the increases in the salary failed to keep up with inflation, pastors were forced to rely more heavily on local sources of income, both in specie and in kind, from their glebe lands and tithes. As Table 8 indicates, the small tithe, the hay tithe, and pasture income in Tübingen district and the hay tithe in Tuttlingen district made large contributions to the specie revenues after the salary. Often the pastor collected the tithes himself. In 1559, the visitor reported that the Tuttlingen city pastor "himself collected each year the fruit, hay, and hemp tithes" that contributed "hay tithe—15 pounds or 10 florins and hemp tithe—4 pounds."[16] Often, however, the tithe would be leased out, as in Neuhausen in 1559, where after all costs the tithe was 354 hectoliters of either sort of grain.[17] Moreover, the tithes collected as specie increased in Tübingen district in 1580, with the small tithe increasing almost threefold and the hay tithe over five-fold. This increase might be related to the trend toward increased taxation in Württemberg during the sixteenth century.[18] These increases were probably accomplished through the more systematic collection of old tithes rather than through the imposition of new ones. Tuttlingen district, in contrast, did not experience any substantial increase in its hay tithe, and the small tithe actually decreased.

We can be fairly certain that the relative abundance of the small tithe in Tübingen, which contributed 10 percent of the specie income in 1559 and over 20 percent in 1580, can be attributed directly to the richness of the soils. In contrast, in Tuttlingen, which was an upland area with a shorter growing season, the hay tithe provided the most important cash contribution after the salary, bringing in 24 percent of the total specie income in 1559 and 33 percent in 1580.

Martin Hasselhorn, apparently unaware of the long history behind this process of the conversion of incomes in land to specie incomes, notes that in the eighteenth century the pastors who collected their own small tithes enjoyed a higher income than those who leased them out: "In the eighteenth century, the small tithe protected the benefices of Württemberg from general impoverishment."[19] Similar conditions must have already existed in the post-Reformation church in Württemberg. In fact, a pastor's diary from the 1570's shows that a pastor could spend much of his time gathering rents and tithes in kind, as well as hundreds of free meals.[20]

As Table 8 shows, the gardens adjacent to the parsonages made only a very modest contribution to the specie income. In 1559, the income records reported pastors' gardens in Tübingen district in more than one-half of the parishes (12 out of 22). These gardens varied in size, from about 1,200 square meters to about 4,700. The Kilchberg and Pfäffingen parsonages were blessed with vineyards. In most cases, the pastor's household consumed the produce of the parsonage garden. The produce could be sold, however, or the garden rented out for cash. Five of Tübingen district gardens were leased out, yielding on the average 1.13 florins for each, while the remainder were used by the incumbents themselves, yielding on the average 3.3 florins of specie income for each. Three parishes collected revenues deriving from their gardens: Altdorf (3.3 florins), Weil im Schönbuch (0.33 florins), and Pfäffingen (0.66 florins and 288 liters of wine from a vineyard).

The 1580 income records for Tübingen district report the existence of gardens and describe their sizes in two-thirds of the parishes, six of which were orchards. Again the size varied from 0.18 hectares to 0.36 hectares. The especially abundant vineyard attached to the living of Breitenholz yielded 5.9 hectoliters of wine a year. The 1580 income records offer little information on the incomes brought in by the gardens, reporting only that the Breitenholz vineyard once again contributed 5.9 hectoliters of wine.

The gardens in Tuttlingen district were somewhat larger. The city parish had a substantial garden of 31.5 ares, and Trossingen of 0.71 hectares. In 1559, the city pastor raised four and two-thirds florins from his garden, while the pastor of Neuhausen brought in two florins. In most cases, though, the produce of the gardens seems to have been consumed by the pastors' households. Öfingen had the smallest garden, with only two Viertel (0.24 hectares). In 1580, only the large Tuttlingen garden is described. The 1580 income records have little to offer concerning incomes from gardens. They are silent concerning gardens other than the one belonging to the city parish.

In 1533, the Wittenberg reformer Justas Jonas suggested that 50 florins should be the minimum annual income necessary to support a Saxon country pastor.[21] Before the Reformation in Württemberg, while the average income of the Tübingen livings was well above this level, 30 percent of the livings had incomes that were equal to or less than this amount. By 1559, the average specie income alone had risen to 53 florins, and only 14 percent of the parishes had a specie income of less than 50 florins. This increase during the first decades of the Württemberg Reformation demonstrates the apparent initial success of the Württemberg dukes in rationalizing and improving clerical incomes.[22] Such growth, however, did not continue in the latter half of the sixteenth century.

Table 8 summarizes the trends in specie incomes between 1559 and 1580. Tübingen district, with its relatively dense population, fertile soil, and vineyards, was substantially richer in specie incomes than the rather thinly populated and isolated Tuttlingen district. In 1559, the average specie income of a Tübingen parish was over one-third greater than that of a Tuttlingen parish. During the next two decades, this disparity increased so that in 1580, the average total cash incomes in Tübingen were three-quarters greater than those in Tuttlingen. The disparity between the two districts shows itself in the range of incomes. In Tübingen district, excluding the rather well paid city clergy, the specie incomes ranged from a low of 25 florins to a high of 130 florins, while in Tuttlingen district, including the city pastor, specie incomes ranged from 2.3 florins to 60 florins.

Although the Tübingen pastors appear to have faced decreasing incomes after 1559, in 1580 they were still better off than their counterparts in the Rhinelands, who, on the average, received 11.5 florins to 18.5 florins a year.[23] Benefiting from the combined resources of the Stift, the Bebenhausen cloister, and the ducal administrator, Tübingen district appears to have started from a position of relative affluence but subsequently declined. Apparently, pastors were unable or unwilling to manage or collect their agricultural revenues, and the duke was unable to make up the shortfall. In contrast, the Tuttlingen livings were as impoverished as those found by Vogler, the average specie salary in Tuttlingen being 15 florins in 1559 and declining to 13 florins in 1580, which reflects the relative lack of resources in this peripheral district. Vogler also found such regional differentiations. In 1560, the district of Bergzabern was affluent, with an average specie income per parish of 33 florins; in contrast, the northwest mountain and plateau districts had an average specie income of 24 florins, and Zwei Brücken had a meager 11 florins.[24] Any consideration of the overall material status of the clergy must consider this diversity in incomes both within a district and between districts.

The same diversity also appears in the revenues received in kind: grain, vegetables, and, in Tübingen, wine. Of the grains, the pastors received spelt and oats most often and rye occasionally. As Table 9 shows, in 1559 the Tübingen parishes received on the average 58.5

TABLE 9

*Average Income in Kind: Wine and Grain
in Tübingen and Tuttlingen Districts, 1559 and 1580*

(in hectoliters)

In-kind income	Tübingen district			Tuttlingen district		
	1559	1580	Net pct. change	1559	1580	Net pct. change
Spelt	58.5	51.4	− 12.1%	63.8	45.7	− 28.3%
Oats	25.5	21.3	− 16.7	38.1	29.8	− 21.9
Wine	5.9	8.8	50.0	0.0	0.0	0.0

SOURCES: Same as for Table 8.
NOTE: Excludes category of miscellaneous (*beiderlei*) grain.

hectoliters of spelt and 5.9 hectoliters of wine. Although the Tuttlingen parishes received about the same quantities of grain, they received no wine at all. The lack of wine would have been quite a disadvantage, since wine not only served as an everyday beverage but also was required for the celebration of communion. As an old church canon states, "The church thirsts not for blood but for wine." According to an estimate from the eighteenth century, a pastor's household alone could consume as much as two Eimer, or about 6 hectoliters a year.[25] By 1580, except for the Tübingen wine income, which increased by 50 percent, total incomes in kind, in both Tübingen and Tuttlingen decreased by about one-fourth. In Tuttlingen, the parishes lost on the average as much as 28 percent of their income in spelt. The slight increase in Tübingen specie income could not have compensated for the decline in grain incomes. The specie income of Tuttlingen district pastors actually decreased. The economic conditions of pastors suffered a decline in the last half of the sixteenth century.

At the end of the eighteenth century, the Stuttgart consistory complained that the tithe had become an eternal source of unholy conflict between pastors and parishioners.[26] Elsewhere in the Empire during the sixteenth and seventeenth centuries, pastors complained of being completely cheated out of their tithes and of receiving inferior grain.[27] However, the investigation of the protocols recovered very few cases of tithe disputes in our sampled areas. During the 40-year period from 1581 to 1621, there were only five complaints by parishioners or pastors concerning troubles with the collection of parish incomes. In 1605, for example, the pastor of Mähringen pointedly observed that the filial church of Yetenbruch was withholding its tithe.[28]

The relatively few cases of tithe withholding that appear in the Tübingen and Tuttlingen protocols appear to have arisen out of ill will toward particular pastors. In 1590, Martin Kärner, pastor of Trossingen, complained that the parishioners were paying the small tithe dishonestly and not giving him the fruit, turnips, onions, and other vegetables to which he was entitled.[29] The consistory recommended that Kärner consult with his superintendent concerning the matter. Subsequently, the consistory transferred Kärner to the city pastorate in Tuttlingen and advised his successor to give prompt notice if he encountered similar problems. In the years following, the Trossingen villagers exhibited an exemplary church life, and there were no further complaints concerning tithes. Kärner seems to have been the focus of some unnamed conflict in the parish, for once he was gone, no indication of problems appears in the record.[30]

II

Apart from the supplements from outside sources, how important to pastoral incomes was the direct exploitation of the glebe lands? Small salaries and ever-changing economic conditions forced the pastors to exploit the agricultural resources of their livings. While the sons of rural pastors would have had the experience of managing farms if not of actual farming, it is not clear how much agricultural experiences pastors from the towns might have had, although, as was true throughout Europe, the connections and interrelations between town and country were very strong in Württemberg.[31] Nonetheless, the students' experience and knowledge of farming and farm management must have been weakened by their long sojourn in boarding schools.

Although there is some disagreement over the extent of the pastors' involvement in tilling the soil and tending livestock—a point addressed later in this section—the incomes derived from the economic exploitation of the glebe lands (*Widumb, Wittum,* or *Widem*) and from the various revenues in kind were very important. In 1559, revenues from the pastors' gardens, fields, and pastures provided 13 percent of their specie income and 36 percent of their grain income in Tübingen district; 23 percent of their specie income and 19 per-

TABLE 10

Percentage of Total Income (Specie and Grain)
Derived from Fields, Gardens, and Pastures
in Tübingen and Tuttlingen Districts, 1559 and 1580

	Tübingen district		Tuttlingen district	
	1559	1580	1559	1580
Pct. of specie income	12.9%	9.0%	23.0%	13.3%
Pct. of grain income	36.0	6.0	19.0	26.0

SOURCES: Same as for Table 8.

cent of their grain income in Tuttlingen district (see Table 10). These revenues in kind, unlike the rather inflexible specie portion of the salaries paid by the patron, were relatively resistant to inflation, since they could be sold at market rate.[32]

Farming, or perhaps more accurately, the management of a farm, must have been very important to the Tuttlingen clergy. But by 1580 they had experienced a setback. Not only did their total specie income decrease significantly but the average area of their glebe lands also decreased, by over 50 percent (see Table 11) and consequently their total grain income decreased. There is no apparent reason for the decrease in area. Had the land been leased out, it would still have been inventoried, and had it been sold, the pastor should have received some kind of supplement to his salary.

In the Württemberg districts under investigation, great regional disparity existed in the productivity of the glebe lands. Although in 1559 the Tuttlingen pastors had on the average ten times more arable fields and almost four times more pastureland than their Tübingen counterparts (see Table 11), the revenue from their own fields was less than twice that in Tübingen, and the revenue from their pasturelands was less than three times that in Tübingen (Table 12). Further, the Tuttlingen pastors depended more on the exploitation of their lands than the Tübingen pastors did (see Table 10).

The size of the glebe lands can also give a rough indication of the economic status of the pastors in the village community. In 1559, the clergy had the use of arable fields and pastures comparable in size to the land owned by the comfortable peasants in 1545. The comfortable peasants with property assessed at 301 florins to 500 florins, possessed over 3.1 hectares (10 Morgen) of fields and pastures. The

TABLE 11

Average Area of Glebe Lands: Fields and Pastures
in Tübingen and Tuttlingen Districts, 1559 and 1580
(in hectares)

	Tübingen district		Tuttlingen district	
	1559 (N = 22)	1580 (N = 24)	1559 (N = 8)	1580 (N = 9)
Fields	1.5	1.2	15.1	6.0
Pastures	1.1	0.94	4.1	2.0

SOURCES: Same as for Table 8.

very rich peasants, who owned property worth over 500 florins, 4.7 hectares to 6.3 hectares (15 Morgen to 20 Morgen) of land. From this latter group of peasants came the ranks of village-office holders, the Schultheissen, court members, and village council members.[33]

While the Tuttlingen glebe lands decreased in size between 1559 and 1580, the Tübingen district livings experienced no great reductions in glebe land (see Table 11). Between 1559 and 1580, the Tübingen clergy's specie income from their own lands increased slightly, from 13 percent to 8 percent of their total specie income, while their grain income from the glebe acreage, although increased by over 0.9 hectoliters, decreased as a percentage of their total grain income, from 36 percent to 6 percent (see Table 10). While only the most affluent of the Tübingen district livings would probably have provided Andreae's young Magister his "fat soups," on the average the Tübingen clergy were much better off than their Tuttlingen colleagues.

The disparity between the highest and the lowest incomes within and between districts suggests that the pastoral estate was somewhat stratified in terms of income if not also status. Some pastors clearly were better off than others. In 1580, the average Tuttlingen district pastor received in specie income only slightly more than half of what his Tübingen counterpart got (see Table 10).[34] Nonetheless, the mediocre economic conditions of the rural Württemberg pastorate should not be overemphasized. Although the material circumstances of the Württemberg clergy did not keep up with the sixteenth-century inflation rates and did not match the expectations of Tübingen theology graduates, the pastors were certainly much better off than the urban and rural poor and probably received a greater annual income than all but the richest of their flock.[35]

TABLE 12

Average Income from Glebe Lands: Fields and Pastures in Tübingen and Tuttlingen Districts, 1559 and 1580

	Tübingen district		Tuttlingen district	
	1559 (N = 22)	1580 (N = 24)	1559 (N = 8)	1580 (N = 9)
Fields (hectoliters)	10.8	4.6	19.3	20.4
Pastures (florins)	6.1	6.0	17.9	3.3

SOURCES: Same as for Table 8.

The 1559 income records provide some indications about the proportion of glebe lands that were rented out. In 1559 in Tübingen district only a minority (18 percent) of the pastors were using their glebe fields, and the majority (59 percent) were leasing either all or part of their acreage. The fields used by the pastors were often quite modest in size, ranging from 0.36 to 0.95 hectares and averaging about 71 ares. In contrast, the pastors leased out on the average about 1.89 hectares of cultivated land.

A larger number of Tübingen pastors made use of their pastureland. In 1559, 54 percent of the clergy were using the pastures while 36 percent chose to lease out their pastures. When they did opt to use rather than lease their pastures, they tended to use all of it, and the average size of the leased pastureland (1.99 hectares) was 7 percent greater than the average size of the pastureland they used (1.85 hectares). The reason that a pastor was likely to use all of his pastureland was either his desire to pasture his own livestock or, more likely, his need to achieve an economy of scale in the harvesting of hay and straw. For example, the living of Bodelshausen had a relatively large amount of pastureland, measuring 3.78 hectares in 1559. This land yielded an abundant nine wagons of hay valued at 1.23 florins each and four wagons of hay valued at 1.43 florins each, totaling 16.8 florins. But each year the pastor had to pay out about 5.6 florins for haying and driving wages, which left him only 11.2 florins after expenses.[36] Thus, expenses consumed about one-third of his harvest revenues.

In Tuttlingen district, the fact that a greater proportion of the pastors were using their glebe lands reflects their greater dependence on local sources of income. In 1559, 50 percent were using at least part of their fields, while 75 percent were leasing all or part. Given the prominence of stock farming in Tuttlingen district, it is not surprising to discover that most (63 percent) of the pastors were using their pasturelands and only a minority (38 percent) were leasing them out.

The pastors commonly leased out the glebe lands for a rent over and above costs. Yet when the pastor himself absorbed the costs of cultivation, as sometimes was the case, either he or his servant had to be farming the glebe lands.[37] It is quite possible too that while it was considered respectable for a pastor to engage in livestock raising, actual dirt farming was considered ungentlemanly. Possible motives encouraging the pastors to keep their pastures could have been the comparatively smaller degree of economic risk involved and the greater return promised by raising livestock.

Regional studies disagree on the extent to which German Protestant pastors were personally involved in farming.[38] This question is significant because of a crucial status distinction in early modern society between those who did and those who did not work with their own hands.[39] The nature of the pastor's participation in farming could influence his relationship with the villagers. Württemberg clerical authorities believed that divorcing the pastor from the land made for a better and more professional minister by increasing his time for study, the preparation of sermons, and the spiritual care of his parishioners and by minimizing the opportunities for disputes between the incumbent and his flock over tithes and rents, which led to social friction and resentment. However, it is likely that in the long term the movement toward cash salaries increased the social and mental distance between the congregation and the pastor, for the clergyman no longer held an economic position analogous to that of the richest peasant landholders.

The authorities' opposition to the pastors' farming was expressed by a visitor in 1559: he opposed their farming because it adversely affected their studies and their ability to fulfill "office and ministry," and approved of their leasing out the glebe lands instead.[40] Similarly, in Schwenningen the pastor and the visitor agreed that by leasing out the glebe lands the pastor could better perform his church ministry than if he farmed it himself.[41] Such complaints about the pastors' cultivation of the glebe lands are intelligible only if the pastors were themselves working them, since there would have been no basis for objection if the work was done by the pastors' servants or hired day laborers. The inspectors had similar objections about the pastors' collecting tithes. They advocated the leasing out of the tithe for a fixed portion of grain because "that then would be more useful to a pastor and more fruitful to his studies."[42] The evidence, therefore, suggests two points. First, some pastors were working their own lands. Many newly ordained rural pastors, dealing with modest salaries and difficult economic conditions, must have been forced to exploit the agricultural resources of their parish lands regardless of past experience with farming. Second, the complaints reveal the strong desire of the authorities to maintain the ideal of the learned pastor whose prime mission was the ministry of the word, requiring long hours of study and sermon preparation.

Contemporary literary evidence from Württemberg suggests that pastors in the Württemberg countryside actively managed their own fields and their collection of tithes in kind. In Andreae's versified practical theology, the new deacon, whose constant refrain is his desire for a parish where "the wine is as abundant as water and the grain is as plentiful as sand," is shocked when he encounters the old incumbent pastor walking through the pastureland with a measuring rod.[43] What the pastor perceives as an important source of revenue the naive deacon sees as simply a beautiful meadow: "Meanwhile, I walked through the green grass because it was in a beautiful meadow valley. There I met an old man . . . who went through the grass with a measuring rod. Since he looked like a pastor, he probably should not have been doing much at all."[44] The pastor's involvement with manual labor offends the deacon's sensibilities. The young man thinks that the pastor should be appreciating art rather than toiling to extract from nature his daily bread: "Indeed, I should have said that you torment yourself with rough work . . . when you probably indeed would prefer to carry an art book."[45]

The deacon presumes to instruct the incumbent in behavior more becoming to his station: "Thereupon I had to place the man on record and once again lead him to school."[46] After a polite exchange of Latin greetings, the old pastor explains his actions with some vexation and a touch of facetiousness: "My lord. . . . I count the grass so that no little blade gets away from me."[47] Because he is owed a tithe from this field and is concerned about possible cheating, he is estimating the probable amount that the harvest will yield.

The new deacon attempts in vain to impress his elder with his university learning. The incumbent pastor, responding somewhat mockingly, gives thanks for his own university professors, but points out that the university did not prepare him to bring forth fruit from the ground by the sweat of his brow: "I thank them for their good teaching. Yet when I came to this place, I had to learn many other things: to break hulls and to get the kernel out with bitter sweat. You shall learn that too some day."[48] The pastor is referring to the threshing of spelt. Spelt, unlike wheat, has a hull that must be removed, and it requires a two-step threshing process. The first step involves separating the grain from the chaff, and the second, separating the hull from the kernel.[49] The incumbent's narration of the economic hardships of a country pastor serves as the prologue to a discussion of the path that eventually leads to true practical theology.

Two important points can be drawn from this story. The material conditions of the typical country parish fell well below the expectations of many candidates fresh from the university. And country pastors, in the experience of Andreae and his readers, participated in the threshing of grain, acquired from tithes in kind and glebe lands, and were concerned about cheating on tithes.

The elder incumbent in Andreae's poem stresses the necessity of farmwork to the young Magister. What exactly did such work entail? A pastor's diary from the late sixteenth century provides a unique insight into the life of a Protestant minister. Thomas Wirsing, an evidently prosperous pastor from Dinkelsbühl, in nearby Franconia, kept a journal recording his day-to-day social and economic activities.[50] During the two months that have been sampled, January and June 1573, Wirsing left the major burden of the farmwork to his servant, Bartel, who was sometimes assisted by various unnamed boys (*Buben*), or hired day laborers. On occasion, some of these day laborers were girls. Wirsing apparently took a largely administrative role in the running of the farm. He would send Bartel off to work while he attended to sundry items of business: making pastoral and social visits, collecting tithes, drinking and eating with friends and various in-laws. A great portion of his time was consumed in litigation, for the Catholic canons of Augsburg cathedral were pressing their claim to the patronage of his living. Apart from his performing the occasional baptism or wedding, there is a conspicuous dearth of references to the more common church functions, such as the Sunday preaching service, the celebration of communion, the visitation of the sick. This might be a result of his apparent desire to keep the journal a business record of expenses, revenues, appointments, letters, travels, and law suits, rather than the result of any actual neglect of his pastoral duties.

Wirsing would assist Bartel in the farmwork only when a particularly large task was at hand. In January, he and Bartel spent the whole morning working side by side collecting and then winnowing a tithe portion of 18 hectoliters of oats.[51] On one occasion, Wirsing and his servant worked together to shoe three horses.[52] And Wirsing once brought morning soup to Bartel while the latter was mowing hay fields.[53] In general, though, Wirsing's involvement in the actual working of the land seems to have been limited to the oversight of Bartel's activities and the time-consuming accounting and collecting of various tithes and incomes attached to his living.

III

By the end of our period, the perceived poverty of the Württemberg pastors exemplified the proverb "Pastors bequeath only books and children." Revenues in Württemberg grew at a relatively slow rate. In Tübingen district, total pastoral revenues increased from about 1,200 florins in 1559 to 1,544 florins in 1580.[54] This increase of over 28 percent would have enabled only those pastors at the upper end of the revenue scale to keep ahead of the rapid rise in prices;[55] the average pastor would have watched his revenues slowly erode in the face of inflation. Reportedly, after the increases in specie salary in 1581, there were no substantial alterations in specie salary until the great revisions of 1814.[56]

The visitors who inspected and inventoried the revenues acknowledged the apparent modesty of the pastors' resources. In Tuttlingen district in 1559, although the living of Öfingen had an above average salary consisting of 60 florins, 71 hectoliters of spelt, and 35.3 hectoliters of oats, the inspector noted that "with such a salary, even with the glebe lands and the garden fully cultivated, not much will remain after the farming costs."[57] An example from Tübingen district further serves to underline the lack of income growth in the sixteenth century. In 1559, the pastor of Lustnau received as salary 53 florins, 21.2 hectoliters of spelt, 18 hectoliters of rye, 18 hectoliters of oats, and a little over 12 hectoliters of wine. In addition he received over 9 florins from the leasing out of the glebe fields and pastures. Two decades later the total income remained almost unchanged. The pastor collected 54 florins from his salary, rents, and tithes, 24.4 hectoliters of spelt, 18 hectoliters of rye, 18 hectoliters of oats, and 12.9 hectoliters of wine.

The apparent poverty of the pastors should be placed in a larger context. The pastors could see themselves as impoverished because they left behind only books and children and were apparently unable to buy and bequeath land. Also, their annual incomes failed to keep up with inflation. But, as noted earlier, the pastors were better off economically than most of their parishioners. The average specie income in Tübingen district of 64 florins in 1580 represents a capital of 1,280 florins at a 5 percent rate of return. Such an income would rank the average pastor with the richest group of landholding peasants, who owned land worth 1,000 florins or more.[58]

A comparison of three late-sixteenth-century household budgets from outside our sampled districts will underline this point. A Rhineland pastor, Michael Formicarius von Hunspach held a living that in 1601 received annually a salary consisting of 44.5 florins in specie and an additional 34 florins' worth of rye, totaling 78.5 florins.[59] Formicarius's total specie salary of 78.5 florins is comparable to the average specie salary in Tübingen district: 64 florins. His household income and expenses are summarized in Table 13. Other expenditures, not included in the table, are outlays for shoes, day laborers, carters, books, and alms. Since his budget showed a deficit, Formicarius complained that he never had any ready money. He also claimed that he had to borrow or sell grain at a poor price to get a penny: "Concerning money, coins never come into my money pouch or remain there overnight, for I have to borrow during the whole year."[60] In addition, although he was provided with a tithe in hay and straw, his parishioners cheated him with a product poor in quality by reaping the plants too soon in order to obtain a more bountiful and tithe-exempt second growth, so he had to purchase these items himself.[61]

Although Formicarius might have felt constrained by his income, his consumption pattern indicates a comfortable level of affluence.

TABLE 13
A Rhineland Pastor's Budget, 1601

Income		Expenses	
	SPECIE (IN FLORINS)		
Salary	44.5	Clothing	40
Sales of 16.5 Malter of rye	34	Meat	30
		Wood	8
		Servant	3
		Salt	3
TOTAL	78.5		84
	IN KIND		
Rye	46.5 Malter	Rye:	
		Sold	16.5 Malter
		Made into bread	26 Malter
		Used for animal feed and shepherd's salary	4 Malter
Spelt	3 Malter	Spelt consumed by household	3 Malter
Wine	2–4 Ohmer	Wine consumed by household	2–4 Ohmer

SOURCE: Tabulated from Vogler, *Le clergé*, p. 185. See the table of measures in Appendix D.

Most of his income was spent on items that were not necessities. Forty-eight percent of his expenditures were for clothing and 36 percent were for meat. In addition, he received enough grain to satisfy his household's consumption with sufficient surplus to sell. In contrast, a mason's family of five people in late-sixteenth-century Antwerp devoted 10 percent of its outlays to clothing and 22.6 percent to meat and animal products.[62] And the sixteenth-century chronicler of the small South German town of Überlingen provides us with a budget for a middling, town-dwelling household consisting of husband, wife, and maid. This household spent only 6.2 percent of its outlays on clothing and 18 percent on meat.[63] Formicarius's proportionally large expenditures on clothing and food reveal that his household was relatively well off. Since his income was comparable to that of the average Tübingen pastor, the Tübingen pastors were probably also better off than the Antwerp mason and the Überlingen townsman.

The relationship of the pastors to their glebe lands appears to have undergone change in the second half of the sixteenth century. The revenues derived from the glebe lands were important in both districts. However, the movement toward the professionalization of the pastors through the conversion of revenues into predominantly cash salaries did not proceed rapidly.[64] Thus in the comparatively prosperous Tübingen district, the actual proportional contribution of the salary to the specie revenues decreased between 1559 and 1580 from 75 percent to 50 percent. Although the income records show that the church authorities attempted to put an end to the practice of pastors' farming their own lands, the sixteenth-century pastors were not yet the gentlemen rentiers they became in the eighteenth century.[65]

The Württemberg pastors were trained to serve in parishes. After completing their studies and passing the ordination examination, most candidates had to leave the university town and take up a post in a rural parish. The rapid inflation of the sixteenth century coupled with the Württemberg state's inability to sufficiently increase cash salaries forced pastors to rely on their most dependable source of income, the land attached to their livings and their small tithes of grain and other produce. They managed their glebe lands, hired day laborers, supervised their servants, collected tithes and rents, took precautions against cheating, participated in the threshing, and cultivated their orchards and gardens.

While the pastor was distinct from his parishioners because of his social origin, his education, and his geographic origin, his role as a farmer could perhaps have served to integrate him into the economic life of the community. But his role as a collector of tithes could easily have offset this effect. Thomas Wirsing probably represents a typical country pastor. He acted as a part-time farmer, part-time preacher and physician of souls, and full-time manager of his revenues and tithes. While the clergy were members of a profession associated with the Ehrbarkeit, consideration of the disparities of wealth and status among the pastors, of the deteriorating incomes of the rural pastors, and of the persistence of some in farming their own glebe lands must qualify any straightforward identification of the pastoral estate with a rising early-modern bourgeoisie. Nonetheless, the pastors in Tübingen district, who received average or above average salaries and had claim to large glebe lands, must have possessed an economic status analogous at the very least to that of the comfortably-off peasant landholders. To understand more fully the role played by the Württemberg church in the local parishes, we must now turn to an analysis of popular religious practices, for only through an examination of the relationship between official church ideals and lay religious practices and attitudes can we assess the nature and character of religious life in the Württemberg countryside.

CHAPTER 4

Popular Religious Practices

In recent years a small debate has erupted over the success or failure of the German Reformation in respect to its impact on the lives of ordinary parishioners.[1] Both sides of this debate have used visitation protocols as evidence for this arguments. The following discussion will attempt to avoid the language of success and failure in an effort to assess conditions in the parishes in terms of the sentiments voiced in the protocols both by the clerical officials conducting the investigations and by the villagers who appear in the records as plaintiffs and defendants. The argument focuses on four aspects of public religious life: the nature and extent of the practice of healing and magic, attendance at various church services, the social importance of the communion service, and the complaints of parishioners themselves.

Although the number of cases of magic in the sampled districts is relatively small, we begin by analyzing the visitation complaints about these illicit practices because the practice of magic and witchcraft has been used by historians as an important indicator of the level of Protestant lay piety. The visitation commissions heard complaints and initiated sanctions against three types of magical practices: magical healing or charming (*Segensprechen*), soothsaying (*Wahrsagen*), and magic *(Zaubern)*. The categories were not mutually exclusive, for sometimes a person could be accused of magic for practicing healing. When all the complaints about church life that occur in the protocols are tabulated for the five-year period 1601–5, cases concerning healing, soothsaying, and magic constitute only 3 percent of the total. This rate parallels the rate in late Reformation Strasbourg from 1555 to 1580: the occurrence of magical

TABLE 14

Complaints About Church Life and Religious Discipline in
Visitation Reports in Tübingen and Tuttlingen Districts, 1601–1605

Reported complaints and causes of disciplinary action	No.	Pct.
Sexual mores and family life	69	30%
Complaints against magistrates	33	14
Marriages with Roman Catholics	27	12
Bad householders	18	8
Drunkenness, profligacy	18	8
Attendance at church and communion	11	5
Transgression of Sunday observance	9	4
Cursing, swearing, slander	7	3
Folk healing, blessing, magic	6	3
Dancing	5	2
Complaints against members of the morals court	4	2
Blasphemy	2	1
Miscellaneous	20	9
TOTAL	229	100%

SOURCES: HStA Bü. 1282 (1601), 1283 (1602), 1284 (1603), 1285 (1605).

practices there was comparatively infrequent.[2] Similarly, in Württemberg, healing and magic cases were among the most infrequently noted types of religious deviance, occurring about as often as improper or illegal public dancing but less often than breaches of the Sunday observance (see Table 14). Of course, we need to distinguish the frequency of complaints from the actual rate of occurrence of these practices and customs among Württemberg peasantry and townspeople, a statistic that probably cannot be recovered. The reports do, however, reveal the official perception of religious and moral behavior as mediated through the records left behind by the visitors and the local church and secular officials. We find that most of the magic practiced is folk medicine and find no evidence of a traditional folk religion at odds with the official religion of the state church.

Although the practice of and recourse to magic was involved in only a small number of cases, the cases appear to have been widely but very thinly distributed, with more prevalence on the periphery of the duchy, in Tuttlingen district (see Table 15). In the 40-year period 1581–1621, no complaints at all about magical practices occurred in 79 percent of the Tübingen district parishes and in 27 percent of the Tuttlingen district parishes. Where complaints did occur,

TABLE 15

Geographic Distribution of Cases Involving
Folk Healing, Blessing, and Magic, 1581–1621

Tübingen district		Tuttlingen district	
Parish	No. of cases	Parish	No. of cases
Tübingen city	3	Tuttlingen city	3
Walddorf	1	Tuningen	3
Öschingen	1	Schwenningen	3
Kilchberg	1	Trossingen	2
Oferdingen*a*	1	Talheim	2
Nehren	2		
Mössingen	1		
TOTAL	10		13
Pct. of total	43%		57%

SOURCES: LKA Stuttgart A1 1581, 1582, 1583I, 1583II, 1584I, 1584II, 1585I, 1585II, 1586I, 1586II, 1587I, 1587II, 1588I, 1588II, 1589, 1590, 1621; HStA Bü. 1282 (1601), 1283 (1602), 1284 (1603), 1285 (1605), 1325 (1601, 1602, 1603, 1605), 1327 (1601), 1328 (1602), 1329 (1603), 1330 (1605).

NOTE: Twenty-one percent of the parishes in Tübingen district and 63 percent of the parishes in Tuttlingen district recorded at least one case during this period.

a A citizen of Oferdingen was accused in the Adelberg visitation. LKA Stuttgart A1 1584I fol. 12*v*.

they generally involved only a small number of people. In one instance alone the visitors find "superstitions and consultations of magicians" to be "very common"; here they suggest that the local magistrates' unwillingness or inability to punish the offenders was at fault.[3]

Although the frontier district of Tuttlingen had one-third the number of parishes and less than one-fourth the population of Tübingen district, almost one-third more cases occurred there.[4] Within each of the two districts there appears to have been no clear-cut pattern to the geographic distribution of the cases. In some cases, though, interconfessional boundaries played a role: on occasion, Protestants would consult healers or soothsayers in Catholic parishes, and in a few cases "strangers," most likely itinerant Catholics, appeared in evangelical parishes to practice their healing arts.[5] Those Protestants who consulted these healers would be accused and investigated during the visitation.

Although the period of our study coincides with the era of widespread interest in demonology and the infamous European witch craze, in our two districts there were no reported cases of witchcraft involving a compact with demonic powers, apparently none resulting in the capital punishment of witches, and only two involving magic that allegedly did physical harm. One finding from our admittedly small sample contrasts significantly with what one would expect given the results of other research.[6] In these two districts the great majority (70 percent) of those accused of magical practices were men (see Table 16). Since we are dealing here with accusations rather than prosecutions, it is likely that the predominance of women in the trials and executions of the sixteenth and seventeenth centuries can be attributed to the greater ability of men to escape prosecution by the courts and the administration of justice because of their higher status.

Among our small group of accused healers and magicians, the occupational groups mentioned most often are those connected to the livestock trade.[7] The seasonal nature of such work and its relative poverty probably increased the attraction of folk healing and magic as potentially lucrative by-employments. Jakob Honer, a shearer, received two or three florins for treating cattle with unchristian means.[8]

There appears to have been no common pattern of religious behavior among the accused. Some healers or charmers were identified as infrequent churchgoers, if not outright reprobates.[9] Others were pious and active members, like Michael Jelin, whose pastor testified that he "lives an honorable life, also attends church, and actively sings the psalms."[10] Despite the characterizations of popular religion and witchcraft as a counterculture totally at odds with orthodox religion such churchgoing "blessers" could be active and pious members of the parish.[11]

TABLE 16

Sex of Those Accused of Folk Healing, Blessing, and Magic in Tübingen and Tuttlingen Districts, 1581–1621

District	Male	Female	Unknown	Total
Tübingen	8	2	0	10
Tuttlingen	8	3	2	13
TOTAL	16	5	2	23
Pct. of cases	70%	22%	9%	100%

SOURCES: Same as for Table 15.

Most of the complaints involved practitioners of magical healing, charmers or blessers (*Segensprecher*), who treated injuries and illnesses with a combination of magic and herbalism. The inadequacies of orthodox medical services in the sixteenth and seventeenth centuries left most of the populace dependent upon traditional folk medicine.[12] The ordinances regarding midwives bear witness to the shortage in Württemberg of academically qualified medical practitioners serving the countryside. Shepherds were forbidden to tend pregnant women for the sake of "Christian discipline" and because their coarse instruments could injure or even kill the mother and child.[13] Meanwhile, citizens of the orthodox and sophisticated university town of Tübingen sought treatment from healers as well. Responding to this need, nuns from the nearby town of Poltringen would come to Tübingen on market day and enter houses and "presume to practice medicine." As a result of a visitation complaint, these nuns were forbidden to practice the "appearance of medicine" and restricted to buying and selling in the public marketplace and to taking short rests in the public inns.[14]

As in the Rhinelands, people from all social classes, both male and female, sought out the practitioners of magic.[15] One successful healing could draw in a whole new network of clients. For example, in 1587, someone advised the sick and lame Hans Baur of Öschingen to seek help from the wise woman (*Segensprecherin*) in Melchingen, almost ten kilometers distant. As Baur improved, other villagers sought out the healer for the sake of their own and their children's maladies with apparent success. The visitor reports matter of factly that "all were blessed and became well again."[16] But the results were not always so favorable, as Peter Weinman of Schwenningen discovered. One of his children, upon whose labor the economic livelihood of the family partially depended, suffered an injury that reportedly "a barber could easily have healed."[17] Weinman had the child blessed by a local healer, but the condition only worsened. Treatment was sought in the large (and Catholic) neighboring town of Villingen, apparently with little success, for at the time of the visitation, the family was receiving alms from the parish poor box.[18]

Like modern-day physicians, some healers specialized in certain maladies. Ehrat Volzecher gave blessings against male impotence and female infertility. Jakob Honer treated night diseases, especially in cattle, and Theis Burck blessed swollen joints in horses.[19] Others were general family practitioners, like Heinrich Würstlin's wife, who went around dispensing holy water as a "wholesome medicine" for all kinds of maladies.[20]

Occasionally, such healers received official license to practice, provided, of course, that they avoided all use of superstitious and magical methods. Although Michael Jelin had demonstrated to his own pastor in the parish of Walddorf that he had used only natural means to heal a boy's goiter, he was summoned to appear before the consistory in Stuttgart to be examined by a doctor of medicine in order to determine "whether he applied natural means or also used magic."[21] The doctor concluded that Jelin had used a "natural and proper treatment and medicine to drive out the goiter."[22] The consistory therefore gave him permission to continue his practice using only natural means. Jelin's healing activities ranged beyond the Tübingen district, for complaints arose five years later when he appeared in the parish of Wangen, in Canstatt district, some 22 kilometers from Walddorf.[23] Once again the consistory called him to Stuttgart for examination, but when he reminded the consistory of their earlier decision, which they confirmed by consulting the protocols, he was released from custody.

Next in frequency after healing were cases involving soothsayers and magicians, who were commonly asked to recover lost and stolen property, to discern malignant spells and cast counterspells, and to treat illnesses and injuries.[24] The magicians and soothsayers, like the blessers, were consulted by members of all social classes, including the urban and village magistracy. Maria, the wife of Michael Kienlin, a Tübingen justice and financial officer of the city hospice, introduced several people to the soothsayer in the Catholic town of Rottenburg for the purpose of "consultations."[25] In 1605, the visitors had to admonish a magistrate of Kilchberg, since he had been "running to a magician."[26]

The magicians were sometimes able to practice for years with relative impunity because of the magistrates' tacit tolerance and often because of the conflicting jurisdictions where Protestants lived alongside Catholics. For years the parishioners of Trossingen were accustomed to visit a cattle herder in the Catholic town of Villingen who had a reputation as a magician and healer. Yet, according to the visitor, the magistrates had tolerated his practice since he used primarily herbs.[27] The magician, however, exceeded the limits of tolerance and came to the notice of the visitation commission when he advised a Trossingen parishioner to take his mother, who was insane, to the village of Laussen and once there "have her sleep three nights in a monk's habit, then she will improve."[28] To the visitor this was evidence that "he did not deal with ordinary means."[29] Consequently, the consistory ordered all the magistrates in Tuttlingen district to forbid the magician the practice of medicine within their jurisdictions.[30]

In one case, a magician from a Catholic town was reportedly involved in some kind of religious enthusiasm or pre-Reformation Catholic practice. In 1588, several villagers from Talheim, including the wife of the village magistrate, were seeking counsel from a magician from Pfarra, in Fürstenburg, whom they all considered "a true prophet."[31] One woman in the group was even accused of ascending the mountain Holy Trinity, where there was reportedly a "house of idols," probably a saint's shrine.[32]

As mentioned above, despite the vogue of demonology and the witchcraft prosecutions that swept Europe in the late sixteenth and early seventeenth centuries, in the two Württemberg districts sampled there were only two cases involving magic that did any apparent harm.[33] Significantly, in neither of the cases was the technical legal term *maleficium*, "harmful magic," used. Nor were the cases involving injury associated with any of the classic characteristics of witch prosecutions. The accused were not women, and there was no mention of demonic pacts. Jakob Honer, a barber, had a diversified practice of healing humans and animals, yet he also claimed to be able to identify those women who were witches. These accusations, understandably, brought "many women into evil suspicion and mistrust."[34] In the second case, the visitor reports that there was a witch (Unhold) in the parish, who was dealt with "with charms."[35] The visitor simply rebuked her use of countermagic and took no further action.[36]

Although the visitors recognized the importance of disciplinary sanctions in suppressing magic and superstition, in practice such punishments were often quite mild and sometimes ineffective. The visitors, assisted by the local magistrates and under the authority of the consistory in Stuttgart, had at their disposal three degrees of sanctions: simple admonitions, accompanied perhaps by a public repentance; monetary fines; and imprisonment. The records are often silent about the punishments. Except for the imprisonment of Michael Jelin, most of the cases resulted in an exhortation by the visitor or the local pastor and the defendant's promise to repent. In Theis Burck's case, the pastor "had admonished him about such [blessing horses], and he had promised to give up such practices."[37] When a whole group of women in Tuttlingen used charms, the pastor admonished them and they promised improvement. The consistory reviewed the case and noted with approval: "Because they have promised improvement and recognized their wrongdoing, for the sake of this, therefore, [the investigation] has been permitted to remain at this stage."[38] But since such admonitions were not always effective, folk healers like Ehrat Volzecher of Tuningen, in Tuttlingen district, who were slow to reform themselves had to be charged by the visitor more than once.[39]

The visitors apparently viewed these instances of the practice of magic as minor misdemeanors rather than serious crimes. They desired not punishment but the moral reformation of the offenders. The repeated reliance on the spoken exhortation reveals that the church officials assumed, perhaps mistakenly, that a common ground existed between their own values and the values of the community, including those of the accused.[40] In contrast, folk healers and conjurers could only be identified, or labeled, and subsequently accused and prosecuted as witches after they had first been viewed as enemies of the moral values of the community and of the church and state. This labeling process is the key to the origins of the waves of witch prosecution in early modern Europe.

One accusation drawn from outside the sampled districts seems to have had an intraparish social conflict as its background.[41] This case concerned a marital dispute caused by the husband's suffering from a real but nonetheless inexplicable malady. In 1620, Martin Küll of Hattenhofen, in Göppingen district, was accused of magical healing, and was consequently imprisoned, for reportedly blessing cattle by baptizing them in the name of an evil spirit and marking them with blood and for allegedly causing injury through magic to other people's animals and property.

When he was again accused of blessing, on the basis of his wife's testimony, which was supported by that of certain local officials, the consistory investigated. They determined that the testimony of Küll's wife, who refused to live with him, and of the others was "in disagreement." Concerning the facts, they uncovered only that Küll experienced apoplexy and choking and concluded that the problem derived more from melancholia than imagined [witchcraft]." Considering the reports by Küll's pastor and the Schultheiss that since his jailing, Küll had lived honorably, no one had suffered injuries, and Küll had presented himself for examination and communion at Pentecost, the consistory took no action against him. They instructed Küll that if he was again struck by melancholia, he should immediately consult his pastor. Moreover, they especially commanded "his wife to cohabit with him and to keep his household in a respectable manner."[42]

This case illustrates at least three significant characteristics of the consistory. First, it shows the consistory's willingness to dismiss supernatural causes for Küll's abnormal behavior and to provide an alternative explanation, melancholia, a natural malady caused by the excess of black bile. Melancholy was included in certain witchcraft theories and was used by Württemberg courts to explain the actions of those accused of witchcraft. The development of this psychological perspective probably contributed to the decline of witchcraft as a crime in southwestern Germany.[43] Second, the case reveals the consistory's willingness to obtain the facts of a case through the inquisitorial procedure and its ability to arrive at decisions that were independent of the judgments of local authorities. Third, the case shows the consistory's recognition of the conflict between wife and husband and its desire to protect the patriarchal family by commanding the wife to return to her husband.

In sum, the practice and patronage of folk healing, soothsaying, and magic were not strongly associated with any strong alienation from the established Lutheran church. Also, very little if any witchcraft was evident. The practices do not constitute evidence of a vigorous folk religion or a religious counterculture at odds with the ideology of the Lutheran Reformation. The practices show, however, that a small number of parishioners, many of them local officeholders or their relatives, would often seek out the folk healer to treat maladies of man and beast and sometimes seek out the soothsayer for answers and magical solutions to personal, family, and business problems. The analysis of the protocols also reveals the official attitude toward magical practices. Both the relative weakness of the sanctions imposed and the willingness of officials to tolerate folk magic in these villages show that the state church did not feel threatened by such practices and was more interested in the moral reformation than the punishment of offenders.

I

While the protocols indicate that magic was practiced and used by a small minority, the most tangible manifestation of the public religious behavior of all members of a village was their attendance at the various church services. The visitors were expressly mandated to evaluate attendance of the village corporation (*Gemeinde*) and the magistrates during their investigation. Their reports often contain qualitative assessments of religious zeal in terms ranging from poor or negligent to very good. The Württemberg protocols reveal a picture of church attendance that is neither as positive as that described for Strasbourg nor as bleak as that depicted in Saxony. In many parishes the visitors found what they considered acceptable levels of attendance. They also discovered that the degree of attendance varied according to the type of service.[44]

After the Reformation, the abolition of saints' days and masses for the dead resulted in a decrease in the total number of religious services, but there remained a cycle of worship and prayer that centered on Sunday. In Württemberg, a communion service was to be held once a month on Sundays and on all feast days. On the eve of the celebration of the Lord's Supper, a vesper service and an examination of communicants took place. When there was no communion, a morning service took its place. In the towns, the morning service, usually held at seven or eight o'clock, would be followed by a second service at midday, the catechism service (*Catechismuspredigt* or *Kinderlehr*), devoted to the instruction of children, servants, and unmarried adults. The third and final Sunday service occurred at vespers, or six o'clock. There were fewer services in the villages, for after the morning service, the catechism service was held at midday.[45] During the week, two services were held in the towns, a preaching service (*Wochenpredigt*) and a service of common prayer (the *Gemeingebet* or *Litanei*), while in the villages there was only the weekday sermon.[46] Since attendance was theoretically mandatory for all, young and old alike, all townspeople were thus required to be in church five times a week and villagers three times a week. The feast day celebrations of the Lord's Supper and specially appointed days of prayer during times of war and plague occasioned yet additional services.

During the 21 visitations over a 40-year period, more often than not the visitors recorded no comment, positive or negative, about attendance at any service by magistrates and parishioners. Entries concerning attendance are found in only 8 percent of the visitation reports for Tübingen district and 38 percent for the Tuttlingen district. In most cases, then, the visitors must have encountered what they considered satisfactory levels of attendance. The greater diligence in church attendance of the Tübingen district villagers is also manifest in the fact that over the years of the visitations 52 percent of the parishes were not mentioned in any entry about church attendance whatsoever and another 32 percent were mentioned only once, while every parish in Tuttlingen district was mentioned in three or more entries about attendance. In contrast to the findings for Saxony, an admittedly larger geographic area, in neither of the two Württemberg districts was absenteeism widespread, though there were significant problems with specific services, especially in Tuttlingen.

In Württemberg, the churches were generally well attended on Sundays and holidays at the principal morning service, perhaps in a greater measure in the larger villages and in places where the magistrates set a good example. During the 1581 visitation of Tuttlingen, the visitor noted: "The citizens from Tuttlingen attend the morning sermon diligently on Sundays and holidays. . . . As churchgoers, the magistrates provide a good example for the common man, for they attend all sermons."[47] In 1605, in the village of Schwenningen, in Tuttlingen district, the parishioners were reported "to be attending church zealously" (gehn fleissig in die Kirchen) and the Vogt and the justices to be attending "the sermons with proper diligence."[48]

The common Württemberger apparently had little interest in attending the Sunday services in the afternoon and evening or the weekday worship. The 1581 report on Tuttlingen continues: "But great negligence is apparent at the other two [Sunday] services; the same also at the weekday sermon; and there is great neglect of the common prayer service."[49] In this case, the visitor's admonition resulted in a temporary improvement, for two years later, during the fall, or Michaelmas, visitation of 1583, only vespers, the third Sunday service, is reported to be poorly attended. Yet by the spring, or

TABLE 17

Negative Evaluations of Church Attendance by Type of Service in
Visitation Reports in Tübingen and Tuttlingen Districts, 1581–1621

Service evaluated	Pct. of negative evaluations	
	Tübingen district (N = 26)	Tuttlingen district (N = 62)
Unspecified	8%	26%
Principal morning	4	3
Catechism	27	50
Sunday vespers	0	5
Weekday	46	6
Communion	15	10
TOTAL	100%	100%

SOURCES: HStA Bü. 1282 (1601), 1283 (1603), 1284 (1603), 1285 (1605); LKA Stuttgart
A1 1581–90, 1621.

St. George's Day, visitation, attendance was once again negligent at
the midday service, a complaint that is repeated in 1585, 1586, and
1601.

There were pervasive problems with the midday, or catechism,
service (see Table 17), which was intended for all parishioners regardless of age or marital status.[50] Despite the continued efforts of
visitors to enforce the attendance of all adults, it was in practice a
service for the young and single, where the pastor read aloud the text
of the catechism, the Ten Commandments, the Apostles' Creed, and
the Lord's Prayer. All children were required to attend "as soon as
they might be capable of learning the same [i.e., the catechism] according to their age and understanding," which meant when they
were probably anywhere from 6 to 8 years old.[51] All adolescents, servants, and single adults up to 30 years of age were also supposed to
attend.[52] Since admission to the Lord's Supper did not end this obligation, each villager in theory was exposed to between 10 and 15
years of catechetical instruction before marriage.[53]

Although the pastors were instructed to teach in a friendly and
gracious manner in order not to frighten the catechumens away, absenteeism was common.[54] Neglect of the catechism service happened
especially when it conflicted with the working hours required by vi-
ticulture, farming, and livestock herding. In 1584, the Tübingen vine
dressers were absent because of their work, while in Tuttlingen, the

boys (*Rossbuben*) in charge of the horse and cattle herds gave frequent cause for complaint in the visitation reports.[55] They attended the morning service, but at midday "they had to be with the horses so they would not run through the grain fields."[56] Occasionally, the Rossbuben were the only group recorded as negligent in attendance, and sometimes the visitor's admonitions resulted in improvement.[57]

In the summer months, the attractions of leisure, not the necessities of labor, prompted the absence of young people from the midday service. In Tuttlingen, the adolescents found irresistible the temptation to pick berries in the surrounding mountains and to play about the houses in town. The visitor reports: "In the summer the young people seldom come to sermons; they are out picking strawberries, similarly playing about the houses."[58] In Tübingen, the young servants were so bold as to attempt "all kinds of foolishness" in the church square during the church services, which surely must have piqued the respectable burghers and clergymen.[59] Adolescent truancy from the Sunday afternoon service was such a problem in the late sixteenth and early seventeenth centuries that it prompted a whole series of decrees and ordinances prohibiting Sunday afternoon fruit picking and dancing and strictly regulating the tending of livestock on Sundays.[60] The changing social environment during the late sixteenth century must have played a role in the complaints about unruly young people. Rapid population growth put pressures on large peasant holdings, and the well-off peasants were forced to protect themselves by tightening their control over land and family resources. In Hohenlohe, the effort by the Reformation church to discipline the leisure activities of youth coincided with the desire of the substantial tenant farmers to manage the inheritance of land and the marriages of their children.[61] The relatively weak sanctions—admonitions by the pastor or the visitor and the imposition of nominal fines—were, for the most part, ineffective and probably reflect either an ambivalent attitude toward these summer pastimes of youth or a realistic cynicism about the efficacy of such sanctions.

While absenteeism from the catechism was the most frequently reported problem in the Tuttlingen district, townspeople in the city of Tübingen continually avoided the weekday service, contributing to most of the complaints regarding that service. The twice-weekly services on Tuesdays and Thursdays were held too late in the morning and too often for the herdsmen and vine growers, who needed to spend as many of the daylight hours out of town as possible. The problem was in fact so severe that the Tübingen's leading churchman, Jakob Andreae, compromised and established a new, earlier Wednesday morning service with a sermon and litany to accommodate those who had to leave early for work in the fields. This arrangement apparently met with success, for the visitor reported that "afterward . . . [the] sermon was diligently attended by the common people."[62]

The Sunday evening vespers service fell rapidly into disregard throughout Protestant Germany. The Franconian pastor Thomas Wirsing recorded in 1573 that although he held vespers, no one came.[63] In Tübingen and elsewhere, the local judicial officers were conspicuous in their absence from vespers. They attended services on Sunday mornings and during the week, but the pastor reported that "few are coming to the vesper sermon on Sundays."[64] In their defense the justices pleaded that "among them are several merchants, who are very often in other towns on Sundays, and attend church in those towns."[65] The consistory, however, was skeptical and recommended to the superintendent that "one should keep watch over this."[66]

To summarize, the protocols show that over the years evaluations of attendance were not the same for each parish during each visitation. Often the visitor made no statement, indicating presumably that the resident pastor had made no complaint about his parishioners' attendance. This underlines the necessity of investigating systematically the reports of successive visitations in order properly to evaluate the level of church attendance. The findings from the two districts of the duchy of Württemberg parallel those for the Rhinelands as well as those for England, which were presented in an analysis of parish life in seventeenth-century Wiltshire.[67] There was, judging by attendance, a general respect for the principal Sunday service, more so in Tübingen than in Tuttlingen. The midday and evening services on Sunday and the weekday services were attended with various degrees of conformity, whereas the vesper services and the weekday sermons fell into disregard, apparently because of economic pressures and the attraction of nonreligious activities.

Although we should avoid the pitfall of equating practice with faith, we should also not disavow completely the significance of outward conformity as an indicator of religious sentiment.[68] The evaluation of conformity in church attendance, while not a measure of intimate spiritual states, does reflect the signs and effects of belief as well as the practices and behavior that belief and religious values inspire. Thus, at least in these two districts, the visitors found moderate levels of attendance at the principal preaching service. In respect to this main and most important service, they did not find widespread disaffection.

II

The religious and social meaning of these evangelical services to their lay participants remains largely unexplored.[69] Theologically, the celebration of the Lord's Supper was the centerpiece of the evangelical cycle of worship, for in the sacrament of communion the promise of justification by faith was made manifest and the faith of the believers was strengthened. The *Augsburg Confession* and the *Apology* teach that the Lord's Supper is God's promise that awakens and strengthens the believer's faith. This concept, when interpreted in social terms, appears very individualistic, since it underlines the importance of the vertical relationship between the faithful and God to the possible exclusion of all other social relations.[70] "In the administration of the sacraments the Gospel is applied personally to every individual."[71]

When we turn, however, to actual late-sixteenth-century practice and the function of this sacrament in Württemberg communities, we see that many Lutheran villagers in Württemberg conceived of the evangelical celebration of the Lord's Supper as an expression of their community's social harmony. They would avoid participating in the rite when they were at enmity or involved in a dispute with members of the parish.[72] This was especially true in Tübingen district, where cases involving intraparish conflicts made up almost half of the complaints concerning absenteeism from the communion service, followed only by charges against Catholics. In the village of Walddorf, the visitor reported in 1601 that "several people did not partake of communion on account of strife."[73] In the city of Tübingen itself, women particularly seem to have refused communion when involved in small feuds with fellow townspeople. The consistory gave thanks to God when it heard that "old Sixten's wife finally received communion before her death."[74] Similarly, in 1590 the wife of Rudolf Riepp refused to attend communion because she was involved in some unnamed affair that had resulted in the imprisonment of her stepchildren.[75]

Severe disputes in a parish, which usually involved business dealings, property, or money, could easily lead to at least one party excluding himself or herself from the periodic celebration of the Lord's Supper and even from weekly worship. In 1603 in the parish of Entringen, a conflict over the propriety of Matthias Schulren's business dealings as guardian for the property of his deceased sister's children caused disagreement among the local justices. One faction induced the pastor to bring charges against the guardian. Consequently, Schulren refused to go to church, having enmity (*Grollen*) toward the pastor "because he had assisted the court of wards when they censured him, Schulren, for such selling, trading, and buying with the property of his sister's children."[76] During the visitation two years later, the same justices complained to the visitor of the pastor's interference in secular affairs, particularly the Schulren case, and the pastor complained of Schulren's long-standing absenteeism.[77] The visitor, apparently ignorant of the background of the case, prudently decided to investigate the complaint. With regard to the pastor, he discovered that "several of the justices had required such [activities] from him" and thus concluded "that all the blame lies more upon the justices than the pastor."[78] When the visitor interviewed the recusant, he evidently suspected him of crypto-Catholicism, for he asked Schulren "whether he felt anything lacking in our religion."[79] Uncovering the cause of the conflict and discovering that Schulren had, in fact, been attending sermons and communion in other parishes, the visitor proceeded to reconcile him with the pastor and restore him to the religious community.[80]

The church authorities also emphasized the significance of participation in the communion service as an expression of the confessional, social, and political unity of the community. To avoid communion was, in effect, to disobey the state.[81] The visitor to Weil im Schönbuch, reported in 1577 that Hanns Conrad Männ, a legal resident of Weil, had refused to receive communion in both Weil, his original residence and where he owned property, and in Reutlingen, where he had married and lived with his wife. He had spent all Holy Week at Weil im Schönbuch, but he had gone to no sermon and had argued against the Protestant religion whenever he met someone. Because Männ was a citizen of and property owner in Weil, the consistory ordered both the abbot and the Vogt at Bebenhausen to summon Männ for an interrogation. At this meeting, the representatives of regional secular and religious power were to remind him of his duties and admonish him with God's word. Finally, the abbot and the Vogt were to submit a written report of the meeting to the consistory.[82]

Although this complaint reveals to us very little about Männ's reasons for refusing communion, he appears to have been a Catholic and a contentious one at that. Since the visitor thought it necessary to mention twice in his report that Männ owned property in Weil im Schönbuch, it is very likely that he was a substantial property owner. His economic position and his apparent dual residence must have contributed to his ability to avoid sanctions against his refusal to attend. Finally, the case shows not only the district overlap of secular and spiritual power, namely, the involvement of both the Vogt and the abbot in Bebenhausen, but also the centralized nature of the Württemberg state church. The Vogt and the abbot could do little without the express consent of the consistory in Stuttgart.

In other cases involving Catholics, the consistory and local authorities sometimes showed themselves tolerant in the face of special, mitigating circumstances. A Catholic journeyman, Christoph Marggraf (or Marquart), lived openly for several years with his aged mother, attending preaching services diligently but always avoiding the communion services.[83] When the magistrates interrogated him in 1582, they asked him why they should tolerate him, "since he was neither a member of the university nor a citizen and demonstrated such unchristian behavior regarding the Lord's Supper."[84] Marggraf explained that his mother's death was expected daily "when God requires that she leave this vale of tears"[85] and petitioned that they have patience with him. The whole procedure repeated itself during the spring of 1583 visitation. Marggraf explained that he refrained from communion because he was a Catholic and asked the magistrates "to bear with him until his mother's death," when he would leave town.[86] This time the consistory seemed less willing to tolerate the situation much longer, for, though they left the resolution of the case in the hands of the superintendent and the magistrates in Tübingen, they recommended that "if he persists and does not want to be of our faith, he should seek opportunity elsewhere."[87] The consistory viewed participation in communion as signifying confessional solidarity. Since Marggraf identified himself as a Catholic and refused to attend communion despite the threat of sanctions, he too must have viewed communion as an indication of religious solidarity.

Marggraf must have realized his time was running short, for by the next visitation, in the following November, he married Agnes Rohr, daughter of a town councillor of Esslingen, and had begun attending communion. The visitor remarks, "It is to be hoped that he will act in a Christian manner and otherwise behave decently."[88] After his conversion and marriage, Marggraf was rapidly assimilated into the community. In 1590, he was appointed financial officer of the city hospice, and in 1596, he was elected to the magistracy as a justice.[89]

In contrast, in Tuttlingen district very few complaints involved absenteeism from communion, and none of them were caused by enmity among parishioners. Almost all of the complaints appeared in the early 1583 and 1584 visitations and involved the maintenance of the old custom of partaking of communion only at Easter. In 1583, the visitor notes that in the parish of Schwenningen the inhabitants were going to communion only at Easter time.[90] That same year in Öfingen, the visitor Erhard Schnepf reports that "there are few going to communion outside of Eastertide." Easter was the only popular communion in Öfingen again the following year and in the neighboring village of Aldingen.[91] Aldingen was somewhat exceptional in that, apart from this practice, "no complaint was brought forth or lack felt in hearing the word of God."[92] The consistory responds simply by recommending that "the pastor diligently explicate the benefit of the Lord's Supper and request them [his parishioners] to attend."[93]

Thus, although Lutheran theology emphasized the Lord's Supper as a sacrament signifying the reconciliation of the vertical relationship between God and the individual, both the church officials and the villagers could perceive communion as a symbolic expression of horizontal social and political relationships. For the villagers, the sacrament represented relationships of friendship and enmity, which in turn reflected dynamics of property and power within the village. In contrast, for the consistory and the visitors, communion represented obedience to the state and the church. Finally, if the case of

Marggraf is representative, both the church and the laypeople viewed participation in communion as a sign of confessional allegiance.

III

Lay demands on and expectations of the established church came to the forefront during the visitations to the filial churches that served small dispersed communities unable to support a resident pastor. Moreover, since these hamlets lacked resident clergy, we could reasonably expect the visitation records of these hamlets to contain evidence of lay attitudes that were relatively free from the influence of local official pressures to conform. Similarly, attitudes expressed in these protocols might be insulated from the coercive powers of political and ecclesiastical authorities and might thereby reveal a greater degree of ignorance of, indifference to, or hostility to the church.

Surprisingly, however, what appears in the sources for several, but by no means all, of the filial churches is that parishioners constantly expressed their desire for the spiritual ministrations of the church. In 1590, the inhabitants of Belsen, a filial of the village of Mössingen, nestled on the edge of the Swabian Alb, complained that the monthly sermons delivered by the pastor in their church were insufficient and requested a pastor of their own. Elaborating, they stated that sick people and pregnant women could not reach the mother church in Mössingen on Sundays because of the distance.[94] While the Belsen parish lies only a few kilometers from Mössingen, the passage involved descending a very steep grade, which was all but impassable in winter. Parochial rivalry was also undoubtedly involved here, for Belsen boasted a church dating back to the twelfth century, while Mössingen had only a late Gothic edifice. The consistory responded by ordering the pastor to preach in Belsen every fortnight, and by 1603 the practice of fortnightly sermons in summer and monthly sermons in winter seems to have been accepted without complaint.[95] Elsewhere, though, the inhabitants of filial parishes requested that services be held more often than monthly.[96]

Filial churches also felt the want of celebrations of the Lord's Supper and funeral sermons. Thomas Durnauer, the pastor of Weil im Schönbuch, who, being advanced in years and burdened with a very large parish of 700 adult communicants, was unable to serve the fi-

lial churches as they desired. In 1590, the inhabitants of Dettenhausen complained: "When someone dies in this filial, no funeral service
is performed for the deceased. Rather, the pastor remembers the de-
parted sometime in his next regular sermon. [The consistory orders:]
the pastor shall preach a funeral sermon to them in their little
church."[97] Similarly, in Reusten, filial of Breitenholz, the lack of a funeral sermon "made the inhabitants suffer terribly."[98] The consistory
dismissed the pastor's excuse that he had already invested a great
deal of time in the filial and received no more than twenty florins a
year for his trouble.[99] The inhabitants of Reusten persisted in their
petitions for better service, asking for their own pastor in practically
every visitation from 1583 to 1590.[100] Residents of the filials also desired the Lord's Supper to be celebrated within their hamlets. The filial villagers complained constantly that the Supper was not offered
in their filial.[101] When the inhabitants of the filial Dettenhausen complained, the consistory ordered the pastor to hold communion three
times a year "for the good of the old people and the pregnant
women."[102]

Not all the filials received such good reports. In Tuningen, an out-
of-the-ordinary sexual dimorphism existed, for, as the visitor reported, "the [male] inhabitants come to the sermon, but their wives
do not."[103] In the summer of 1586, while the parishioners of the
mother church of Öfingen received a good report, their counterparts
in the filials Oberbaldingen and Biesingen were picking cherries, ha-
zelnuts, and berries during the church services.[104] Yet nineteen years
later, conditions had improved, and the inhabitants of the filials
were judged to be more diligent in attendance than those of Öfingen.[105]

In Biesingen the parishioners petitioned that the pastor come to
them every fourteen days to hold a catechism service, since with so
many young people in the hamlet it was "burdensome to travel to
Öfingen."[106] The inhabitants of Reusten also manifested a desire for
the catechism service. They complained repeatedly that the increased number of musket shoots, held on Sunday afternoons at
some distance from home, prevented the militiamen from attending
the catechism service.[107] These complaints are somewhat extraordi-
nary, considering the lack of interest in the catechism exhibited by
other parishes. Possibly, the villagers were playing two institutions

of territorial power against each other by appealing to the sacred requirements of the duke's church in order to avoid the call of his secular military service.

On the other hand, the members of a mother church could complain when they felt that the pastor was giving too much attention to a filial. The parishioners of Kilchberg thought that their pastor, Primus Truber, had neglected their sermons in order to preach in the filial Bühl. They found it especially lamentable that Truber had canceled their Saturday vespers on the eve of the Festival of the Circumcision of Christ in order to examine communicants and to preach in the filial.[108] This complaint is significant, because it shows not only that some laity desired the Saturday evening vesper service, which was falling into disuse at this time, but also that the precommunion catechism examination was still taking place. Truber's diligent ministry in the filial seems, however, to have been an exception to the rule, for he received a separate income from the local lord for serving the hamlet.[109]

Insufficient revenues seem to have been the principal cause of the poor and infrequent service for the filials. There was certainly no lack of qualified pastors, for since the 1570's, the Tübingen Stift had produced a yearly surplus of educated theologians and the duchy had become, in effect, a net exporter of ministers to other evangelical territories.[110] Some pastors, indeed, cited insufficient income as the reason for their lack of attention to the filials. Peter Mendlin, pastor of Öfingen, petitioned boldly for a raise.[111] Jakob Dürr, minister in Breitenholz, took a less direct approach and complained that he received not more than twenty florins for serving the filial Reusten.[112] Dürr's request seems justified, since Reusten, with its 170 communicants and 50 children, was almost as large as the mother church of Breitenholz, with 230 communicants. The visitor acknowledged in his report the unhappiness of the situation, writing that if Reusten were to have its own pastor, as it had repeatedly requested, "an excellent Christian youth could be brought up there." The marginal comments, added during the consistory's review of the reports in Stuttgart, show that the consistory considered monthly or fortnightly sermons by the pastor of the mother church sufficient for the filial.[113] It is, however, doubtful whether pastors were generally able to meet even this minimal requirement. Weil im Schönbuch, for example, had more than 700 adult members and three filials. Only a very energetic or conscientious pastor would have been able to fulfill the many duties required of him: administering his church lands, gathering revenues and tithes, performing marriages and weddings, mediating and settling disputes, holding thrice-weekly services and monthly communion at the mother church, and preaching fortnightly and examining communicants monthly at each of the filials.

The visitations reports of the filial churches have revealed that by the end of the sixteenth century, 50 years after the introduction of the Reformation in Württemberg, the laity could have positive attitudes toward the territorial church. It is very likely that only the voices of the most pious of parishioners have been heard here. But the findings show that even in these remote areas outside the tightly knit social structure of the nucleated village, insulated by distance from the local and territorial magistrates, and without benefit of resident clergy, the laity earnestly desired the ministrations of the church. The reports also show that the laity were moderately diligent in attending the main Sunday service, although they tended to neglect many of the other services.

To summarize, evidence gathered from the 30 or so parishes comprising Tuttlingen and Tübingen districts suggests that the magic practiced in late-sixteenth-century Württemberg consisted primarily of folk healing and does not reflect a folk religion at odds with the established church. Also, although the visitors viewed magic and superstition as a nuisance, they did not necessarily perceive it as behavior that was hostile to the church. While evening and weekday services were falling into disuse, moderate levels of attendance occurred at the main Sunday morning service. Moreover, the attitudes of individual villagers are very revealing. Some parishioners had specific attachments to Protestant worship and ritual. Attendance at the communion service could express one's solidarity with other villagers. The Protestant services and rites of communion, catechism, and funerals were so important to some villagers that they complained when these events did not take place in their local church.

These findings have at least two important implications. First, they suggest the involved and intricate level at which problems concerning the historical evaluation of local religious life need to be addressed. Patterns of local and regional diversity can be recovered only by examining serial sources like protocols. Second, these findings show that large-scale generalizations for all of Protestant Europe might prove misleading. Given the indications of territorial, district, and intraparish diversity and variation, it is perhaps necessary to move beyond the polarity of "success versus failure" when speaking of the Reformation in Europe.

The French social history of European religion, as exemplified in the works of Bernard Vogler and Michel Vovelle, is far ahead of its German counterpart. The French findings reveal the difficulty of explicating and generalizing historical trends in piety even at the regional level. For example, on the basis of his examination of wills and bequests, Vovelle measured the decline of religious practice in eighteenth-century Provence. He found that several variables influenced what he calls dechristianization: gender, social and professional group, literacy, access to Enlightenment culture, social instability, and Protestant-Catholic or Jansenist-Catholic conflict. But Vovelle found that these factors only indirectly affected the decline of religion, since they were very dependent on specific contexts. Vovelle found only one direct cause. Those groups active in the marketplace tended to become dechristianized.[114]

To account for the regional diversity in late-sixteenth-century and early-seventeenth-century Germany, we should perhaps speak of territorial and civic Reformations in the plural rather than Reformation in the singular and concentrate on the political, social, and cultural factors that encouraged or discouraged the process of reform and the establishment of the new religion. The powerful social and political influence of the city of Strasbourg on its rural dependencies could not help but affect the reasonable levels of conformity that the visitors approved of. Similarly, in Württemberg, the visitors found acceptable conditions, which must have been determined in part by the centralization of the state church, the strong support of the prince, the church's exceptional practice of frequent and local visitations, and the close cooperation of secular and ecclesiastical authorities at all levels of government.

CHAPTER 5

The Reformation of Society

The Protestant Reformation intended not only the reform of theology and liturgy but also the transformation of lay moral life according to evangelical principles.[1] Some investigations of the social and cultural impact of the German Reformation have represented Luther's movement to reform the medieval church as a particular case of a large-scale cultural conflict taking place in the sixteenth century. In fact, it has been argued that the evangelical message was an alien ideology fundamentally opposed to the folk customs and mentality of the lay population.[2] While this thesis of cultural conflict offers a valuable approach to many aspects of the social history of early modern Europe, evidence from the Württemberg protocols indicates that conflict is not the whole story. The recognition of cultural differentiation, if not outright conflict, should not cause us to overlook areas of common culture—shared values, ideals, and interests—that could unite certain groups of lay parishioners with church officials.

In Württemberg, the struggle to reform and christianize society in the decades following the Reformation went forward by means of distinct but interrelated processes. In the secular sphere, the police regulations were promulgated, periodically revised by the central authorities, and enforced in the localities by magistrates and the courts.[3] In the ecclesiastical realm, three means were used: catechesis and preaching, especially explication of the table of duties (Haustafel); the morals court (Rügegericht); and the periodic visitations. These institutions and the laws behind them were not unique to the Reformation era. In Württemberg, on the eve of the Reformation Duke Eberhard the Bearded had supported moral discipline through his laws and ordinances. The first Territorial Ordinance (Landesord-

nung), in 1495, prohibited blasphemy and drunkenness and placed such transgressions under the penal authority of the district court (*Vogtgericht*).[4] In the sixteenth century, the Württemberg reformers and their secular allies built on this tradition but were also motivated by the new evangelical views on Christian living.

The following analysis focuses on the visitations as an example of the moral and social ideal that the Württemberg reformers and dukes supported. In the parishes, the visitors heard and investigated complaints, imposed sanctions, and referred cases to other jurisdictions, such as the village morals court, the district court, the district superintendent, or the Stuttgart consistory.[5] Four facets of this moral and social vision are of special concern: sexual mores and family life, public decorum, the sanctity of Sunday and other holidays, and social relations among neighbors. We shall see that the visitations had at least two goals: the discipline of both public and private behavior for the sake of godly living, and the protection and maintenance of patriarchal families in the face of the economic, social, and moral permutations of the late sixteenth and early seventeenth centuries.

These subjects are consonant with the moral and social concerns of the Ten Commandments. While a full explication of Luther's understanding of the place of moral law in the life of the Christian would exceed the scope of this study,[6] it is important to note that Luther emphatically rejected the medieval distinction between evangelical precept and evangelical counsel, which reflected a basic hierarchical understanding of Christian society, and called for clergy and members of religious orders to live up to a moral standard higher than that of the laity.[7] This spiritual hierarchy was closely associated with the theological framework of merit and righteous works.[8]

Luther and his Protestant successors expected all Christians to be held accountable to the moral standards of the law, particularly the Decalogue. Luther rejected the "sophists" who taught that Christ abolished the law of Moses so far as ordinary Christians were concerned and made the commandments into "counsels" on being a perfect monk.[9] For Luther, Christ's words, like all Scripture, applied to everyone equally, perfect or imperfect. "For perfection and imperfection do not consist in works. . . . They exist in the heart, in faith and love, so that those who believe and love the most are the perfect ones."[10] This is the root of the Protestant *innerweltliche Askese*: the moral standard of a godly life, hitherto expected only of the perfect—the monks cloistered apart from the world—now became expected of all Christians living in the world.

Luther envisioned that beginning with the catechism, people would be taught the law and learn that the commandments are "of the most high God."[11] "When men consider this, there will arise a spontaneous desire to do God's will. . . . we are to keep them incessantly before our eyes and constantly in our memories, and practice them in all our works and ways."[12] The Württemberg theologian Jakob Andreae summarized in the *Formula of Concord* (1580) the threefold purpose of the Lutheran teaching concerning the purpose of biblical law and the Decalogue: to maintain external discipline against unruly and disobedient men; to lead men to a knowledge of their sin; and to give the reborn Christian a definite rule according to which he should pattern and regulate his entire life.[13] The Decalogue, supplemented by what might be termed Pauline morality, provides the theological basis for the evangelical view of family life and social mores.[14]

I

The following discussion aims to show that the visitations and church discipline served as a means of protecting the family and affirming Protestant moral standards. The protocols show that the religious elites attempted to project their new ideals (and restatements of traditional ones) upon the larger society. The sources contain, however, many opinions, attitudes, and expressions of self-interest of common parishioners that have been mediated through the representatives of the official church. The records reveal a great deal about popular attitudes and behavior in those areas that were of concern to the visitors. The parishioners seem to have resisted or ignored certain aspects of church discipline. On the other hand, certain groups among the laity could view church values as consonant with their own self-interest, and use church authority and sanctions in order to preserve the moral and economic stability of peasant households.

Table 14, which was discussed in the previous chapter, summarizes the disciplinary cases involving sexual mores and family life from the visitations conducted during the five-year period from 1601 to 1605. Given the respective populations of the two districts, the total number of reported cases appears quite low. The number of cases reported for Tuttlingen is substantially higher (25 percent) than the number for Tübingen, perhaps because of less disciplined conditions in the district of Tuttlingen or greater zeal on the part of the Tuttlingen superintendent. Distance from the central power is often considered an important factor in the ability of princely government to impose its will and exercise sanctions in the localities. Possibly, the greater frequency of disciplinary cases in Tuttlingen may be attributed to its relative remoteness from the centers of state and ecclesiastical power and the inability of the church to exercise control.[15]

The visitors often heard complaints about illicit sexual activity. Although sexual offenses came under the jurisdiction of the morals court, the court's findings and operation were under the review of the visitation commission. The 1559 Church Ordinance provides a pithy but comprehensive list of the concerns of the morals court judges that covers most areas of private, public, and economic morality from adultery to usury.[16] Obviously, the number and kinds of cases reported could vary according to the diligence and disciplinary fervor of the moral censors and to their relationships with their fellow parishioners and the other magistrates. For example, it was not uncommon for the visitors to find that the censors were too soft in executing their duties.

The most prevalent form of censured sexual behavior, prevalent since it was the most difficult to conceal, was the bearing of illegitimate children.[17] Some of the young women named as having given birth to bastards in both districts were working as servants outside their hometowns or villages. The accusation, though, was recorded in their hometown. Despite the presumed in loco parentis role of the master, single women were vulnerable outside their own village not only to the temptations of the flesh but also to sexual coercion by male members of the household of their employers. In fact, the assertion is frequently made that domestic service was the school for vice in the premodern period.[18] Many (but not all) researchers agree that there was a general respect for ecclesiastical law and Christian sexual morality in the early modern period. Others have argued that no young woman would have become an unwed mother by choice. Since these servant girls were not accused of prostitution or whoredom, it is probable that they had engaged in intercourse in the belief that it might lead to marriage, although the possibility of violent rape or other forms of sexual coercion cannot be ruled out.[19]

Possibly, these Württemberg servant girls accused of bearing bastards are analogous to the young women appearing in the marriage court records of Reformation Basel, where many cases of fornication involved single men who had carried on with women servant girls or prostitutes.[20] In Württemberg, when the fathers of illegitimate children are known either by name or occupation, they most often appear to be members of itinerant occupations. This could imply that the greater physical freedom provided by such employment liberated these young men from moral and social constraints of the settled community.

In some cases where the father could be identified, the visitors were concerned that he contract to fulfill certain financial obligations to the girl that would enable her to support the child.[21] For example, in 1605 the daughter of Conrad Nopper of Öfingen was pregnant by someone from Dürra "who, however, supports her with money that she might keep the child."[22] It is not exactly clear what happened to the mother and child when such arrangements could not be made.

Similarly, the man who impregnated Gallin Spitznagel's daughter contracted to provide for her. When the child died, all obligations ceased and the daughter went into service in the town of Talheim, an arrangement that had the double benefit of physically removing from her family an economic dependent as well as a possible source of dishonor. Whether rumor of her previous condition followed her to her new residence is not known.[23]

The next most prominent category of sexual offenses was prenuptial cohabitation, or sleeping together too soon, as established by a birth too soon after the church wedding.[24] The accusations forthrightly demonstrate both indifference to the Protestant view of marriage and the persistence of the pre-Reformation understanding of marriage.[25] Medieval custom—and, to an extent, the practice, if not the precept, of the church up to the Council of Trent—had been to treat marriage as consisting essentially of the private consent of two individuals to marry. According to the Protestant reformers (and their Catholic counterparts in the sixteenth century) this view of marriage had led to such abuses as clandestine engagements, premarital intercourse, and the seduction of young women by men who did not keep their promises. The repeated cases of prenuptial cohabitation in Württemberg are significant, for they indicate a discrepancy in values: some villagers were conserving the old pre-Reformation understanding of marriage and resisting the attempts by church and state to enforce the new view. The officials seem to have accomplished only mixed results with their efforts.

The complaints must have originated from the villagers. In rural England, the village wives kept a close eye on the courting behavior of their single sisters.[26] The parents and guardians of the accused are a likely source of the Württemberg accusations, especially if they wanted to express their displeasure with an unapproved match. In Württemberg's neighbor, the county of Hohenlohe, peasant family elders used Protestant marriage laws and courts as part of their strategy to control the youth. In Hohenlohe, the parents and guardians of young people brought most contested engagements to the attention of the courts.[27]

In Tübingen district the problem of sleeping together too soon appears to have been very widespread. One woman even had her first born "a half-year too soon,"[28] that is, three months after her nuptials. In Ofterdingen, Bodelshausen, and Jesingen, the protocols note simply that "several married couples" had slept together too early, had confessed to the crime, and had been punished. In Tübingen district, the apparently greater frequency of prenuptial conceptions reflects greater efforts by local officials to control marriage.

The recording of some of the Tübingen complaints manifests a marked double standard. Although in law both parties were culpable for such sexual crimes, in several cases only the woman is cited as the offender, though, of course, she is named as the wife of her husband.[29] For example, "Anna, the wife of Jerg Ulrich, had slept with [her husband] prematurely."[30]

The prevalence of these complaints would appear to show that the reformers were not totally successful in influencing the sexual behavior and attitudes of all members of the community some 30 years after the restoration of Protestantism in Württemberg. Young parishioners seem to have considered their marriages to have begun before the church service, that is, with intercourse and the exchange of promises at some earlier date, possibly with the consent of their parents.[31] It is indeed possible that it was the pregnancy itself that prompted these marriages, but the evidence is silent on this point.

Although the sixteenth-century magistrate's positive social role in exercising discipline and maintaining the limits that defined a community's principles has not gone unrecognized, the tendency remains to view the church officials as imposing alien norms and values.[32] This predilection is understandable since it is reinforced by the nature of our sources. The visitation records reflect the professional concerns of the secular magistrates and ecclesiastical officials as disciplinarians, representing the suasive and coercive power of the state, who desired to institute certain standards of moral and social behavior. But the social reality reflected in the protocols is not so one-sided. Although the visitors represented ecclesiastical and secular power external to the village, in some cases certain groups among the villagers brought the complaints before the officials, apparently out of a desire for discipline and order to be enforced in their communities.

Greater detail concerning church discipline cases can be gleaned from the records of the consistory itself in those instances where such records survive either as the full protocol of deliberations of the consistory's own investigation or as the local Vogt's report to the consistory about a case. For example, in 1587 the Stuttgart Vogt reported to the consistory the results of his investigation into an allegation of adultery between a young servant, Hans Jeylin, and Dorothea, the wife of his master, Andreas Sattler. By examining several people, the Vogt determined that the allegation had substance. Andreas Sattler, from Dettingen, a weaver by trade, had married Dorothea about a month before the investigation and moved to Stuttgart in order to obtain legal residence there. Shortly thereafter he had journeyed to Dettingen to make arrangements regarding the estate left behind by his parents, leaving his wife at her mother's house, along with the servant Hans. There "the said unmarried servant, Hans Jeylin, [servant] of the said weaver's wife, . . . had drunk with her [and] the following two nights lain with her in bed, and thus they committed adultery with each other." Andreas returned three days later and, knowing nothing, slept with his wife that night. What was unknown to the cuckolded husband was common knowledge to the whole neighborhood, for he testified to the visitor that "as soon as he had been informed of the unchastity committed the other day, since by then the clamor or rumor [*Geschrei*] about it had been very vulgar throughout the neighborhood, he separated himself from her."[33]

Another case of alleged adultery also underlines the importance of rumor and gossip and their role in bringing cases to the visitation's attention. In this instance, local rumor also prompted the husband's initial accusation. In 1584, the Schultheiss of Nehren, suspecting his wife of adultery, beat her cruelly and petitioned for a divorce. This caused "a common rumor in Nehren and the surrounding hamlets." The visitor, a conscientious and careful investigator, discovered that shortly before this incident the Schultheiss had attended the annual fair with his daughter (the wife's stepdaughter) in order to buy his wife a fine fur. The fifteen-year-old girl asked him, "Why are you buying such a fur for the whore ([I, the visitor, am] reporting this with obedient reverence)?"[34] Astounded, the father reportedly threatened and scolded his daughter to tell him what she had seen. She related that her stepmother had ordered the servant to wake her early in the morning. "The daughter, while she was lying in her bed, had then heard a noise from the leather couch."[35] Others gave testimony that contradicted the girl's story that she had found the accused persons in the act of adultery. Pointing out that only the daughter corroborated the story, they accused the Schultheiss of lying, and reported, at the same time, that he was wont to beat his wife cruelly. The Schultheiss testified that when he learned of his wife's alleged misdeed, he wanted to divorce her. The visitor notes: "I therefore had to report such a matter, [especially] since at Nehren and the surrounding villages there is a great and widespread clamor." The consistory, in the person of the general superintendent, replied that because nothing was certain and agreed upon and because the case could not proceed upon a young girl's accusation alone, the visitor (the district superintendent) should submit the matter to the magistrates, who could investigate and set a fine.[36]

At least two observations can be made about these cases. The first involves the role village rumor played in bringing problems to the attention of the visitation. Evidently, behavior that the church would see as a lapse in proper conduct would not have come to the attention of authorities if gossip had not grown into a rumor that passed beyond village limits. "Rumor" or "outcry" is distinguished from simple gossip (*Geschwätz*) in being so widespread that it comes to the ears of officials and substantial citizens outside the village and forces the local officials to act on the reported misconduct.[37] While villagers would not share gossip with a visitor and were capable of concealing many things from the church's inspection, scandalous rumors, by definition, were beyond the village's control and came to the attention of outside authorities like the visitor.

A second point concerns the visitor's attitude toward his subject. His reference to the use of the word "whore" speaks eloquently of the official sense of the need for objective detail, since it was the very application of this evocative pejorative that allegedly prompted the husband's suspicions. Moreover, the visitor's polite apology for having cited the evidently offensive term manifests the increasingly moralized sensibility of the late-sixteenth-century European court and officialdom.[38]

There is no discernible pattern to the geographic distribution of the cases other than the lack of reports from the central administrative towns, a paucity probably attributable to the visitations' tendency to concentrate on rural problems. Also, visitors were usually superintendents, and hence aware of the disciplinary problems and the quality of religious life in the district towns, where they resided. Six cases of adultery were reported in Tübingen and only one in Tuttlingen. In all the cases except two, the married party was a woman, usually charged with a sexual liaison with a servant. In 1601 in Schlaitdorf, two women, probably prostitutes, were charged with illicit behavior with mercenary soldiers.[39]

Despite the small number of cases, most of the rural social groups and occupational classes were represented in the complaints, from the top of the village social hierarchy on down. The Schultheiss of Dusslingen was not only accused of adultery but also suspended from office for visiting an inn on St. Stephen's Day, behaving suspiciously, and committing adultery with a woman who had separated from her husband.[40] In Mössingen, a poor married householder with a wife and child was seen in the fields with a servant girl and the two of them were reportedly acting like married people and otherwise carrying on.[41] In the town of Schwenningen, a persistent servant was found dallying with the wife of a citizen in the fields. The fields were apparently a common, but perhaps not sufficiently secret, locale for such trysts.[42]

Not surprisingly, the protocols reveal that the villagers considered the most intimate aspects of the sexual and marital life of all members of the community, even the village Schultheiss, matters of public knowledge. Early modern village life was open and public, and "everyone had a right to know what everyone else was doing."[43] Such openness and inquisitiveness might appear to be a tyranny of local opinion but such sanctions served to maintain the unity and integrity of the family as a social and economic unit. When Jakob Penslin came before the visitor on account of his adultery, the visitation commission (and presumably the community), noting that he was poor, married, and the father of a child, considered his family obligations and economic condition. These circumstances not only underlined his immoral and irresponsible action but also complicated the punishment. Penslin made things worse by refusing to confess his sin, which compelled the visitor to refer the case to the magistrate for disciplinary action: fines and imprisonment. This course of action could only have imposed further hardship on Penslin's innocent dependents, which the visitor seems to have realized.[44] The stress on Penslin's failure to confess is significant, for it underlines the visitation's self-consciously spiritual function. Confession was the first step in the church's disciplining process. If Penslin admitted his error, and accepted the pastoral admonition, the matter would presumably have then been considered resolved. The local morals court would have administered the appropriate secular penalty.[45]

Historians have given little attention to the subject of sexual violence in early modern Europe.[46] The Württemberg ecclesiastical regulations on rape are brief but straightforward. They leave the judgment and punishment of rapists to secular law and concentrate on the moral character of the crime and its consequences for marriage law. Rape was considered to have occurred when a man forcefully violated a woman whom he could not legally claim as his wife and when a man ravished an unwilling woman who did not desire to live with him as a concubine or as a wife.[47] In the minds of the churchmen, there were, therefore, three components to the definition: the use of force, the lack of consent, and the absence of a valid betrothal or marriage. The man's use of force and the woman's lack of consent were important to the clergy in their efforts to ensure that the sexual union involved in rape had no legal or moral connection with betrothal or marriage. Seduction of a naive woman through devious means or through a go-between was also considered the equivalent of rape.[48] If the woman was a minor, all promises that she might have made or that were made to her were invalid. If she was of age, then any promises concerning marriage must have occurred secretly and illegitimately and thus were void, and the seducer should be seriously punished.[49] The laws against seduction also protected patriarchal authority over engagement and marriage. The ordinances emphatically identified rape along with all the other forms of seduction and deception as contrary to legitimate engagements and marriage.[50]

If single women—daughters, widows, and abandoned wives—claimed to have been raped (by "soldiers"), they had to testify under the promise of silence before their pastor and a magistrate within one month of the alleged act, otherwise they were to be regarded as whores and punished accordingly. This prescription does not indicate how the women were to go about proving that they had been raped. The pastor and magistrates were not likely to accept the woman's unsubstantiated word; perhaps there was some kind of examination by the local midwife. The ordinance's concern specifically with single women, the emphasis on the one-month time period, and the skeptical observation that "sometimes dishonesty and deceit play a role therewith" suggest that this instruction was intended to deal with false accusations from single women who had conceived out of wedlock and then claimed, after the fact, to have been raped.[51]

Despite the probable skepticism of the authorities, the protocols show that accusations of rape or seduction were at least investigated. For an unequivocal example, one Jerg Seuter, a young journeyman (*Gesell*), after appearing before the marriage court (*Ehegericht*) with the daughter of the Schultheiss on account of some unspecified marital matter, subsequently, since he "still did not want to yield," forced his way into the house where "he [wanted] to have the Schultheiss's daughter by force."[52] While crimes of violence were by definition not in the purview of the visitation, it is not coincidental that this woman who appears in the records as the victim of sexual violence was the daughter of a magistrate. Other, less well connected victims probably had no opportunity of pressing a successful allegation. The complaint against Jakob Koler less clearly concerns a forced assault. Koler had taken advantage of his position as the master's son to seduce and impregnate his father's maid. There is no indication of any damages having been paid, and the woman had to leave service and return to her hometown, in nearby Catholic Fürstenberg.[53] Both cases have in common the issue of the father's authority over the sexuality of all household dependents: sons, daughters, and servants.

Just as the parishioners considered every aspect of the life of each member of the community subject to scrutiny, so too was the visitor concerned with uncovering all matters about life and worship within the limits of his mandate. His purview extended even into the birth chamber. After Conrad Birkenhans's wife brought into the world three stillborn babies in succession, the rumor spread that she was guilty of inducing abortions. When report of this reached the visitor, he interviewed the midwives and the women of the village and ascertained that there were no grounds to the charge, which apparently laid the rumor to rest.[54] When Georg Schwaldorffer's wife and her in-laws disposed of a frightfully deformed baby, the visitor apparently judged that he was dealing with a case of illicit and indecent burial rather than infanticide, for he imposed a stiff two-florin fine and admonished the parish to avoid "a similar impropriety."[55]

One unmarried, semi-itinerant, and probably impoverished woman was accused of and imprisoned for infanticide. After living for six years in Hungary, she returned to her village in Württemberg and became suspect because she looked as though she had recently given birth to a child. The visitor notes simply: "This, unfortunately, was true." After confessing that she had murdered her baby, she was imprisoned. The unhappy plight of this poor woman and her lack of status and place in the village are evident in that the visitor was given no name to record for her, he simply left a blank space in the hope of entering her name later.[56]

An even more heinous crime occurred in Trossingen. Hans Honer (or Homer), a married man, shearer, and citizen of Trossingen impregnated the daughter of the old schoolmaster Georg Wurtt. Since the pregnancy was not evident, Honer attempted to remove the evidence of his adulterous relationship by giving the young woman a poisonous draft "without a doubt, in order to put to death the mother and the child." The poison induced a premature birth, and the child died soon thereafter. The mother, though, injured her mouth and throat so badly that she had difficulty eating the rest of her life. Honer quickly left Württemberg for Hungary, evidently abandoning his wife.

Without success, the Württemberg authorities petitioned the Austrian and the Hohenberg governments to send Honer back. The visitor believed that the unpunished misdeed of this criminal might result in others suffering some kind of retribution, for he remarks that while the authorities awaited Honer's repatriation, there might be "misfortune" among the family and friends of Honer because the victimized daughter still lived "under their supervision."[57] How sensitive all members of Honer's family would have been to the possibility of divine retribution is perhaps open to doubt, for at least one scion of the clan, Jakob Honer, lived outside the boundaries of respectable God-fearing society, coming before the visitor the following year accused of practicing folk medicine and carrying on with witches (Unholden).[58]

Sexual behavior in premodern times should not be separated from other social relations. In the Reformation era we find that problems of illicit sexual activity can be intimately related to conditions in the household. In 1603, Adam Speyren (or Speyer) complained to the consistory about the sad situation of his daughter, Margaretha, who had hitherto been living with a mercenary soldier but was now living at home; she stubbornly refused to work, which distressed the whole family.[59] This anxiety would have been more than simply moral, for Speyer is explicitly identified as a poor man, and Margaretha's refusal to contribute to the family's economic livelihood would have been burdensome. Such poor households were experiencing severe difficulties in face of the economic conditions of the early seventeenth century. Two years later in 1605, Margaretha was ordered to leave the village, for she was living with yet another man. The visitor reported, moreover, that Margaretha had given birth to a child as the result of an illicit liaison with a mercenary.[60]

While the report stresses Margaretha's dishonor, we know little about how this dishonor manifested itself in the village, if it did at all. The French historians of *mentalité* tell us that the medieval popular mind conceived of honor externally, in reference to the judgment of other people, rather than as verdict of one's own conscience.[61] The reformers in Württemberg, however, tended to identify honor with conscience. In fact, their reports continually associate the attributes of being Christian and being respectable or honorable. While research on English court records has indicated that there was not necessarily any stigma attached to bearing bastards during the sixteenth and seventeenth centuries, we are still ig-

norant about the processes by which reformers, Protestant and
Catholic, might have succeeded in having their parishioners adopt
and internalize the reformed notions of Christian conduct.

Most of the incidents about marital strife and domestic disputes
that merited the attention of the magistrates and the church authorities would have been dealt with by the marriage court that sat in
Stuttgart.[62] Yet a few cases do appear in the protocols that show that
the visitors could act as domestic peacemakers.[63] For instance, they
were able to reconcile a quarrelsome husband to his wife by moral
suasion and without the use of corporal or fiscal discipline.[64] The
visitor made every attempt to be comprehensive and thorough in his
investigations. When a wife was abandoned by her husband, the
case was discussed by the ducal chancellery and was recorded both
in the visitation protocol and the list of morals cases (*Vogtzettel*).[65]

In some instances, we can obtain a rather brief glimpse into the
nature of conflicts among members of a household. In Tuningen in
1602, a young tailor living and working at home was disciplined for
abusing his father and beating his mother.[66] During the next visitation, the visitor heard a story about the cruelty practiced within another Tuningen household. The adult males of the Hauser family
had recently let one of their brothers freeze to death by leaving him
to lie in the cold without even straw for his bed.[67] While we know
little of the efficacy of the visitor's discipline, such cases must have
been brought to the attention of the authorities by villagers who felt
that the accused had exceeded the tolerable limits of intrafamilial violence.

As is evident from Table 14, the third most prevalent complaint
about religious deviance involved the marriage of Protestants to
Catholics. The late Reformation in Germany is usually conceived of
as the age of religious conflict and rigid confessional boundaries that
are often assumed to have established themselves according to the
dictum *cuius regio, eius religio*.[68] Throughout the Empire, however,
and especially in Württemberg, Catholics and Protestants continued
to live in close proximity in areas where territorial sovereignties
were very splintered. This lack of territorial and confessional integrity rendered possible economic, social, and even spiritual (godparent) relationships. The number of interconfessional marriages evidenced in the protocols is simply one manifestation of what must
have been a larger network of complex interrelationships. Both the

prescriptions against marriage to nonevangelicals and the enforcement of those prescriptions reflect the Protestant conception of companionable marriage. While the ordinances emphasize the need for spiritual harmony in the family, the visitations condemn the use of marriage as a strategy to maintain the family property by going outside the confessional church.

All but two of the cases of interconfessional marriage involved daughters or female wards to Roman Catholics who resided either in parishes adjacent to the evangelical parishes in Tuttlingen district or elsewhere in the Swabian Alb. Of these, all but one of the women married with their parents' or guardians' consent. This one exception might very well have been a marriage of love, since the visitor expressly noted the lack of the parents' consent and their absence from the wedding.[69]

The interests, goals, and values of the peasant elders could conflict with those of the church officials. The fathers considered the marriages to be matters of property, but the visitors strongly condemned the use of marriage simply as a means to preserve a family's estate. For example, Stigel Martin was admonished for marrying his daughter to a Catholic solely for the sake of "shameful" property, especially since his daughter "could otherwise have married very well," presumably to an evangelical with property.[70] When Dies Oetter married his daughter to a Catholic, he sponsored a sumptuous wedding celebration in Nordstetten, the groom's hometown, and gave his daughter a princely marriage portion of 200 florins. The pastor had previously cautioned him against the marriage, but he had replied that "no one would ever want to cut off his own head." While there were suitable hometown matches for his daughter, they would have involved giving away some share in the family's property and privileges. His goal was clearly stated in the complaint. By marrying his daughter outside of Tuningen and to a Catholic, "thereby the farm, the business, and the tenure might remain to his own son alone."[71]

Perhaps in competition with Oetter's sumptuous wedding, another Tuningen resident, Jakob Heldt, married his daughter to a Catholic in a princely fashion.[72] Similarly, a small merchant from Tuttlingen married his daughter against her will to a young man from Villingen in order to keep his city property intact. This wedding prompted even greater controversy, for many citizens traveled to. Villingen for the marriage ceremony and attended the Roman mass afterward.[73] Such incidents were not uncommon in the late Reformation. It would, however, be very interesting to know whether evangelical parishioners were able to discern the fine theological distinctions treasured by the higher clergy between the evangelical worship service and the Catholic mass.[74]

For the Württemberg parishioners, the nuptial masses fulfilled the need to demonstrate solidarity and joy with the newlyweds. Large, convivial wedding celebrations were just one of several festive or ceremonial occasions that the church disapproved of. In the Villingen case, the wedding gave evangelical parishioners the opportunity to drink and dance with their Catholic neighbors. It is noteworthy that the accusations concern only attendance at the mass. No parishioner is accused of actually partaking of the transubstantiated elements, which would have indicated a total disregard for the theological distinctions between the two confessions and a total lack of confessional consciousness.

II

While the effort to discipline interconfessional marriages seems to have been a unilateral concern of the authorities, both the parishioners and their clergy were concerned to limit and discipline the excesses of the bad or poor householders (*böse Haushalter*), the drunkards and profligates whose problems with drink and other excesses caused them to shirk their work, hindered them from fulfilling their familial responsibilities, and threatened their households with financial ruin. The disciplining of the offenses of drunkenness, profligacy, vice, wastrelness, and gambling was not simply a matter of lay or clerical elites imposing from above new ideals of order and discipline upon a carefree and irreligious populace. Certain groups of parishioners, in some cases the blood relatives and in-laws of the bad householders, turned to the church authorities and requested sanctions and exhortations because they hoped to mitigate very severe social problems and to protect property from being squandered. (The word "bad" has been consciously chosen to translate *böse* in order to stress moral overtones.)[75]

For example, during the Spring visitation in 1601, Georg (Jerg) Lauffer is cited as a "bad householder" who was a drunkard (*zerhaft*) and very much in debt. The severity of his problem with alcoholism is evident in the complaint that since St. Michael's Day, seven months earlier, he had not been sober for more than eight days in a row. "He is a lazy good-for-nothing, he leaves everything for his servant to do."[76] The next year Lauffer was again identified as a "bad householder" and a wastrel.[77] And in 1603, he was described in terms of even greater opporbrium as a bad, useless householder who had incurred many debts. Not only was Lauffer an alcoholic who consumed his family's income, but he also abused his wife and caused his child to run away from home. The situation was so desperate that both his in-laws and his blood relations requested that the magistrates take action.[78] Another inhabitant of Schwenningen, Balthass Bentzinger, was found to be a spendthrift and a bad householder. Although still a young man, he "lies about every day in drunken dissolution." In this case, it was the reprobate's own wife and father who registered the complaint.[79]

Sons of Schultheissen and former Schultheissen were relatively prominent among those accused of bad householding, appearing in 3 of the 23 complaints between 1581 and 1605 and in three of the eight Tuttlingen parishes within five years.[80] These complaints intimate the type of parishioner who supported the discipline of drunkards. Village officeholders came from the group of peasants who had large holdings. Such peasants would be particularly interested in the disciplining of bad householders in their families as a way to control family wealth and manage resources in the face of the rapidly increasing demographic pressures of the late sixteenth and early seventeenth centuries.[81] In this case, the church officials were allying themselves with a social group in the parish that had very specific interests.

The accusation of being a bad householder overlapped with other accusations of social deviance, such as being a profligate or drunkard (*zerhaft*) and wastrel (*Verschwender* or *Vertuer*). For example, one of the Tobel brothers of Aldingen was noted in 1603 not only for bad householding but also for his profligacy and swearing.[82] In 1605, Michael Schatz's own children charged that he was totally drunk and in debt to the innkeeper. Moreover, he lay about almost daily in the public house and apparently did no farmwork.[83] Additionally, the son of the Schwenningen Vogt, who was found to be a bad householder in 1602, was accused of profligacy in 1601.[84]

The battle against the bad householders embodies a vision of the good, respectable, useful householder. He is sober, does not drink to excess, and causes no scandal by beating his wife. He does not gamble and is an industrious and diligent worker. Most important, he manages his farm and servants well. This vision is moral, but it also reflects a fundamental attitude about the stewardship and management of property. In fact, one possible punishment for the bad householder was the restriction of his legal rights and privileges. In the city of Tübingen, several of the useless, bad householders had legal actions brought against them and were declared legally incompetent.[85]

One Württemberg profligate was not without an earthy sense of humor. In 1603, Michel Runhart caused a fight at the local public house with a smith's apprentice when he managed to switch the smithy's beer glass with one full of Runhart's urine.[86] Runhart was neither submissive nor teachable. In 1604 and 1605, he was again cited for being a bad householder and was even imprisoned by the justice. Moreover, he had violated the sanctity of a holy day, the Annunciation of Mary, by working all day long.[87]

The prevalence of profligacy and drunkenness does not appear to be any indication of the general level of religious practice in a community. For example, the visitor notes that in Schwenningen many were bad householders, yet the pastor had no complaint about church attendance, reporting that the parishioners "came as time afforded to the services."[88]

It would be a mistake, however, to consider these examples of deviance as representing the behavior of the average Württemberg peasant. Michel Runhart and the other bad householders seem to have been members of small subpopulations consisting of friends and relatives who were equally inclined to imbibe alcohol so frequently and in such quantities that they were unable to attend to their farmwork. In 1601, Runhart and his brothers, Jakob and Caspar, were named, along with the Kieffer brothers, as bad householders who disturbed the peace with their drunken carousing. They had been challenging each other in a beer-drinking contest, a custom still practiced today among the Swabians, especially university students.[89] The Kieffer brothers, first charged in 1602, appeared again in 1603 "all as wicked, useless heads of households" and were again punished without effect. Another profligate, Jakob Honer, the brother of Hans, appeared several times before the visitors.[90] His regular companions included Melcher and Martin Tobel. Their meeting place, naturally, was the local inn, and they always desired the companionship of their fellows, for, as the visitor reports, "if one of them is in the public house, the other also wants to be there."[91]

The social history of the public house in early-modern Germany remains to be written. Although public houses represent an important social nexus in the village, we know very little about them. The public houses serve as a refuge from respectable, God-fearing society.[92] They also provided a gathering place for youths and a venue for opposition to patriarchal and village authority. For example, Dies Burck, the "disrespectful, disobedient" son of the Trossingen Vogt, would become inebriated and then wrestle and argue with the other public house patrons.[93] Martin Spett, identified as a complete drunkard, was accused of drinking the night away with several young men in self-willed defiance of the Schultheiss.[94] Melcher Eisenhart could not be kept away from the public house. Once when he was brought home to sober up, he was put to bed without clothes on, presumably to hinder any more excursions. Despite these precautions, he sprang out of the house naked, borrowed some clothes, and returned to the inn.[95]

Nor were women immune to problems with drink. A midwife, the widow of Conrad Göttin, was cited as a complete drunkard and debtor. Even more reprehensible was her habit of crawling to village houses whenever she was called for in an emergency.[96] It seems noteworthy that the only woman to appear accused of profligacy and drunkenness was not only a widow but also a midwife, one of the few economic activities that a married woman could carry on outside the male-dominated household. Göttin's position was thus singular and exposed in two respects: as a widow she was without a mate, and as a midwife she had to be active outside the household. Her problems with alcohol were aggravated by, and were more noticed by the village authorities because of, her exceptional position.

Magistrates and justices were also prone to drink. The Schultheiss of the filial of Pfrondorf caused a great scandal when he visited the village of Lustnau. There he became so drunk that he was unable to ride his horse, and when the innkeeper brought him wine, he spilled half of it and then cursed and blasphemed over his clumsiness. The drunkenness of the Schultheiss was not as shameful as his rowdy and scurrilous behavior and the waste of wine. When the village pastor arrived and attempted to talk sense into him, the Schultheiss responded by abusing the clergyman with "wholly impudent words and [he] intended something offensive."[97] Complaints were also registered against the Schultheiss of Dusslingen, since he was a profligate and an innkeeper who encouraged drunkenness and excess and had economically exploited at least one parishioner.[98]

In Württemberg, as well as in the rest of early modern Europe, magistrates were accustomed to conducting their official business with the assistance of such amenities as food and drink. In Talheim, both the Schultheiss and the justice appear to have indulged in too much drink, for it was reported that they were apparently drunk and not respected because they were too easy in their punishments. Setting such a poor example, they were thus not able to accomplish anything in the morals court.[99]

Those individuals whose lifestyles were most reprehensible in the eyes of the church were called Epicureans. These people, always male, had no connection whatsoever with the classical materialist philosopher; rather they distinguished themselves by profligacy and drunkenness, compounded by godlessness and resistance to authority. None of them was identified either as married or as a head of household, and it would be of great interest to know more about the social and economic status of these extreme deviants from respectable society.[100]

Relatively few cases of blasphemy were recorded, either because in fact the Württembergers were reluctant to blaspheme their God or, more likely, because it was such a common practice that only the most severe and injurious instances were disciplined. The church ordinances themselves distinguish between the cursing and blaspheming that could result from an outburst of anger and the more self-conscious and premeditated dishonoring of God's name. In disciplining blasphemers, the church authorities seem to have been blind to social position. One of the justices of Gönningen was cited for slander and blasphemy, and similarly, the common parishioner Conrad Buck was disciplined for blasphemy, slander, and profligacy.[101]

In certain villages, blasphemy seems to have been a quite common practice. In Aldingen, although the general population attended the Sunday services at an acceptable level, enough male parishioners indulged in blasphemy for the visitor to remark, "The blasphemy almost became rooted there," which suggests that the practice was widespread.[102]

In their fear of moral scandal and unchastity, the church authorities waged a long and evidently unsuccessful war against dancing and other festive gatherings, especially those involving the young, unmarried men and women of the village. Many of the dances that the ecclesiastical authorities complained about were allowed by the local secular officials.[103] In 1603, the Schultheiss of Kirchheim, in the district of Tübingen, allowed a public dance at a church fair that angered the neighboring villages. Ostensibly, the neighbors were morally offended, protesting "for the sake of decency," but there could well have been not a little envy behind their complaints.[104] This same Schultheiss also gave cause for complaint because he failed to abolish the wintertime spinning bees (*Spinnstuben*) or candle rooms (*Lichtkarzen*), where, it was believed, the teenagers were sleeping together.[105] Here we seem to have two contrary perspectives on what constituted appropriate behavior. On the one hand, we have the view of the Schultheiss, who apparently saw nothing wrong with dancing and the unchaperoned congregation of young people. On the other hand, we have the complaints that probably represent the views of the well-educated and cultured pastor Philip Heiland, a Tübingen master of arts and son of a Stift official. Heiland had spent five years at the university, a length of study well above the average. While he seems to have been committed to parish ministry, serving his whole life long in village churches, he remained oriented toward the culture of town and academy. He promoted no fewer than five of his sons to the university and preferment in the church.[106]

Other Schultheissen also tolerated the festive gatherings of young people. In the village of Nehren the Schultheiss was admonished for not abolishing the spinning bees.[107] The village magistrates were not cooperating with the church's desire to end the opportunities for unmarried youths to gather together. In Weilheim am Neckar, both the Schultheiss and the justice allowed the young single men to hold a dance on Shrove Tuesday without the consent of the pastor. The objection was raised not so much against the dance itself as against the lack of consultation with the pastor, "because it is but a part of discipline, whether and when we should allow dancing." The magistrates were instructed to consult with the pastor in the future.[108]

Some individuals even made a habit of sponsoring all-night gatherings in their homes. Michael Barhowen and the widow of Gallin Schrenken were disciplined for shamelessly holding dances in the night.[109]

The church's battle against the festive leisure activities of youth has a larger social context that lies largely hidden from the view of the visitation protocols. In order to establish the Protestant idea of courtship and marriage, both church and state wanted to eliminate the opportunities for youth of both sexes to meet together, engage in sexual activity, and form private engagements. But more than unchastity was involved here. Using the ideology of the household, both the church and the state were breaking apart the larger corporate kinship system of tradition. The attack on dancing was connected with a strategy of disciplining illegal festivities for baptism and marriage that were also occasions for social gatherings. The result was to increase the importance of the family and to displace the claims of the village and larger kinship networks. This process had begun even before the Reformation. In 1432, the Council of Basel had complained of the parceling of churchyards into family plots.[110] But in the mid and late sixteenth century, both the Protestant vision of the family's centrality to Christian moral development and demographic pressures contributed to the decline of older, corporate relationships.[111] But this interpretation must be qualified. The protocols show that many of the village officials tolerated the illegal festive gatherings. Since these Schultheissen came from the ranks of the most substantial peasants, their tolerance or encouragement of spinning bees and dances would not serve their apparent economic self-interest: the control of family resources through the regulation of courtship and marriage.

III

A related and significant problem in the eyes of the clergy was the maintenance of the sanctity of Sunday and the other holy days by disciplining disorder, prohibiting work, and placing strict limitations on weddings and other celebrations. The success of their efforts is difficult to evaluate, since the visitation records cease in 1605 and do not begin again until 1621, when the emphasis of the visitations shifted to an exclusive concern with the lifestyles and ministry of pastors and schoolmasters and occasionally magistrates. These protocols record few complaints concerning the deviancy of laypeople from evangelical norms.[112]

The clergy did have a different conception of how the laity should celebrate the high feast days of the evangelical religion. On Easter Eve 1602, many of the inhabitants of the village of Gönningen were in the streets acting unchastely, swearing, and otherwise making merry. The clerical authorities were not amused and disciplined them.[113]

A more frequent complaint centered on the public houses. In the city of Tuttlingen, the magistrates had to be admonished, for although they patroled the town to find delinquents from the Sunday services, they did not report the contemptuous inhabitants whom they found in the public houses.[114] The innkeepers were required by law to close their doors during the hours of the church services, yet some continued to serve customers, both resident villagers and transient guests, during the services and at other illegal hours, which encouraged disturbances.[115]

Common, too, was the parishioners' habit of using the Sunday morning hours for necessary and sometimes not so necessary fieldwork and errands, especially during the harvest season. The parishioners of Derendingen protested that they had to go out on Sunday mornings to harvest and load cattle fodder, for the cattle would not eat the fodder once it was a day old.[116] Similarly, in Weilheim am Neckar, the parishioners went out to harvest the fodder, load it on wagons, and transport it back to the village. All this activity in the fields on Sunday mornings disturbed and angered the neighboring Catholics, who apparently were not harvesting on the holy day.[117] In this case, the evangelical visitors acted upon a complaint originating from the other confession. The Catholics, for their part, were not always so respectful of Sundays and holy days, for on the Annunciation of Mary in 1603, "old George's son," a man from nearby Catholic Denkingen who was apparently well known by the evangelical parishioners of Aldingen, reportedly worked in a field near Aldingen. Although he was admonished to depart, he nonetheless continued working. The Aldingen villagers remarked that "they would not allow us [to work] on their holy days."[118]

The activities associated with the transporting, hulling, and milling of grain also gave frequent cause for complaint in Neuhausen and Aldingen. Some parishioners would travel to the mill on Saturday and stay overnight there. Others would leave on Sunday morning before the service, and many would include special side trips on their way to and from the mill, all of which promoted negligent church attendance.[119] In Neuhausen, the bakers made bread on Sunday mornings, breaking the Sunday observance. Even the village schoolmaster, whose house stood right next to the church, brazenly allowed people to bake bread in his oven during the sermon.[120] The pastor would not have been pleased to have the distracting aroma of baking bread wafting through his sanctuary while conducting the service. In Neuhausen, despite an apparently average church attendance, the impression is of a great deal of coming and going on Sunday mornings during services.[121]

IV

The visitors had within their purview not only religious and moral offenses but also what we would consider today social and economic crimes or misdemeanors, such as slander and usury. When Georg Lauffer slandered the justices, apparently in response to his being disciplined for profligacy, his offense was recorded in the protocol.[122] The magistrates, in fact, often appeared as the object of abuse, and sometimes it seems to have been justified. It caused a great scandal when the justice Simon Tremmel and his servant borrowed, on their own signatures, 40 florins from the village. Consequently, the reputation of the justices began to be smeared, and "the common man talks about it disgracefully."[123] The insults concerning Tremmel were perhaps merited, for he had a previous record of financial misdealings while holding public office. Two years earlier, it had become known that during his term as Bürgermeister, a sum of 63 florins had been collected in taxes but had not been reported to the Schultheiss.[124] The visitors were not concerned with disciplining only those who slandered magistrates, for commoners, such as Conrad Buck, were cited for multiple social offenses: slander, profligacy and blasphemy.[125]

The battle against usury represented another struggle of theologically centered values against worldliness, a struggle that appears to have been doomed to failure. Württemberg law expressly condemned the lending of money or goods at interest, defined as "when someone lends another money, and the borrower must put down in writing a larger sum that was borrowed."[126] In the parish of Nehren at the beginning of the seventeenth century it was common practice to engage in usurious contracts, and the clergy appear to have been powerless to put a stop to it.[127] During the economic hardship of the Thirty Years War, a visionary Württemberg vintner named Hans Keil protested the practice of usury. Generally, villagers did not have much sympathy for the theoretical, official, pastoral concern to limit the exploitive business loans, nor did they perceive that it might be in their interest to support the condemnation of usury. In practice, those who had the capital to lend, for example, the farmers of substance and the Württemberg dukes, must have agreed with the consistory that usury was both necessary and tolerable.[128]

v

As we have suggested, both cultural agreement and cultural conflict are evident in the attempts by the Württemberg state church to reform social morals. Admittedly, the ideal of the evangelical godly life originated during the sixteenth century among members of the elite culture, in the minds and hearts of theologians like Luther, and amid the lecture halls of universities like Wittenberg and Tübingen. Motivated by new evangelical notions of the Christian's moral, family, and social life and by a desire to protect the family unit from economic ruin caused by drunkenness and profligacy, the church officials worked to enforce standards of decent and godly life, sometimes with the cooperation of parishioners and sometimes in the face of lay indifference.

While the villagers probably had other formal and informal means of dealing with delinquency and deviancy that do not appear in the records of the church visitations, this investigation has shown that the values manifest in the church's discipline could overlap with the communities' own conceptions of acceptable behavior. In response to an activist church discipline, the typical village divided into those desirous, those indifferent, and those actively hostile to the reformation of life and manners. The parish youth resisted many aspects of the Reformation, such as the catechism and the attempt to discipline dances. Certain other groups, especially those concerned to protect family property, seem to have agreed with the clergy that the parish and the family were basic units of moral and political order, and they used the church's discipline to further their own ends. The most easily identifiable social group of villagers are the Schultheissen, who were recruited from among the richest class of peasants. With the discipline of bad householders, this group appropriated the visitation's discipline to serve their own interests. Members of this group at other times, however, tended to tolerate the traditional festive activities of youth that the church was especially concerned to control.

The church played many social roles in the village. One such role was the resolution of conflicts, especially in association with the most important and powerful village interest group, the substantial peasants. The results suggest that the practice of mediation and compromise was just as important to the church's social function as the exercise of hegemony and power.[129] At times the lay conception of household morality and order differed from that of the church. This was the case with prenuptial cohabitation and many of the leisure activities of the young people. The village youth seem to represent a group strongly indifferent to the Reformation. There were also areas of substantial agreement between certain groups of laity and the clerical officials. Often, members of the laity who saw that their interests coincided with those of the state church called upon the visitors to resolve conflicts and implement order.

Conclusion

Examination of the Württemberg sources has revealed a very complex and nuanced tableau of religious life. On the whole, the evidence reveals not only indifference to the church's discipline but also a moderate degree of outward conformity to the evangelical church. Parishioners of the filial churches expressed positive attitudes toward the rites and services celebrated by the Protestant church in Württemberg. There is no evidence of widespread disaffection from the state church nor of the existence of an alternative folk religion.

The pastors' social origin, culture, and education tended to separate them from their parishioners. This factor might have been mitigated by their day-to-day contacts with the parishioners and their long tenure in one living. While there were areas of conflict between the clergy and the villagers, the late Reformation pastors in Württemberg were not gentry patronizing plebeian congregations. They were educated in the literate, Latin-oriented, territorial culture of sacred and profane letters and subsequently lived, worked, and raised their families amid the German-speaking, local, particular culture of their parishes.

The intellectual culture and theological education contributed to certain attitudes of the Württemberg pastors that distinguished them from their parishioners. The protracted length of their studies, extending upward of ten years, and the segregated residence in the educational institutions, the cloister schools and the Tübingen Stift, furthered the socialization of a homogeneous professional group. The intellectual content of the curriculum and the quasi-monastic, moral discipline of the cloister schools and the Stift encouraged the development of a specialized intellectual sensibility, a feeling of group consciousness, and a sense of vocation.

This vocation was to serve in a parish. After graduating from the university at Tübingen and passing the central ordination examination, candidates had to leave the hub of Württemberg learned society and take up a post in an often remote parish. The pastors were outsiders, but circumstances forced them to become familiar with their parishes. A few pastors might have acted like Andreae's old pastor and dispensed with erudition in order to bridge the social distance between themselves and their parishioners. Since the most dependable of their sources of income was the land attached to their living, economic necessity in the face of the rapid inflation of the sixteenth and early seventeenth centuries forced them to exploit their holdings. Economics thus integrated the pastors into the social life of the agrarian community. Many of the country pastors must have lived like Thomas Wirsing, townsmen by origin, acting as farmers, tithe collectors, and preachers and physicians of souls. Also, although the economic mediocrity of the average pastor's income neither kept up with inflation nor matched clerical expectations, most pastors, except for those who held the poorest positions, were better off than many of their parishioners.

While the weekday morning service and Sunday afternoon and evening services fell into decline, parishioners showed moderate zeal in attending the principal Sunday morning service. Communion was supposed to be celebrated monthly and several times a year at the high feast days, but many of the parishioners seem to have felt that an annual participation in the Easter communion fulfilled their religious obligations. Young people and single adults were apparently more likely than other parishioners to be negligent in their attendance, sometimes because of the demands of seasonal agriculture, but more often because of indifference toward the church, if not active resistance to its efforts to discipline their festive pastimes such as dancing and berry picking. In contrast, the reports deriving from the visitations of the filial churches reveal that even in remote areas without benefit of resident clergy, laypeople earnestly desired the spiritual ministry of the church.

The visitations were used to discipline the clergy and the laity through exhortations, warnings, fines, and, in rare cases, imprisonment. Members of the community from all walks of life came under inspection: the incumbent, the schoolmaster, the Schultheiss, the folk healer, the semi-itinerant shepherd, and the town drunk. The system of sanctions and persuasions had only mixed success in inhibiting unchristian behavior.[1] When the church's interest in discipline coincided with the interests of groups within the village, such as the desire of the relatives of Schultheissen to restrain profligacy, the church might have had greater success. It should be clear, however, that evangelical church discipline cannot be reduced to an attempt by the urban elites to impose foreign mores and manners upon uniformly indifferent parishioners. The values manifested in the discipline could reflect the conceptions of appropriate behavior held by special groups within the village. Some parishioners, probably most often the substantial householders, used the church's discipline to resolve conflicts, establish order, and protect the economic integrity of families.

Although the examination of the protocols and other archival materials has shed new light on the extent of the impact of the Reformation on religious life, the investigation itself has raised new questions. Particularly useful would be a means of analyzing degrees of religious commitment, hierarchically within individual communities and comparatively between different localities. Insofar as religious piety is an immanent human characteristic or trait, it is reasonable to assume that when adequately measured throughout a population, it should appear in some kind of distribution, perhaps even a classic normal one. Different levels of outward religious practice might correspond to varying degrees of inward spiritual commitment. Such terms as the godly, the lukewarm, the indifferent, the godless, and the reprobate naturally come to mind. As we have seen, similar or analogous terms occasionally appear in the sources.[2] Because there are no records concerning individual attendance at sermons and communion, we cannot hope to quantify levels of religious practice throughout a community as contemporary French sociology has done. It might be possible, nonetheless, to conduct a comparative analysis of various parishes by examining the reports from several administrative districts.[3] The qualitative assessments of lay religious life by the visitors and the local pastors could then be analyzed and some general geographic patterns of differential piety could be established.

The subsequent history of the church in Württemberg suggests a legacy for two of our findings: the nominal conformity that the visitations desired and enforced and the distance between clergy and laity created by the recruitment, education, and socialization of the clergy. By the mid-seventeenth century, in response to what was viewed as widespread irreligion and in the face of clerical opposition, Johann Valentin Andreae established individual parish consistories modeled on the Genevan pattern throughout the land to exercise discipline at the local level. He accomplished this with the help of local groups of devout laity.[4] At the beginning of the eighteenth century, the Pietist movement sought to bridge the gap between the academic world of the clergy and the less learned world of the laity. Tübingen vine dressers expressed a desire for religious education to which the teaching assistants from the Stift responded in the hope of promoting faith, not merely to display erudition.[5]

On a more general note, historians of the early-modern church should not be too hasty in making generalizations about the nature of sixteenth-century Protestantism. For instance, although the effectiveness of Lutheran preaching and catechesis has been seriously questioned, we should remember that such efforts at evangelization and pedagogy were not unique to the early-modern territorial church in Germany. It was not the first time that a Christian movement led by city-trained, literate clergy attempted to convert the countryside.[6]

The recent historiography of sixteenth-century religion and society has done much to enrich our understanding of Reformation religious life and to free traditional religious historiography from many inherited and often self-serving confessionalist preconceptions. The tendency has been, however, to paint a very pessimistic portrait of the fruitless attempts of the reformers to make pious evangelical Christians out of the laypeople of Europe. Though this view is a refreshing and necessary correction to generations of sugary, hagiographic, and optimistic accounts of the Reformation, it has perhaps misread the very nature of the Reformation and the goals and intentions of the reformers. Although Luther would have perhaps preferred congregations of like-minded godly people, he did not think it possible to gather enough real Christians in all of Germany to form one congregation.[7]

Perhaps a rapprochement could be reached between the diverse pessimistic and optimistic views by recognizing the twofold nature of the German territorial churches: they were spiritual creations, brought forth, as the reformers claimed, by the voice of the Gospel, as well as political entities, administered by the prince through his officers by virtue of his being chief member of the church.[8] The same duality exists in the twin emphases on consolation and discipline manifest in the visitation itself: the visitor could both encourage and exhort a repentant sinner to good works, or he could recommend imprisonment for a recalcitrant reprobate.

Appendixes

Parishes and Filials in Tübingen and Tuttlingen Districts, 1581–1621

Tübingen District	
Altdorf	Mössingen with Belsen
Bodelshausen with Oberhausen	Nehren
Breitenholz with Reusten	Oferdingen with Rommelsbach
Derendingen with Kressbach	and Altenburg
Dusslingen with Stockach	Ofterdingen with Alten Sickingen
Entringen	Öschingen
Gönningen	Pfäffingen
Hagelloch	Schlaitdorf with Häslach
Jesingen	(shared with Walddorf)
Kilchberg with Bühl	Talheim
Kirchentellinsfurt	Walddorf with Häslach, Gniebel,
Kusterdingen	and Reibgarten
Lustnau with Pfrondorf	Weil im Schönbuch with
and Steinbös	Dettenhausen, Breitenstein,
Mähringen with Jettenburg,	and Neuweiler
Immenhausen, and	Weilheim am Neckar
Ohmenhausen	

Tuttlingen District	
Aldingen	Schwenningen
Hohentweil	Talheim
Neuhausen auf Eck	Trossingen with Schura
Öfingen with Oberbaldingen	Tuningen with Sunthausen
and Biesingen	Tuttlingen

APPENDIX B

Tübingen Clerical Families

The lefthand columns of numbers give genealogical information; "III 5 (2)" means third generation, fifth child (son or daughter of the second child of the previous generation). A, B, or C after a family name indicates a different family.

The following abbreviations are also used:

b.	born
d.	died
dtr.	daughter
J.D.	Juris Doctor (Doctor of Law)
m.	married
M.A.	Magister; having the Master of Arts degree
matric.	matriculation or inscription at the University of Tübingen
N.N.	name not available
supt.	church district superintendent

The data are gathered from Seigel, "Anhang III: Alphabetisches Verzeichnis der Mitglieder von Gericht und Rat," in his *Gericht und Rat*, pp. 170–299; Sigel, "Das evangelische Württemberg . . . Magisterbuch"; and LKA Stuttgart A1 1581, 1582, 1583I, 1583II, 1584I, 1584II, 1585I, 1585II, 1586I, 1586II, 1587I, 1587II, 1588I, 1588II, 1589, 1590, 1621.

ANDREAE

I	1	Jakob. Reformer.
II	2	Jakob, M.A., b. 1549, d. 1630. Pastor in Hagelloch 1569, Dusslingen 1573–89, Metzingen 1589, Kirchentellinsfurt 1617–30.

	4		Johann, b. 1554, d. 1610. Pastor in Hagelloch 1576, Mössingen 1578.
III	5	(2)	Eberhard, M.A., b. 1583, d. 1635. City pastor and supt. in Tuttlingen 1617–21.
	6	(2)	Regina. M. 2nd to Johann Ulrich Scholl, pastor in Breitenholz.

BIDEMBACH

I	1	Eberhard. Abbot of Bebenhausen.
II	2	Johann.
	3	Eberhard, M.A., b. ca. 1561, d. 1591. Deacon in Tübingen 1587–91. M. in 1588 to Maria, dtr. of Sebastian Vogler of Tübingen. (Vogler was senator 1588, 1605; justice 1596; d. 1605.) Maria m. 2nd in 1597 to Johann Philip Khonberger, Bürgermeister of Schorndorf.

BOLLINGER

I	1		Johann. Pastor in Wangen am Neckar.
II	2		Ulrich, b. 1569, d. 1612. Pastor in Schlaitdorf 1600–1610. M. 1st in 1596 to Anna née Machtoff, widow of Georg Otto, pastor. M. 2nd after 1602 to Lea Brenz, widow of Markus Löffler, dtr. of Sebastian Brenz of Calw, a shoemaker. Her 3rd marriage in 1612 was to Matthaes Vogel, pastor.
III	3	(2)	Johann Gottlieb. Pastor in Wangen am Neckar.

CLESS

I	1		Martin. Supt. in Knittlingen.
II	2		Valentin, b. 1561, d. 1634. Pastor in Weil im Schönbuch 1590–1634. M. to Anne Magerlin, dtr. of Bartholomäus Magerlin, M.D., professor of medicine at Tübingen University.
III	3	(2)	Johann Jakob. Pastor.
	4	(2)	David. Pastor.

CLEBER

I	1		Michael, b. 1565, d. 1611? M. in 1594 to Susanna Burckhardt, b. 1578, dtr. of George Burckhardt, professor of logic at Tübingen University.
II	2	(1)	Michael. Pastor.

3 (1) Esajas. Pastor.

GEBHARDT

I   1   Ludwig, d. 1606. Silk tailor. Town councillor 1596, 1606.
II   2   (1) Nicolaus. M. in 1607 to Anna Maria, dtr. of Martin Haag, pastor.
     3   (1) Jakob, d. 1577.
     4   (1) Ludwig, M.A., matric. at Tübingen University in 1591. Pastor in Kusterdingen 1597–1615. M. in 1597 to Maria Scholastika, dtr. of Israel Wieland, pastor in Dusslingen.
III 5   (4) Israel Ludwig. Pastor.
     6   (4) Johann, b. 1603, M.A. 1620. Pastor and dean (*Dekan*) of Rötteln in Markgrafschaft Durlach 1654–86.

HAAG

I   1   N. Haag in Tübingen.
II   2   (1) Jakob, b. ca. 1505–10, d. 1564?–1571. Town councillor 1564–71. M. in Hausen an der Zaber ca. 1535 to Ann, dtr. of Hans Moralt, Schultheiss of Hausen an der Zaber.
III 3   (3) Martin, M.A., b. ca. 1552 in Tübingen, d. 1616. Pastor in Siegelmingen, Nehren. While in Tübingen, m. to Agnes, dtr. of Martin Ganz, pastor in Geradstellen.
IV   4   (3) Jakob, M.A. Pastor in Kusterdingen 1615–24, Weilheim 1624–35. M. to Margaretha N. Her 2nd marriage was to Philip Ludwig Majer, pastor in Bodelshausen 1635–53.
     5   (3) Ludwig Friedrich, b. 1585 in Siegelmingen, d. 1647. Surgeon, barber. Town councillor 1635, 1636; member of the city court 1646, 1647; justice 1647. M. 2nd in 1636 to Dorothea, widow of Ulrich Hanselmann, M.A., pastor in Bottnang.
     6   (3) Anna Maria. M. in 1607 to Nicolaus Gebhardt, pastor (see under Gebhardt).

HEERBRAND

I   1   Jakob. Professor of theology and chancellor of Tübingen University.
II   2   (2) Christoph, b. 1549, d. 1609. Pastor in Weilheim am Neckar 1576–1609. M. in 1574 to Margarete Schnepf, dtr. of Theodoric Schnepf.
III 3   (2) Johann Wilhelm. Pastor.

4 (2) Agnes. M. 1st in 1597 to David Heckmayer, Hofgerichtsad-
vokat in Tübingen; m. 2nd in 1622 to J.D. candidate Eberhard Schultheiss of Halle.

5 (2) Margarete. M. in 1611 to Samuel Bansorius, J.D., Hofger-
ichtsassessor, Tübingen.

HEILAND

I   1   Samuel. Administrator of the Stift (Stiftsephorus)
II 2   Georg Philip, b. 1570 or 1571 in Tübingen, d. 1605. Matric.
1586, M.A. 1590. Repetent 1593; deacon in Göppingen
1594, 1596–99; pastor in Kirchentellinsfurt 1599–1605,
Mössingen 1605.
III 2 (1) Samuel.
2 (2) Johann Dietrich.
2 (3) Andreas, M.A., b. 1600. Pastor.
2 (4) Markus Philip. Pastor.
2 (5) Sebastian, b. 1664. Pastor.

KIENLIN (A)

I   1   Stefan, d. 1570. Tanner. Justice 1558; Bürgermeister 1561,
1570.
II 2 (1) Josef, d. 1619. Justice 1578, 1618; Bürgermeister 1578, 1617.
M. in 1566 to Anna, dtr. of Hans Katz from Remmingheim.
3 (1) Sixt, d. 1608. M. 1st in 1570 to Anna, widow of Bastian
Neuffer; m. 2nd in 1572 to Ursula, dtr. of Endriss Reutter.
4 (1) Stefan, d. before 1583. Pastor in Lustnau. M. in 1558 to
Maria Kaiser from Entringen.
III 5 (3) Stefan, M.A., matric. at Tübingen University in 1589. Pastor
in Kirchentellinsfurt 1602–10, Weilheim 1610–20, Lust-
nau 1620–29. M. in 1600 to Katherina, widow of Hans
Reustlin, Hofmeister at Lichtenstein.

KIENLIN (B)

I   1   Bernard, d. 1586. Tanner. Justice 1568, 1585, 1586; Bürgermeister 1568, 1585. M. 1st to Margaretha, d. 1575; m.
2nd to Sara, widow of Kaspar Haas from Kirchheim unter
Teck.
II 2 (1) Hans.
3 (1) Maria. M. in 1579 to Anastasius Kommerell, M.A. (see under
Kommerell).

4   (1)   Jakob, b. before 1558, d. 1610. Town councillor 1596. M. in 1579 to Barbara, dtr. of Daniel Keppler, town councillor in Weil der Stadt. She was the aunt of the astronomer Kepler.

KIENLIN (C)

I   I   Lorenz. M. 1st to Agnes, who d. between 1568 and 1582. M. 2nd in 1582 to Sara, widow of Jakob Speiser and dtr. of Mathis Rieker, Stuttgart. Her 3rd marriage in 1590 was to Nikolaus Kommerell (see under Kommerell).

II   2   (1)   Lorenz (son of Lorenz and Agnes), b. 1568, d. 1648. Justice 1615, 1616, 1628–45. M. to Rosine, dtr. of Kaspar Haas, Kirchheim unter Teck.

III 3   (2)   Sara. M. in 1616 to Christoph Stark, deacon in Dettingen/Urach.

4   (3)   Agnes. M. in 1634 to Balthes Kreutter, M.A., pastor in Tailfingen.

KIES

I   Johann. Hauptmann at Hohen-Neuffen.

II   Johann, b. ca. 1584, d. 1664. Pastor in Schlaitdorf. M. in 1610 to Agathe Hafenfeffer, dtr. of Matthias, pastor and Frühprediger in Tübingen 1612–17.

III   Ludwig. Pastor.

Johann David. Pastor.

Agathe. M. to Georg Hausch, Pastor.

KOMMERELL

I   I   Fabian, b. ca. 1504, d. 1594. Baker. Citizen of Tübingen 1592. Reported to have been town councillor.

II   2   (1)   Anastasius, M.A., b. 1551, d. 1611. Pastor in Kirchentellinsfurt 1594–99, Kilchberg 1599–1611. M. in 1579 to Maria Kienlin (see under Kienlin [B]).

3   (2)   Nikolaus, b. ca. 1550, d. 1610. Clothmaker. Town councillor 1596, 1609; Lehenträger of the Hospice, 1596. M. 1st to N.N.; m. 2nd in 1590 to Sara Speiser, widow of Lorenz Kienlin (see under Kienlin [C]); m. 3rd in 1592 to Barbara Zehen.

MOCKEL

I   I   Sebastian of Beilingreis, b. 1537, d. 1606. Pastor in Ofterdingen 1569–1606. Tübingen supt. until 1591.

II   2   Matthaeus, b. 1571, d. 1637. Pastor in Ofterdingen 1606–
              37.
     3   Johann Theodorich. Pastor.
III 4   (2) Johann Bernhard. Pastor.

NEOBOLUS OR NEUHELLER

I   1   Jodokus or Jost, d. 1572. Deacon in Tübingen 1538–40,
              Augsburg 1540; pastor in Entringen until 1568.
II   2   (1) Johann, b. 1542, d. 1610. Pastor in Entringen 1568–1610.
III 3   (2) Jeremias. Pastor in Pfäffingen 1624–32.
     4   (2) Johann Jakob. Pastor.

NOCKER OR NOCKHER

I   1   Sebastian. Silk tailor in Stuttgart.
II   2   (1) Johann Georg, matric. at Tübingen University in 1590. Pastor
              in Lustnau 1602–20, Dusslingen 1620–39. M. 1st to Mar-
              garete; M. 2nd to Margarete.
III 3   (2) Johann Georg II.

OSIANDER

I   1   Andreas. Court preacher in Stuttgart.
II   2   (1) Andreas, M.A., b. 1590, d. 1635. Deacon in Balingen 1613,
              Calw 1614; pastor in Nehren 1616–35.
III 3   (2) Gottfrid Nikolai. Pastor.

PREGIZER

I   1   Lucas of Bregenz. Kunstmaler.
II   2   (1) Johann Ulrich I, b. 1537, d. 1597. Pastor in Kusterdingen
              1571–97. M. to Charitas Rhoner.
III 3   (2) Johann Ulrich II. Deacon in Tübingen 1606–12; pastor in
              Lustnau 1624–39.

RUCKER

I   1   Johann. Pastor.
II   2   (1) Johann, b. ca. 1558 in Königsberg. Pastor in Oferdingen
              1586–1615.

SCHAD OR WAGNER

I   1   Martin of Neuenstadt, b. 1549, d. 1616. Pastor in Öschingen
              1571–1616.
II   2   Johann, b. 1577, d. 1634. Pastor in Mähringen 1608–26.

3 N.N. (dtr.). M. to Johann Ziegler, pastor (see under Ziegler).

SCHMID OR FABRI

I 1 Wilhelm Schmid (or Fabri), b. in Weinsberg, d. 1555 in Jesingen. Pastor in Jesingen. M. to Barbara.

II 2 (1) Hans, Bärenwirt, Tübingen. M. in 1568 to Maria Steinholber, dtr. of the Schultheiss of Belsen.

  3 (1) Jakob Fabri, M.A., d. 1573. Pastor in Dusslingen. M. in 1563 to Agathe, dtr. of Hans Widmann of Tübingen.

III 4 (2) Martin, b. 1569, d. 1627. Vogt in Tübingen. M. 1st to Judith, dtr. of Johann Brenz, the reformer M. 2nd in 1590 to Katherina Beer.

  5 (3) Johann. Professor at Tübingen University.

  6 (3) Jakob Fabri, M.A., d. before 1641. Pastor in Corb bei Waiblingen.

IV 7 (4) Johann Martin, M.A., b. 1596, d. 1672. Pastor in Kilchberg 1621, Mössingen 1643.

SCHOLL OR SCHODEL

I   Scholl. Burgvogt in Göppingen.

II 1 Sebastian Scholl, M.A., b. ca. 1573. Matric. 1590, M.A. 1594. Deacon in Hailerbach 1597; pastor in Degenfeld 1597, Neuweiler 1598, Jesingen 1619–36. Resigned in favor of his son-in-law in 1636.

SCHWARZ

I 1 Johann Thomas I. Preceptor in Grossbottwar. Pastor in Altdorf until 1591.

II 2 (1) Johann Thomas II. b. 1551. Pastor in Altdorf 1591–1616.

III 3 (2) Jeremias, b. 1598, d. 1643. Pastor in Altdorf 1616–43.

SIGWART

I 1 Johann Georg, b. 1554, d. 1618. City pastor and supt. in Tübingen 1587–1618; professor of theology at Tübingen University 1587–1618. M. to Margareta Rappelbeck.

II 2 (1) Johann David. Pastor.

  3 (1) Gideon, b. 1592, d. 1638. Pastor in Derendingen 1617–38.

  4 (1) Martin. Pastor.

STEEB

I 1 Michael, d. after 1573. Cartwright in Tübingen.

II   2   (1)   Johannes, M.A., b. 1546, d. 1615. Pastor in Bodelshausen.
             M. 1st in 1573 to Anna, widow of Hans Wolff, Heimsheim.
             M. 2nd in 1614 to Margarete, widow of Hans Georg Lösch.
             Her 3rd marriage in 1616 was to Hans Kratzer.
III 3   (2)   Elias, b. 1578, d. 1625. Schultheiss in Boldelshausen. M.
             before 1604 to Ann N.
IV   4   (3)   Johann, b. 1605, d. 1668. Sheepfold administrator in Tübin-
             gen. M. ca. 1628 to Agnes N.
V   5   (4)   Elias, M.A., b. 1631 in Bodelshausen, d. 1699 in Bodelshau-
             sen. Pastor in Weiler bei Hornberg, Bodelshausen. M. in
             1652 to Maria Cleophe, dtr. of Jakob Fischer of Hornberg.

TRUBER

I   1   Primus I, b. 1508.
II   2   (1)   Primus II, b. 1552, d. 1591. Pastor in Kilchberg 1587–91.

VITUS

I   1   Georg of Metzingen, b. 1560, d. 1616. Pastor in Lustnau
             1591–1602. M. dtr. of Balth. Bidembach.
II   2   (1)   Eberhard. Pastor.
     3   (1)   Georg Friedrich. Pastor.

WIELAND

I   1   Johann. Preacher in Vaihingen.
II   2   (1)   Israel, b. 1542, d. 1633. Pastor in Weilheim am Neckar 1568–
             76, Dusslingen 1589–1610.
III 3   (2)   Maria Scholastika. M. to Ludwig Gebhardt (see under Geb-
             hardt).

ZIEGLER

I   1   Johannes of Backnang, b. 1582, d. 1610. Deacon in Sulz am
             Neckar; pastor in Talheim 1609–10. M. to dtr. of Martin
             Schad (see under Schad).

APPENDIX C

School Attendance in
Tübingen District, 1601

Parish	Communicants	Catechumens	School-children	Ratio of catechumens to school-children
Mössingen[a]	730	400	70	18%
Gönningen	340	357	38	11
Nehren[b]	250	220	33	15
Öschingen	230	150	27	18
Talheim	276	70	25	35
Bodelshausen	330	200	35	18
Weilheim[c d]	110	56	—	—
Schlaitdorf	280	160	70	44
Oferdingen	480	160	48	30
Derendingen[d]	290	51	55	29
Mähringen[e]	320	180	38	21
Kusterdingen	180	110	19	17
Walddorf[f]	700	730	44	4
Dusslingen[g]	600	305	49	16
Altdorf	280	260	40	15
Lustnau	550[h]	300	66	22
Weil im Schönbuch[i]	700	354	93	26
Ofterdingen	350	160	30	19
Entringen	520	300	50	17
Breitenholz	242	48	26	56
Jesingen	350	160	40	25
Hagelloch[j]	160	80	—	—
Kilchberg[d]	83	80	—	—
Kirchentellinsfurt	218	85	50	59
TOTAL	8,569	4,976	946	
Average pct. of catechumens attending school				19%

SOURCES: HStA Bü. 1282 (1601), 1328 (1602), 1329 (1603).

NOTES: The communicants represent the adult members of the parish. The catechumens represent the children as well as young unmarried adults and some servants.

[a] Includes Belsen.

[b] Data are for 1603.

[c] Includes Kressbach.

[d] Weil and Kilchberg children attended school in Derendingen. The catechumens from Weil (56) and Kilchberg (80) were added to those from Derendingen (57) to calculate the percentage of catechumens in the three-parish area attending school in Derendingen.

[e] Includes Jettenburg (also called Yettenbruch) and Ohmenhausen.

[f] Includes Häslach, Gniebel, and Riebgarten.

[g] Includes Stockach.

[h] Data are for 1602.

[i] Includes Dettenhausen, Breitenstein, and Neuweiler.

[j] There was no school in Hagelloch.

Money and Measures in Sixteenth-Century Württemberg

MONEY				
1 Pfund	=	20 Schilling	=	240 Pfenning or 376 Haller
1 florin	=	30 Schilling		
1 florin	=	1.5 Pfund		
GRAIN				
1 Scheffel	=	8 Simri	=	1.77 hectoliters
1 Simri	=	4 Vierling	=	22.15 liters
1 Viertele	=			0.17 liters
LIQUIDS				
1 Fuder	=	6 Eimer	=	17.63 hectoliters
1 Eimer	=	16 Imi	=	2.94 hectoliters
AREA				
1 Morgen	=			0.315 hectares
1 Jauchert or Mannsmahd or Tagewerk	=	1.5 Morgen	=	0.472 hectares
1 Viertel	=	0.25 Mahnsmahd	=	0.118 hectares

SOURCE: Adapted from *Die Archivpflege*, pp. 79–90.

Reference Matter

Notes

The following abbreviations are used in the Notes. Complete authors' names, titles, and publication data are given in References Cited.

HStA   Hauptstaatsarchiv, Stuttgart, A281 Visitationsberichte
KO 1559   *Württembergische Grosse Kirchenordnung 1559*
LKA   Landeskirchliches Archiv, Stuttgart
WA   Weimarer Ausgabe: Luther, D. *Martin Luthers Werke*

Introduction

1. The thesis of the Reformation's failure is not new, however; see Holl, "Luther und das landesherrliche Kirchenregiment." Strauss's important book on Reformation pedagogy and church visitations, *Luther's House of Learning*, started the more recent debate. Strauss argues that the evangelical message, especially in the later phase of the development of princely territorial churches, was an alien ideology that saw little or no merit in folk customs and the popular mind. Because of the distance between the theology of the Protestant clergy and the mentality of the people, and the repeated failure of Lutheran methods of catechetical pedagogy, the Reformation caused "little or no change in the ways in which ordinary men and women conducted their lives" (p. 299). Consequently, Strauss concludes that "the burden of proof ought now at last to be placed where it belongs: upon those who claim, or imply, or tacitly assume that the Reformation aroused a widespread, meaningful, and lasting response to its message" (pp. 307–8). Strauss's challenge prompted Kittelson to publish his own investigation of the visitation reports from the rural Strasbourg parishes in the late sixteenth century. Kittelson argues that, at least in the environs of Strasbourg, the Reformation did fundamentally alter the religious behavior of the people. See Kittelson, "Confessional Age," pp. 361–74; and his "Successes and Failures," pp. 153–55, 174. For an analysis of the changing role of both Cath-

olic and Protestant clergy, see Burke, *Popular Culture* p. 271; Bossy, "Counter-Reformation." Burke finds that during the sixteenth century Protestant and Catholic clergy participated in a general withdrawal of the elite and educated classes from popular culture. The view of the Reformation's alleged failure and of the inherent opposition, if not hostility, between the sixteenth-century shepherds and their flocks has gained widespread support. Scribner accepts it as a commonplace in *For the Sake of Simple Folk*, his illuminating study of popular propaganda in the sixteenth century, in which he judges that the Reformation achieved only mixed success in its propaganda efforts, and perceptively observes that questions about the Reformation's effectiveness in communicating its ideas "lead to wider questions about the nature of the Reformation itself" (p. 249). Similarly, Brady accepts the thesis of a massive, successful resistance by the common people against the introduction of literate piety and a religion of social obedience. He accordingly sees the Lutheran Reformation as urban Christianity's unsuccessful war against the durable, old-fashioned, sociable, more permissive, and intrinsically popular form of medieval religion. See Brady, "Social History," p. 171.

Strauss's findings have been criticized by others than Kittelson. Oberman wryly observes that Holl responded to similar criticisms several decades earlier. Oberman attempts to refute Strauss by arguing, on the basis of Luther's doctrine of the two kingdoms, that Luther never intended a moral transformation of the German people and that therefore there was no failure. Quoting Elert, Oberman concludes that "the antichrist plays a role whenever ethical progress is equated with the kingdom of Christ." Elert, *Morphologie*, vol. 1, p. 451; Oberman, "Martin Luther," pp. 91–94, 119. Although both Strauss and Kittelson use visitation reports as their principal source, Kittelson overlooks and Strauss mentions only in passing the one major investigation of the Protestant protocols: Vogler's three-volume dissertation, "Vie religieuse." With an admitted sympathy for the reformers and their theology, and while recognizing that some parishes and regions remained relatively backward religiously, Vogler argues in his study of the religious life of the Rhinelands that the Reformation "profoundly altered the common mentality of the German world" (vol. 1, p. iii). See also vol. 2, p. 1051. Although he acknowledges the new culture of the Protestant ministers, Vogler believes, in contrast to Burke, that the pastors remained close to the people because of their lifestyle and their daily contact with parishioners (vol. 1, p. 521).

2. See the summary in Delumeau, *Catholicism*, pp. 134–40.

3. Molitor, "Frömmigkeit," pp. 18–19. For a summary of German research into post-Tridentine Catholic visitations, see Zeeden and Molitor, *Die Visitation im Dienst*. For research into the Protestant protocols, see Société Savante d'Alsace, *Sensibilité religieuse*.

4. See note 1, above. Some dissertations supervised by Zeeden at the universities of Freiburg and Tübingen have investigated mainly Catholic protocols. See also Tietz, "Das Erscheinungsbild." Since Zieger was unable to use Prussian visitation records, his monograph, *Das religiöse und kirchliche Leben*, is primarily an examination of church ordinances. See also Theiss, "Pfarrer und Gemeinden." The *Sonderforschungsbereich* 8 at Tübingen published a repertory of the Hesse protocols, which is the first volume of a projected series covering all of the West German visitation reports from the sixteenth and seventeenth centuries. See Zeeden et al., *Repertorium der Kirchenvisitation.* A somewhat out-of-date list of the unprinted sources for Catholic and Protestant protocols is included as an appendix to Zeeden and Molitor, *Die Visitation im Dienst*, pp. 92–126.

5. These early protocols are printed in Rauscher, *Visitationsakten.*

6. Conversation with Gerhard Schäfer, director of the Archive of the Evangelical Church in Württemberg. For a summary of the institutional history of these visits and an analysis of the underlying secular and ecclesiastical ordinances, see Brecht, "Les visites pastorales."

7. The moving force behind the surge of visitation activity throughout the 1580's appears to have been the consistory, whose members included such eminent Württemberg divines as Johannes Magirus and Dieterich Schnepf.

8. The inhabitants of Bodelshausen complained as early as 1581 that they were being overrun by beggars; see LKA Stuttgart A1 1581 fol. 6ʳ. See also LKA Stuttgart A1 1583I fol. 8ʳ, 1584II fol. 3ʳ, 1586I fol. 2ʳ, 1587I fol. 8ᵛ, 1588II fol. 3ᵛ, 1589 fol. 3ʳ, 1590 fol. 48ᵛ; and HStA Bü. 1284 (1603).

9. See Sabean, *Power in the Blood*, pp. 6–8; and Robisheaux, "Origins of Rural Wealth," pp. 55–56, 91–99.

Chapter 1

1. For Saxony, see Drews, *Das evangelische Geistliche*; and Karant-Nunn, *Luther's Pastors.* For Prussia, see Zieger, *Das religiöse und kirchliche Leben.* Other investigations include Klaus, "Soziale Herkunft"; and Vogler, *Le clergé.*

2. Zeeden has summed up the importance of this historical period: "The development of confessional churches is one of the main events in the history of Europe, especially in Germany during the sixteenth and seventeenth centuries." Zeeden, "Grundlagen and Wege," p. 67. See also Kittelson, "Confessional Age," pp. 361–62.

3. The main sources of the geographic and social origins of the Tübingen and Tuttlingen pastorates were the Tübingen University matriculation records, which exist in two different compilations, an eighteenth-century edition by Stoll (*Sammlung*) and a modern version by Hermelink (*Die Ma-*

trikeln). In addition, the present study made use of Binder, *Kirchen- und Lehraemter*; and Sigel, "Das evangelische Württemberg."

4. "Pfarrer hinterlassen nur Bücher und Kinder." Hasselhorn, *Der alt-württembergische Pfarrstand*, p. 19.

5. See Ch. 3 for the economic condition of the Württemberg pastorate. For the social and political function of the parish pastor, see Bader, *Das Dorf*, pp. 182, 193, 210–13, 280–81; Hasselhorn, *Der altwürttembergische Pfarrstand*, pp. 56–65; and Sabean, *Power in the Blood*, pp. 8–9, 11, 17. Vogler reports that pastors' wives served as baptismal sponsors. Vogler, *Le clergé*, p. 209.

6. See Brecht, "Herkunft und Ausbildung." One of Brecht's major sources is the index file of the as-yet-unpublished "Württembergisches Pfarrbuch" being compiled by Otto Haug. The section for Franconian Württemberg has already been published as *Pfarrbuch Württembergisch-Franken*.

7. Brecht, "Herkunft und Ausbildung," p. 165.

8. Ibid., p. 170.

9. *KO 1559*, fol. cxx^r.

10. "Arme und unuermügliche Landkinder." Ibid., fol. clix.

11. "Das nit nach Gunst, Muet oder Gab sonder allein der Erudition unnd unuermüglicheit nach gehandelt werde." Ibid., fols. clxiii^r, clxiii^v. For further discussion of the officers of the Stift, see Ch. 2.

12. LKA Stuttgart A13 Zeugnisbücher, no. 1, vol. 1 (1614–79), fol. 24^r, p. 76 (the volume begins with foliation and shifts to pagination.) See also Ch. 2. In certain cases, a candidate who achieved a mixed result could still obtain promotion. For example, in 1615 Leonard Flackher, the preceptor of Freudenstadt, was found to have a bad sermon and a passable examination, but he was promoted to a parish living (fol. 7^v). Other candidates, fresh from the university with their master's degrees, were not so fortunate. In April 1615, although Jo[h]ann Wilhem Liebler was found to be satisfactory in his preaching and his examination, he had to return in October of the following year as well as in February 1617 to repeat his examination. After the third try he was offered a position, which he "accepted with thanks." Similarly, both Georg Koch and Christian Bausch had to repeat their examinations twice before receiving appointments (fol. 10^r). Ducal intervention could save a candidate from a lifetime in the Stift. Gottfried Curbin failed his examinations in 1616 and 1617. In 1621, Duke Johann Friedrich nominated Curbin to a living in Wittlingen, where he apparently remained as late as June 1656, when he was judged to preach "somewhat softly, but well, with method and substance," and transferred to a new position (fol. 16^v).

13. Hermelink, *Geschichte*, pp. 116–18.

14. LKA Stuttgart A13 Zeugnisbücher, no. 1, vol. 1 (1614–79), fol. 27^r.

15. Hermelink, *Geschichte*, pp. 124–25, 165.

16. The Württemberg visitation protocols are extant and complete for the following years: 1581–90, 1601–3, 1605, 1621, and 1641.

17. Brecht, in "Herkunft und Ausbildung," gives a figure of about 2,700 Württemberg clergy. This figure is valid for our period because the number of positions remained relatively stable in the late sixteenth century. Of these, 140 pastors served in Tübingen and Tuttlingen districts from 1581 to 1621, including the clergy of the Tübingen *Stadtpfarrei* (city parish), i.e., St. Georgen and the *Stiftskirche* (foundation church), and excluding the clergy and preceptors of Bebenhausen. If positions are counted rather than clergy, the clerical sample considered here accounts for about 6 percent of the total positions. Brecht has counted 600 livings, or positions, in Württemberg, excluding teaching positions in the Stift and the cloister schools. Tübingen had 27 parish positions, and Tuttlingen had 9.

18. The three pastors whose origin is unknown were all in place during the 1560's. Two of them, Jakob Eisenkopf and Johann Thomas Schwarz, appear in the records at about the time of the Interim, and possibly belong to the first generation of Württemberg pastors. Although the geographic data are in a sense a subset of Brecht's, the information has been gathered independently and is superior to Brecht's because a greater percent of origins has been recovered and the total number of clergy is known.

19. Christoph Heerbrand and Johann Neobolus were the sons of friends of Luther. Neobolus's father, Jodokus or Jost, living in Wittenberg with Luther from 1535 to 1538. Luther recommended him to the Württemberg church, where, from 1553 to 1540, he was deacon in Tübingen. After serving a year in Augsburg as deacon, he took up the pastorage in Entringen, outside Tübingen. The highlight of Jodokus's career came when he was appointed theological advisor to Württemberg's secular ambassadors to the Council of Trent. In 1568, Jodokus retired from office and his son succeeded him. Sigel, "Das evangelische Württemberg." The two converts, Johann Kölner (b. 1534) and Primus Truber (b. 1508), were the oldest of the pastors in place in 1581. The offspring of early Württemberg reformers included Theodorich Schnepf and Johann Dieterich Schnepf, Erhard's son and grandson; and the three sons of Jakob Andreae, Jakob II, David, and Johann, and Eberhard, son of Jakob II. (See Appendix B.)

20. Sigel, "Das evangelische Württemberg."

21. Elze, *Die Universität Tübingen*, pp. 29–30.

22. Sigel, "Das evangelische Württemberg."

23. For a general study of the Reformation and the cities, see Brady, *Turning Swiss*, pp. 151–221. For a case study of the Reformation in one Swabian city, see Rublack, *Eine bürgerliche Reformation*.

24. These data are compiled from the figures cited in Hermelink, *Die Matrikeln*, vol. 2, pt. 1: Register, pp. xiii–xxiv.

25. Decker-Hauff, "Führungsschicht," pp. 62–63.

26. Brecht, "Herkunft und Ausbildung," p. 170.

27. Vogler, *Le clergé*, p. 18

28. Vann, *Making of a State*, pp. 41, 43, 172. Cf. the earlier analysis of this political class by Decker-Hauff, who defines the group much more broadly to include ducal officials and churchmen. Decker-Hauff, "Die Entstehung der altwürttembergischen Ehrbarkeit, 1250–1534" (diss., Univ. of Vienna, 1946), cited by Seigel, *Gericht und Rat*, p. 48, without page reference.

29. Brecht, "Herkunft und Ausbildung," p. 172. See Vogler's tabulation of Brecht's findings in Vogler, *Le clergé*, p. 18.

30. Vogler, *Le clergé*, p. 19.

31. See Appendix B.

32. In 1580, the Bodelshausen pastor received a specie salary of 63 florins, which was almost the average for Tübingen district (64 florins). LKA Stuttgart A12, no. 41, 1580 Kompetenzen, fols. 279ʳ–280ʳ.

33. LKA Stuttgart A12, no. 41, 1559 Kompetenzen, fol. 661ʳ.

34. For purposes of comparison the following table summarizes the data on social recruitment in the next century (1700–1800) as presented by Hasselhorn, *Der altwürttembergische Pfarrstand*, p. 30. Hasselhorn's totals and percentages are corrected here. Higher clergy include those ranked dean or superintendent and upward. Teachers in German schools are teachers without university education.

Profession of father	No.	Pct.
Unknown	141	4.4%
Pastor, deacon	1,106	34.6
Low official	535	16.7
Artisan	305	9.5
Higher clergy	246	7.7
High official	183	5.7
Merchant	136	4.3
Bürgermeister	126	3.9
Preceptor of Latin schools	98	3.1
Doctor and apothecary	86	2.7
Surgeon	72	2.3
Innkeeper	49	1.5
Teacher in German schools	47	1.5
Military officer	21	0.7
Vine dresser	18	0.6
Musician	16	0.5
Other modest profession	7	0.2
Peasant	6	0.2
TOTAL	3,198	100.0%

35. The situation in the district of Tübingen appears to correspond nei-

ther with that described by Vogler for the Rhinelands, where the desire for social mobility and the attraction of studies prompted sons of artisans to enter the ministry, nor with conditions in Ernestine Saxony. Karant-Nunn describes a process in Saxony whereby the sons of artisans were co-opted into bourgeois society. In Vogler, *Le clergé*, p. 19; Karant-Nunn, *Luther's Pastors*, p. 13.

36. Seigel, *Gericht und Rat*, pp. 203, 210, 280.

37. Vann, *Making of a State*, pp. 117–21. Cf. Decker-Hauff, as quoted by Seigel, *Gericht und Rat*, pp. 48–49.

38. Excluding the untypically high incomes of the Tübingen city clergy, the average specie revenue of a Tübingen district benefice was 64 florins. Two of the three benefices under the patronage of the court had above average incomes. In 1580, Derendingen received 74 florins, Weilheim am Neckar 67 florins. The third parish, Kusterdingen, had a slightly below average income of 62 florins. LKA Stuttgart A12, no. 41, 1580 Kompetenzen, fol. 269. See Appendix B for the list of families. See also Seigel, *Gericht und Rat*, pp. 63–64.

39. Seigel, *Gericht und Rat*, pp. 63–64.

40. Seigel reports that a total of sixteen Tübingen city magistrates were sons and three were grandsons of clergymen in the sixteenth and seventeenth centuries. Seigel, *Gericht und Rat*, p. 64.

41. *Grundherren*, p. 28.

42. See Appendix B. Although the patronage was in the hands of the members of the town court, most of the pastors appointed from magistrate families came from among the town councillors, the comparably larger group.

43. Seigel, *Gericht und Rat*, p. 65; and Sigel, "Das evangelisch Württemberg," vol. 12, p. 491.

44. For an overview of the growth of early modern princely government and the increase of its tasks, see Oestreich, *Verfassungsgeschichte*, pp. 83ff.

45. *Das Königreich Württemberg*, vol. 2: *Schwarzwaldkreis*, pp. 313–15. For Enzlin's story, see Bernhardt, *Die Zentralbehörden*, pp. 263–70; and Vann, *Making of a State*, pp. 70, 84.

46. Vogler, *Le clergé*, p. 19.

47. Strauss, *Luther's House of Learning*, p. 285. For a survey of elementary education in Württemberg during the sixteenth century, see Schmid, *Geschichte des Volkschulwesens*, pp. 5–87.

48. LKA Stuttgart, A1 1581 fols. 2^r–12^v.

49. Ibid., fols. 41^r–44^r.

50. LKA Stuttgart, A1 1590 fols. 46^v–52^r, 1621 fols. 30^r–32^v.

51. See Appendix C. Although the *Schulordnung* (school ordinance) of 1559 (*KO 1559*, fol. cxii^r) assumed that both boys and girls would attend the village schools, in fact only boys seem to have attended. The evidence for

this is the visitors' repeated use of the words schoolboys (*Schulknaben*) and pupils (*Schüler*) interchangeably. Despite Schmid's contention that *Schüler* was an inclusive term for boys and girls, the visitors of the Tübingen and Tuttlingen districts seem to have encountered only schoolboys, with one exception. In 1588, they reported that 49 male pupils (Schüler) and 8 girls (*Mädlin*) were attending the Tuttlingen city school. Although Tuttlingen was a city, its school was primarily a German school. In 1588, the visitor notes that the school "has only one pupil who is learning Latin, but 49 boys and 8 girls are learning German. In the summer, school attendance is neglected because the children are needed for the harvest." LKA Stuttgart 1588I fol. 44ʳ. Cf. Schmid, *Geschichte des Volkschulwesens*, p. 19. A separate school for girls taught by a schoolmistress existed in Tübingin. LKA Stuttgart A1 1581 fol. 2ᵛ, 1582 fol. 2ʳ, 1583I fol. 1ʳ. Cf Furet and Ozouf, who believe that there was no necessary correlation between school attendance and literacy rates, *Reading and Writing*, pp. 235–37.

52. The practice of German elementary schools contrasts with that of French parish schools, where pupils learned first to read Latin, since it was believed to provide the pedagogical basis for learning French. Furet and Ozouf, *Reading and Writing*, pp. 75–76, 80.

53. See Stahlecker, *Geschichte der Lateinschule*, pp. 163–64. The candidates were originally required to submit testimonies that they could not financially support their studies. *KO 1559*, fols. clxii;ʳ–clxiiᵛ; see also fol. clxiiᵛ.

54. WA Tischreden, vol. 5, no. 5252, pp. 27–29. Moreover, Luther thought that although they might later practice a trade, all schoolboys, present and former, after studying Latin, would always stand in reserve to serve the church as pastors or preachers. WA 30², pp. 546–47. Evidently, Luther had Latin schools in mind.

55. Vogler, *Le clergé*, p. 19.

56. According to Brecht's compilations, the sons of nobility constituted 0.6 percent of all pastors of known origin, a proportion that is probably high, since modern genealogists have been more apt to trace noble ancestry, and the contemporary record keepers were more likely to have noted and recorded it. Brecht, "Herkunft und Ausbildung," p. 175. See also Vogler, *Le clergé*, p. 18.

57. Hermelink, *Die Matrikeln*, vol. 2, pt. 1: *Register*, pp. xxi–xxiv.

58. Vann, *Making of a State*, p. 84. Cf. Decker-Hauff, "Führungsschicht," pp. 56–58.

59. Brecht, "Herkunft und Ausbildung," p. 172. See also Vogler, *Le clergé*, p. 18.

60. "Dieweyl der Kirchendiener Kinder vor andern der Kirche wieder dienen konnen." Cited in Vogler, *Le clergé*, p. 21 n. 23.

61. Brecht, "Herkunft und Ausbildung," p. 172. See also Vogler, *Le clergé*, p. 18.

62. Vogler, *Le clergé*, p. 21. The Württemberg pattern of self-recruitment does not appear to reflect the origins of a *gentes theologicae*, like that described by Léonard, because it was not a group limited strictly to families and close friends of academics. See Léonard, *History of Protestantism*, pp. 214–15. See also Vogler, *Le clergé*, pp. 23–24.

63. In the sampled districts, the families with three or more generations of pastors were Andreae, Bollinger, Cless, Heerbrand, Heiland, Mockel, Neobolus, Osiander, Schmid, Scholl, and Schwarz. See Appendix B. For the situation in the Rhinelands, see Vogler, *Le clergé*, p. 21.

64. Pastors succeeded by their sons were Matthaeus Mockel, Johann Neobolus, Jacobus Erhardt, Kerner in Trossingen, and Maurer in Hausen an der Zaber. The Schwarz family in Altdorf held the same living for three generations.

65. See Ch. 3. While Clasen reports that almost every village had some rich peasants with property valued at over 500 florins, only a few villages had rich peasants who owned over 1,000 florins of property. Clasen, *Die Weidertäufer*, p. 209. At a conservative rate of return of 5 percent per annum, the yearly income of such a rich peasant would have been about 50 florins. In Lamenburg district, in the nearby county (*Grafschaft*) of Hohenlohe, only 4.8 percent of the population possessed more than 100 florins of wealth. Robisheaux, "Origins of Rural Wealth," p. 267, table 2.18.

66. Hasselhorn has argued that the churchmen enjoyed the "right," as did all members of the Ehrbarkeit, to have ecclesiastical revenues pay for the theological education of at least one son. Hasselhorn, *Der altwürttembergische Pfarrstand*, p. 33.

67. Sigel, "Das evangelische Württemberg."

68. LKA Stuttgart A3, 7 (1651–58) Konsistorial-Protokolle, pp. 412, 415, 424.

69. Although Kolb seems correct in pointing out the paucity of evidence about the social origins of pastors' wives, this subject merits further analysis. Kolb, "Zur Geschichte des Pfarrstands," pp. 149–50.

70. "In Andern Ländern regiere der Dativus, aber in Württemberg der Genetivus." Cited in Kolb, "Zur Geschichte des Pfarrstands," p. 84 and p. 84 n. 7. Yet, as Kolb observes, the practice of giving gifts was not unknown in Württemberg.

71. Brecht counts about 600 ecclesiastical livings and about 100 positions in Latin and cloister schools. Brecht, "Herkunft und Ausbildung," p. 164.

Chapter 2

1. "Unsere Jünglinge werden in der wichtigsten Periode der intellektuellen und moralischen Entwicklung in Wäldern und Einöden begraben. Sie wissen sich in den schönsten lateinischen Phrasen auszudrücken, aber wenn

sie mit einem Menschen zusammen kommen, der nicht ihr täglicher Gesellschafter ist, so sind sie wegen der paar deutschen Worte verlegen. . . . Jene Blödigkeit [d.h. Verlegenheit] die näturliche Folge des klösterlichen Zwangs, verliert sich selten." From "Einige Wünsche die Wirtembergische Geistliche betreffend," quoted in Hasselhorn, *Der altwürttembergische Pfarrstand*, pp. 41–42.

2. Kittelson, "Confessional Age," pp. 368–69. The discussion in this chapter was greatly improved by the cogent comments of James Vann and David Sabean.

3. *KO 1559*, fol. cxix^r.

4. "Gemeinlich herrschaffende Underthonen." Ibid., fol. cxx^v.

5. Stahlecker, *Geschichte der Lateinschule*, pp. 245–47. According to Stahlecker, in 1603–4 the Tuttlingen school had 8 Latin pupils, 75 German pupils, and 19 girls in attendance (p. 246). On the relationship between the Latin and German schools, cf. Stahlecker and Keck, *Geschichte der Mittleren Schule*, pp. 39–40.

6. The Latin schools were established so that the children "von jugent auff von iren Elementis, per gradus dester ehe und fürderlicher zu den nutzlichen Sprachen, wie dann das alt Testament in Hebraischer unnd das new Testament in griechischer Sprachen geschriben seien, unnd dann von selbigen zu rechter Theologie, unnd anderen hohen notturfftigen Künsten, Regimenten, Aemtern und Hausshaltungen gerhaten unnd kommen mögen." *KO 1559*, fol. cxix^r.

7. "Wie die blinden Ethnici von Gott und seinem Wort nichts gewisst. . . . Darneben ein exemplum unnd testimonium sacrae Scripturae anzeigen, wie Gott der Herr dise Laster grewlich straff." Ibid., fol. cxxviii^r.

8. Ibid., fol. cxxxi^v.

9. For example, phrases from Terence were to be drilled in Latin and "in good German." Ibid., fols. cxxviii^r, cxxxi^v.

10. Non-university-bound students often outnumbered the students intending to become pastors, lawyers, or doctors. See Stahlecker, *Gerschichte der Lateinschule*, p. 180. Stahlecker observes that the urban officialdom consisted of Latin school alumni and that the schools must not have been considered merely as preparation for the university, because the city of Tübingen would not then have invested the financial support that it did.

11. "Gutte unnd fruchtbare Ingenia." *KO 1559*, fol. cxliii^r.

12. Ibid., fol. cxliii^v.

13. "Oder unser Paedagogium zu Stutgartten zu promouieren weren." Ibid. Keck gives this age range for candidacy for the examination in *Geschichte der Mittleren Schule*, p. 41.

14. See Grafton, who observes not only the linguistic vitality and accessibility of Latin but also its social function. Facility in Latin was "a means of winning advancement (and, of course, keeping those unfit by birth and po-

sition from winning advancement in their turn)." Grafton, "Polyhistors," p. 36.

15. In general, the role that the structure of elementary Latin and German education played in determining the urban character of the Reformation needs illumination. For a survey of the recent research on cities and the Reformation, see Greyerz, "Stadt und Reformation," p. 35.

16. Duke Ludwig combined the schools of Anhausen, Denkendorf, and Lorch into one. The six abolished schools in Murrhardt, Alpirsbach, St. Georgen, Herrenalb, Königsbronn, and Hirsau. Stahlecker, *Gerschichte der Lateinschule*, p. 2. For the history of the Württemberg cloister schools, see Stahlecker.

17. The church treasury became a constant point of contention between the estates and the duke. Vann, *Making of a State*, pp. 53, 67, 149. Cf. Keck, *Geschichte der Mittleren Schule*, p. 41 n. 69. For the history of the appropriations, see Deetjen, *Studien zur Württembergischen Kirchenordnung*.

18. Luther recommended towns rather than cloisters or collegiate churches (*Stiftskirchen*) as the location for prospective Brandenburg high schools. Luther to Margrave Georg von Brandenburg, July 18, 1529, in WA Briefe, vol. 5, no. 1452, p. 120. For Brenz's proposal to use the rural convents as humanistic schools, see "Ordnung des Kirchendiensts, so in den Stifften und Clöstern furgenommen werden möcht (1 June 1529)," in Brenz, *Anecdota Brentiana*, ed. Pressel, no. X, pp. 33–39. See also Ehmer, "Bildungsideale und Bildungspolitik," p. 15.

19. Ehmer, *Valentin Vannius*, p. 219 n. 33; Reyscher, *Vollständige*, vol. 2, p. 126. According to Nicodemus Frischlin, at one time there were a total of 193 students in cloister schools. Frischlin, *Elegiarum Liber Quartus: Monasteria Ducatus Vvirtembergici*, cited in Ehmer, *Valentin Vannius*, p. 219 n. 35.

20. *KO 1559*, fol. cl^v.

21. Ibid., fol. cl^v, fol. cxliii^r. Apart from the exceptions specified in the cloister ordinance, the particular school ordinance provided that the preceptors were to hold exercises on the style and usage of Latin in the fifth form of the principal cloister schools and in the fourth form of the grammar schools so that the pupils might come to a right understanding and practice of the Latin language and to a fear of God (fol. cli^r).

22. The set books authored by Melanchthon were the *Grammaticae Philippi*, the *Erotemata Dialecticae*, the *quaestiones* from his *Grammaticae*, and, for rhetoric, his *Rhetorica*. Ibid., fol. cl^v. The readings from Cicero were the *Epistolae Familiares*, the *De Officiis*, and the *Libellos de Amicitia et Senectute* (fol. cl^v–cli^r). For the prescribed historical readings, see fol. cli^r.

23. The *lectio theologica* occurred weekday mornings during the first hour, and two hours on Saturday were devoted to the Gospel text for the following Sunday. All the remaining hours of instruction, that is, late morn-

ings and afternoons on weekdays, consisted of liberal arts subjects. *KO 1559*, fols. cl^r–cli^r.

24. "Nach dem vermögen ires verstands, beid in Grammatica & Theologia bericht werden." *KO 1559* fol. cl^v.

25. Ehmer, *Valentin Vannius*, p. 220. Heerbrand's *Compendium* first appeared in 1573; Ehmer suggests that the *Margarita Theologiae* of Spangenberg might have been in use earlier (p. 220).

26. The second set history reading was the *Historia Tripartita*. See Ehmer, *Valentin Vannius*, p. 210. While Spitz observes the importance of ancient and contemporary history to the Protestant reformers, Hahn notes that none of the early school orders incorporated either Luther's or Melanchthon's suggestions about the importance of church history. Spitz, *Protestant Reformation*, p. 377; Hahn, *Die Evangelische Unterweisung*, p. 51.

27. Vannius's theological compendium, the *Sylva Locorum*, is described in full in Ehmer, *Valentin Vannius*, pp. 220–21. Vannius set five rules. (1) The pupil should have six volumes of blank books, with a specified number of pages for each locus. (2) The part devoted to each locus should be divided into three parts, one-half for biblical entries, one-third for church authors, and one-sixth for secular authors. (3) Each of these three divisions should be subdivided into two parts, the first for commandments and promises, the latter for examples and histories. (4) Entries should be made only in key words. (5) During the readings, the dialectical and rhetorical method should be respected, but the pupil should make use of, not simply write down, observations from the past (p. 221). This method of compiling a book of commonplaces was the one previously developed by the Strasbourg gymnasium. See Sohm, *Die Schule Joh. Sturms*, p. 221. The church ordinance also recommended the use of copybooks in the Latin schools. *KO 1559*, fols. cxxiii^r–cxxiii^v. Ehmer judges Vannius's method to be scholastic because Vannius used the Bible as a reservoir of prooftexts for dogmatics. Ehmer, *Valentin Vannius*, pp. 221–22.

28. The term *Novizen* (novices) in the 1559 church ordinance was changed to *Klosterschüler* (cloister students) in the 1582 edition, possibly because of the former's Catholic overtones. See Ehmer, *Valentin Vannius*.

29. *Württembergische Klosterordnung vom Juli 1535*, summarized in Deetjen, *Studien zur Württembergischen Kirchenordnung*, pp. 214, 216–18.

30. The phrase *mit ernst straffen* (e.g., in *KO 1559*, fol. clvi^v) in the cloister school's disciplinary ordinances could perhaps mean use of the rod, but the same phrase is used in the ordinances of the Stift and in the visitation protocols to mean a monetary fine.

31. The first ordinance was probably authored by the Upper German Ambrosius Blarer with the help of the more conservative Lutheran Erhard Schnepf. Such theological cooperation was most likely due to the influence

of Duke Christoph. Despite Blarer's predilection for radical reform, the order embodies the medieval monastic spirit of *laborare et orare*, following the time-honored Benedictine pattern of the *opus dei*. See Deetjen, *Studien zur Württembergischen Kirchenordnung*, p. 214. The 1556 cloister ordinance has been reprinted in Christoph Friedrich Sattler, *Geschichte des Herzogtums Württembergs unter der Regierung der Herzogen*, cited in Ehmer, *Valentin Vannius*, p. 210. The 1559 cloister ordinance can be found in *KO 1559*, fols. cxlii-clxi. Ehmer discusses the drafting of the ordinance on p. 217.

32. "Allein auff die Theologie, damit ich mit der Zeit in der Kirch Gottes zu einem Diener nach seinem Göttlichen Beruff gebraucht werden möge." *KO 1559*, fol. cxlv^v. Cf. Leube. "Die Zweckbestimmung," p. 161.

33. See Leube, "Bursa und Stift," pp. 5–6. Ariès has observed that such a regulated common life in a college was in fact a late medieval phenomenon, epitomized by the 1501 reforms of Standonc at College Montaigu. Ariès, *Centuries of Childhood*, pp. 167, 170.

34. "Eines zimmlichen allters ungefahrlich sechzehen oder sibenzehen Jar." *KO 1559*, fol. clxii^r.

35. Sigel, "Das evangelische Württemberg." Cf. Leube, who states that students matriculated at the university between the ages of 13 and 15. Leube, "Bursa und Stift," p. 1. According to Jens, students entered the lower cloister at 14, the higher cloister at 16, and the Stift at 18. Jens, *Eine Deutsche Universität*, p. 110.

36. In 1594, there were 153 students attending the Stift, some of whom lived in other households. Leube, *Geschichte des Tübinger Stifts*, p. 231.

37. Stoll, *Sammlung*.

38. "Aber die Stipendiaten, so Theologiam zustudieren schuldig, und deren alter und geschicklichkeit zu disem thüchtig ist, Söllen zu der Theologischen leere auch in der selben Facultet zuprocedieren und fürtzefarn bey verlierung ihrer Stipendia angehalten werden." Ulrichs zweite Ordnung vom 3, November 1536, printed in Roth, *Urkunden*, p. 190.

39. "Wer ein theologus will werden, der hatt erstlich ein grossen vortheil: er hatt die bibel. Die ist nun so klar, das ers kann lesen an omni impedimento. Darnach lese er darzu locos communes Philippi. . . . Das gibet im denn eloquentiam et copiam verborum." (Whoever wants to become a theologian has a great advantage. He has the Bible. The Bible is so clear that he can read it without any impediment. After the Bible, he should read Philip [Melancthon]'s *Loci*. . . . This reading will give him eloquence and a wealth of words.) Tischreden, vol. 5, no. 5511, p. 204.

40. The reviews served to prepare students for examinations. Melancthon had published for this purpose his *Examen Ordinandorum*, which enjoyed wide distribution. *Libri Philipi Melanthonis, Corpus Reformatorum*, vol. 23, pp. xxxv–civ, 1–102. The 1660 church ordinance speaks of the in-

tent on the part of the authorities to choose as teaching assistants those destined to become future doctors of theology. *KO 1660*, p. 276.

41. "Zu dem fürnämlichen alle publicae Lectiones . . . in Artibus, Autoribus et Theologia gelesen, repetiert werden, damit man also eigentlich, unnd gewisslich befinden mög, ob sie unsere Stipendiaten denen fleissig obgelegen, die wol verstanden, und solche zu nutz eingebildet, und memoriert haben, oder nit." *KO 1559*, fol. clxvi^v. See also Leube, *Geschichte des Tübinger Stifts*, p. 67.

42. *KO 1559*, fol. clxviii.

43. This arrangement is stated in the *Ordination der Universität* (1561), which respects the prescription of the 1559 church ordinance concerning doctoral candidates. Leube, *Geschichte des Tübinger Stifts*, pp. 62–63.

44. "Damit sie der rituum ecclesiae dester bass exerciert und berichtet werden." *Ordination der Universität* (1561), quoted in ibid., p. 63. Research into French colleges of the early modern period indicates that the longer a student remained in school (and the higher his last degree), the more prestigious was his socioprofessional origin. See Frijoff and Julia, *Ecole et société*, pp. 56–58.

45. "So sollen neben dem Magistro Domus, noch sechs Magistri, ausser unsern Stipendiaten, die zum geschicktesten, gelertesten einer Gravitet, und hierzu am tauglichsten, von unsern Superintendenten, des Stipendii, auch Magister Domus erwölt, deputiert unnd verordnet." *KO 1559*, fol. clxvi^r.

46. Leube, *Geschichte des Tübinger Stifts*, p. 63.

47. Leube, *Geschichte des Tübinger Stifts*, p. 63–64.

48. The titles listed were Apophthegmata Erasmi, Elucidarium Vocabulorum, Copia Verborum, Dictionarium, Confabulationes Erasmi, Dialectica Caesarii, Laurentius Valla, Tabulae Moselani, Terentius, tria volumina orationum Ciceronis, and Declamationes Graecae Erasmi. Ephoratsregistratur des Evangelischen Seminars (Stifts) Tübingen, printed in Leube, *Geschichte des Tübinger Stifts*, p. 76.

49. The library holdings of Martin Meglin, an evangelical pastor from Kitzingen in Hohenlohe, also demonstrate the continued importance of Erasmus in the intellectual life of the Lutheran clergy in the early modern period. Included as part of an inventory of bequest, the library contained 96 titles, 8 of which are books by Erasmus. The only author more treasured by Meglin was Martin Luther, with 10 titles. "Verzeichnis der Bücher Martin Meglins," in Demandt and Rublack, *Stadt und Kirche*. See Vogler's findings concerning the place of Erasmus in Rhineland pastors' libraries during the sixteenth century. Vogler, *Le clergé*, pp. 240–53. Among the Rhineland clergy, the *Adagia* and the *Colloquia* were Erasmus's most popular works. Grafton has argued that Erasmus and his colleagues determined the form of humanism that focused on Latin rhetoric and the interpretation of Latin texts and that influenced German intellectual life until deep in the eighteenth

century. Grafton, "Polyhistors," pp. 34–35. In a similar vein, Evans has stated that Christian humanism was the fundamental characteristic of the intellectual culture of the Empire after 1540. Evans, "Culture and Anarchy," pp. 15–16.

50. See Brecht, "Die Entwicklung," p. 19.

51. Ibid., p. 15.

52. Ibid., pp. 15, 18.

53. Ibid., p. 18.

54. Ibid. The interest of the Lutheran clergy of Württemberg in Reformed works is comprehensible in light of the initial Upper German character of the Württemberg Reformation, the proximity of the duchy to Reformed lands, and the Württemberg penchant for polemic in the late Reformation. For example, see the condemnation of the Calvinist doctrine of the Lord's Supper in article 7 of the Solid Declaration of the *Formula of Concord. Die Bekenntnisschriften*, p. 973:2. Kolb observes that commentaries by Calvin, Bullinger, Musculus, Oecolampadius, Bucer, Gwalther, Hemmingius, and others were in use at the end of the sixteenth century. Kolb, *Die Bibel*, p. 130. See also Kolb, "Luthertum und Calvinismus," esp. pp. 137–39; and his "Zur Geschichte des Pfarrstands," p. 90.

55. HStA Bü. 1282 (1601), 1283 (1602), 1284 (1603), 1285 (1605).

56. Leube notes that in the first decades of the Stift, the sermon practices were held in the Stiftskirche. The 1559 church ordinance says nothing about sermons during meals. When the change occurred is not known. During Frischlin's time, the Magister were still preaching in the church. See Leube, *Geschichte des Tübinger Stifts*, p. 83 n. 1.

57. Ephoratsregistur des Evangelischen Seminars (Stifts) Tübingen, printed in Leube, *Geschichte des Tübinger Stifts*, p. 83.

58. According to Crusius, *Schwäbische Chronik*, vol. 2, p. 384.

59. *KO 1660*, p. 284. Cited by Leube, *Geschichte des Tübinger Stifts*, p. 164.

60. The Komplenten were candidates for a master's degree, whereas the novices were candidates for the baccalaureat.

61. Leube, *Geschichte des Tübinger Stifts*, pp. 167–68.

62. "Und wolcher Stipendiat under dem Gebett und lesen, ob dem Tisch schwetzen, oder sonsten sich mit ungeberden erzeigen oder vom Tisch, ehe man das *Gratias* gesprochen, lauffen würdet, derselbig soll, so oft das geschicht, seines Weins des tags beraubt, oder dem verwircken nach, mit Gefencknuss gestrafft." *KO 1559*, fol. clxxiᵛ.

63. See Müller, "Prüfungs und Anstellungswesen."

64. According to Fritz, the Württemberg examination had a standard for passing higher than that in other parts of Germany. Fritz, "Der württembergische Pfarrer, pp. 230–31.

65. *KO 1559*, fol. clxxiiiiᵛ.

66. Ariès, *Centuries of Childhood*, pp. 241–43.

67. "Er soll auch darneben in der Wochen unter den Stipendiaten in der geheim etliche auffsehr anrichten, jedes unfleiss und verhandlung wider die Statuten bey iren Aiden ime dem Magistro zu rügen, und was gerügt oder sonst erfunden, alle Sonntag das nach essens erörttern, und was zustraffen, das den Statuten nach, gleich bar büssen und zalen lassen, und kein straff auffziehen." *KO 1559*, fol. clxxxiv^v. Cf. Leube, "Bursa und Stift," p. 6.

68. *KO 1559*, fol. clxx^r–clxx^v.

69. Ibid., fol. clxx^r. In the preface to the statutes of the Stift, the authors use forms of the word *Zucht* (discipline) and *Ordnung* (order) even more often than invocations of various persons of the Trinity or references to the godly prince (fol. clxviii^v).

70. Strauss, *Luther's House of Learning*, pp. 180–81. The lack of provision for corporal punishment is noteworthy, since Ariès has argued that the history of college discipline in the early modern period was marked by the extension of the use of the rod, a punishment formerly restricted to the youngest children, and the institution of a humiliating system of discipline, marked by whippings and spying. Ariès, *Centuries of Childhood*, pp. 261–62.

71. "Landkinder, . . . die gern studiren wölten, sich Armut halber nicht erhalten mögen." *KO 1559*, fol. clxxxi^r.

72. "In allen Statutis gleichsam andern Stipendiaten halten." Ibid.

73. "M. Schaubel hat allhie Schulden gemacht und um derselben willen heimzuziehen um Fastnacht copiam begehrt, welches ihm erlaubt worden. Als er aber kein Geld aufbringen können, ist er, als wir berichtet worden, nach Ulm gezogen und alda zu eimem Laden hinuasgefallen, darauf er bald Tods verschieden." Quartelbericht (des Stifts) Georgis 1594, printed in Leube, *Geschichte des Tübinger Stifts*, p. 57.

74. "Die ganze Zeit krankte an sittliche Defekten." Leube, *Geschichte des Tübinger Stifts*, pp. 30, 171–72.

75. Cf. Vann, *Making of a State*, p. 29.

76. See Leube, *Geschichte des Tübinger Stifts*, p. 74.

77. Chr. Fr. Schnurrer, *Erlauterungen der württembergischen Kirchenreformations- und Gelehrtegeschichte*, 1798, cited in Leube, *Geschichte des Tübinger Stifts*, p. 58 n. 1.

78. *KO 1559*, fol. clxv^v. Leube, *Geschichte des Tübinger Stifts*, p. 67.

79. Leube, *Geschichte des Tübinger Stifts*, p. 78, citing Visitationsrezess 1618. Kolb, *Die Bibel*, pp. 145–49.

80. Instruction wegen dess Ordinis Studiorum, 1688, reprinted in Leube, *Geschichte des Tübinger Stifts*, p. 221.

81. "Hierzu war ich nun wohl gerüst't: / Denn alle Künst' ich mich wohl genist. / Ich hatt' durchlernt der Logik Strick' / Und der Rhetorik Büchlein dick, / Ich hatt' erlernt des Himmels Sphär / Und was von Sitten Ethik sagt, /

Und was Homerus einhertagt: — / Das konnt' ich gar, —als wärs nur Kraut— / Kein Bau'r hätt's mir zugetraut." Andreae, *Praktische Theologie,* p. 4.

82. Ibid., p. 9.

83. "Bis dass verschwind't der Luft Gebäu, / Bis dass verdaut der Pappenbrei, / Bis dass verraucht des Hirnes Dampf, / Bis dass vertobt der Witze Kampf / Und nur die Praktik kommt zu Haus, / Die all' Theorik treibet aus." Ibid.

84. "Wie, sag ich, sollt' der geistlich Stand / Von Bauern haben sein'n Verstand? / Soll nit die hohe Schuk uns weisen / Wie wir bezähmen die Unweisen / Was wäre denn die Theologie / Anders, als eine Baurn-Kirchweih." Ibid. On the social distance between pastors and parishioners, cf. *Hasselhorn, Der altwürttembergische Pfarrstand,* p. 63; Fritz, "Der württembergische Pfarrer," p. 296; and Fulbrook, *Piety and Politics,* p. 78.

85. See Strauss, *Luther's House of Learning,* p. 101.

86. See Davis, *Society and Culture,* p. 241. Languedoc, Scotland, and Bohemia are some of the examples cited by Burke to illustrate the withdrawal of the upper classes. Burke, *Popular Culture,* pp. 271–72. Strauss remarks: "It comes as a surprise to conventional assumptions about preponderant illiteracy to discovery that schools were common in villages and small towns across the duchy [of Württemberg]." Strauss, *Luther's House of Learning,* pp. 18, 314 n. 70.

87. Frijoff and Julia have made the case for school attendance rates as a reliable indicator of literacy, *Ecole et société,* pp. 15–17. This assumption has been criticized by Furet and Ozouf in *Reading and Writing,* pp. 235–37, 302–3. Furet and Ozouf's data, however, derive from the nineteenth century, when conditions might very well have been radically different from those three centuries earlier. In the sixteenth century, both Catholics and Protestants established parish schools and emphasized literacy. For the school attendance rate in 1601 in Tübingen district, see Appendix C and Ch. 1.

88. Brecht, "Herkunft und Ausbildung," p. 169. Hasselhorn has characterized the eighteenth-century Stift as "the great life insurance of the honored class." Hasselhorn, *Der altwürttembergische Pfarrstand,* p. 44. Vogler observes that the development of a pastoral caste in the Rhinelands after 1580 was stopped by the Thirty Years War. Vogler, *Le clergé,* p. 22. Léonard argues that Protestant pastors married and tended to form dynasties with ministers and theologians belonging to family groups "so that the views of the father, father-in-law, or uncle were adopted by sons, sons-in-law, nephews, connexions, and like an heirloom were carefully guarded and implemented." He cites the development of a gentes theologicae in Germany, consisting of the likes of the families Fabricus, Feuerlein, Leyser, Olearius, and Osiander. Léonard, *History of Protestantism,* pp. 214–15.

Chapter 3

1. "Als ich in meinen jungen Tagen, / Oft hört' von guten Pfründen sagen: / Wie dass nicht feist're Suppen wären / Als die man gäb' geistlichen Herren." *Praktische Theologie*, p. 3.

2. "Wo wär' Wein, Korn, Obst, Holz und Weid'? / Ich hört nit all'weg guten Bescheid. / Da wollt das Pflaster in den Flecken / Mich auch zuweilen lassen stecken; / Da g'fiel mir nit der Kirchenthurn, / Dort waren nit recht gericht die Uhr'n.— / Bald wollt das Pfarrhaus mir nit ein: / Bei mir sollt's wohl ganz anders sein!" Ibid., p. 6.

3. Brecht describes the reforming work of Andreae in Württemberg in his *Kirchenordnung und Kirchenzucht*, pp. 53–82. Scholars do not agree on the material condition of evangelical pastors in early modern Europe. For the early Reformation in Thuringia, Karant-Nunn reports the following on Saxon pastors' incomes: "It is apparent from the visitation protocols that incomes increased considerably, sometimes severalfold, between the first general visitation in 1527 and the fourteenth in 1554–1555." Karant-Nunn, *Luther's Pastors*, p. 45. In contrast, Vogler has made a convincing case for the poverty and economic mediocrity of the Rhineland curés during the late Reformation (1560–1609). See Vogler, *Le clergé*, pp. 149–89. For general observations on the social status of sixteenth-century pastors, see Leibel, "Bourgeoisie," pp. 301–3. Stone has observed that in early-modern England the highest ranks of the clergy were regarded as inferior in status to the highest ranks of the legal profession. He also notes the low incomes of the lower clergy, especially the vicars and curates. Stone, "Social Mobility," pp. 20, 27.

4. LKA Stuttgart A12, no. 41, 1559 Kompetenzen, 1580 Kompetenzen. All data in this chapter from 1559 and 1580 are from these sources.

5. Kreidte, *Peasants*, p. 48.

6. Cf. Karant-Nunn's discussion of the Saxon clergy, where she argues that the clergy became increasingly bourgeois in the sixteenth century. She also observes that increasing incomes attracted pastors from middle-class backgrounds and provided a standard of living that met their class-conditioned expectations. Karant-Nunn, *Luther's Pastors*, p. 52.

7. Vogler finds that specie could make up to 80 percent of a parish's total income. Vogler, *Le clergé*, p. 151.

8. LKA Stuttgart A12, no. 41, 1559 Kompetenzen. The patronage of Tuttlingen dates back to Carolingian times. About 800, Gerald, Charlemagne's brother-in-law, gave the town to Reichenau. Nau, *Die Münzen und Medaillen*, p. 108.

9. Lau and Bizer, *Reformationsgeschichte*, pp. 166–70.

10. LKA Stuttgart A12, no. 41, 1559 Kompetenzen, fol. 449ʳ.

11. See Vann, *Making of a State*, pp. 53, 67. Cf. Lemp, *Der Württem-*

bergische Synodus, pp. 24–25; Hermelink, *Geschichte*, pp. 78–79, 94; and Deetjen, *Studien zu Württembergischen Kirchenordnung*, pp. 67–68.

12. LKA Stuttgart A12, no. 41, 1559 Kompetenzen, fol. 775ᵛ.

13. Ibid., fol. 748ʳ.

14. In 1580, Kirchentellinsfurt and Kilchberg were receiving 112 florins and 75 florins respectively in specie revenue.

15. Vogler, *Le clergé*, pp. 155–57.

16. "Den frucht-, hew- und hanff-zehndt samblett er allen jaren selbst ein." LKA Stuttgart A12, no. 41, 1559 Kompetenzen, fol. 773ʳ.

17. Ibid., fol. 775ʳ.

18. See Sabean, *Power in the Blood*, p. 7.

19. Hasselhorn, *Der altwürttembergische Pfarrstand*, p. 11.

20. I am grateful to David Sabean, who referred me to Thomas Wirsing's journal (*Tagebuch*) and to Eberhard Elbs of the University of Constance, who kindly lent me both his microfilm copy of this diary and a transcript for the months of January and June 1573. Two of the extant volumes are in the Fürstliche Fürstenbergische Hofbibliothek: Donaueschingen ms. nos. 676a and 676b.

21. Staatsarchiv, Weimar, Abteilung Feudalismus reg. Ii 690, fol. 6, and Walter Delius, *Justas Jonas, 1495–1555* (Berlin, 1952) p. 75, both cited in Karant-Nunn, *Luther's Pastors*, p. 51 n. 95.

22. See LKA Stuttgart A12, no. 41, 1559 Kompetenzen. See Table 8. See also Deetjen, *Studien zur Württembergischen Kirchenordnung*.

23. Vogler, *Le clergé*, p. 153.

24. Ibid., pp. 151–52.

25. Hasselhorn, *Der altwürttembergische Pfarrstand*, p. 6.

26. Kolb, "Zur Geschichte des Pfarrstands," p. 173.

27. The Saxon visitors found frequent instances of such deficiencies during the late sixteenth century. Sehling, *Die evangelische Kirchenordnungen*, p. 404. See Theiss, "Pfarrer und Gemeinden," p. 42. For a discussion of conditions in Thuringia in the 1520's, see Boles, "Economic Position," p. 99. For the Rhinelands, see Vogler, *Le clergé*, pp. 163–65. For Saxony, see Drews, *Der evangelische Geistliche*, pp. 70–74. For a discussion of tithes in sixteenth- and seventeenth-century France, see Hoffman, *Church and Community*, p. 69; and Goubert, *French Peasantry*, pp. 161–62, 164.

28. HStA Bü. 1285 (1605).

29. LKA Stuttgart A1 1590 fols. 48ʳ–49ʳ.

30. In 1601 parishioners were coming "in a satisfactory number," not only to the Sunday services but also during the week. In 1602, they were found to be blameless and attending both the sermon and the Lord's Supper. HStA Bü. 1327 (1601), 1328 (1602).

31. Bader observes that there was a great deal of coming and going be-

tween town and country, with town dwellers working in the country and peasants doing business in the towns. Bader, *Das Dorf*, p. 329.

32. The leases were usually a fixed portion of the harvest, commonly one-third to one-half. LKA Stuttgart A12, no. 41, 1559 Kompetenzen, fol. 781ᵛ.

33. The distribution of wealth in sixteenth-century Württemberg villages is summarized by Clasen, *Die Wiedertäufer*, pp. 208–9. See also Franz, who argues that only the upper levels of the German rural classes were true peasants, in that they owned and tilled land. Franz, *Geschichte des deutschen Bauernstandes*, p. 228.

34. Vogler found two classes of benefices in the Rhinelands during the late sixteenth century: the richer ones, located in areas of prosperous agriculture, especially the wine regions of the Palatinate; and the poorer ones, usually situated in sparsely populated areas or isolated mountain regions. Vogler, *Le clergé*, pp. 151–54.

35. In 1567, a male servant in Nuremberg, for example, received a yearly salary of 4 florins. Dirlmeier, *Untersuchungen*, p. 95. Also see Dirlmeier for a discussion of wages and prices in sixteenth-century Germany. On the commonplace tale of clerical poverty in seventeenth-century Catholic France, see Goubert, who notes that although the priests were not poor relative to the income of rural laborers, some were less well off than their colleagues. Goubert, *French Peasantry*, pp. 162–63.

36. LKA Stuttgart A12, no. 41, 1559 Kompetenzen, fol. 657ʳ.

37. Ibid., fol. 790ʳ.

38. Vogler believes that the Rhineland pastors had to remain apart from the farmwork and used the labor of their wives, children, and servants in order to preserve a status superior to that of the peasants. Vogler, *Le clergé*, p. 176. Drews judges that the evangelical pastor was not a farmer even though he occasionally handled a few sheep or cows. Drews, *Der evangelische Geistliche*, p. 26. In contrast, Tietz has suggested that evangelical pastors, in Saxony at least, were involved in farming. Tietz, "Das Erscheinungsbild," p. 56. Theiss's investigation of pastoral incomes finds that the glebe lands in the erstwhile archbishopric of Magdeburg were often farmed by the pastor himself. Theiss, "Pfarrer und Gemeinden," p. 38. Karant-Nunn's discussion also seems to indicate that pastors were personally active in farmwork. She cites examples of the Saxon clergy resisting the authorities' attempts to convert their incomes into specie payments by leasing out the glebe lands. The Saxon pastors objected that they would then neither know how to maintain themselves nor be able to teach their children husbandry. Such objections suggest that the pastors were personally working their farms, although it is possible that only the raising of livestock was in question. Karant-Nunn, *Luther's Pastors*, p. 34. Since many Württemberg pastors tended to keep for their own use the greater portion of their pastureland

while leasing out most of their fields, it seems probable that pastors were more likely to tend livestock than to seed, plow, and harvest fields of grain. Possibly the holders of the poorer benefices tended to farm their own glebe lands.

39. Stone, "Social Mobility," p. 17.

40. "Dass gemellte Widumb also verlihen werden, bedunck mich und den pfarrer dasselbst nutzlich sein, den dass er sie selbst baw, wart seines Ampts und Ministerii." LKA Stuttgart A12, no. 41, 1559 Kompetenzen, fol. 784^v.

41. "Dass auch solche widumb zwo gehortten gestalet verlihen, bedunket mich und pfarrer, seinen kirchen dienst zuverrichten, besser sein dan dass er sie selbst bauwen sollte." Ibid., fol. 787^r.

42. "Dass dan auch einem pfarrer Nutzlicher und zu seinen studiis fruchtbarer." Ibid., fol. 782^r.

43. "D'rauf zog ich ins gelobte Land, / Da Wein wie Wasser, Korn wie Sand." Andreae, *Praktische Theologie*, p. 5.

44. "Indem reis't ich durch's grüne Gras, / Weil da ein schönes Wiestal was [war]: / Da traf ich an eine alt' Person, / . . . Die gieng mit einem Rechenstiel / Im Gras, —thät doch nit gar viel,— / Ein'm Pfarrer sie sich wohl vergleicht,—." Ibid., p. 6.

45. "Doch hätt' ich g'meint, sie hätt' sich gescheucht, / Mit grober Arbeit sich zu plagen . . . / Und möcht doch wohl ein Kunstbuch tragen." Ibid.

46. "D'rauf muszt' ich den Mann registriren, / Und in die Schul' erst wieder führen." Ibid.

47. "Mein Domine! . . . das Gras ich zähl, / Dass mir kein Hälmlein komm' davon!—" Ibid.

48. "Ich dank' ihn'n ihrer guten Lehr'; / Doch wie ich kommen bin heirher, / Hab ich viel Anders müssen lernen: / Die Hülsen brechen und den Kernen / Mit bitterm Schweisz herausgewinnen, / Das werdet Ihr auch noch einmal innen." Ibid., p. 8.

49. I thank David Sabean for sharing with me his insights into sixteenth-century agricultural practices.

50. Wirsing, Tagebuch. See n. 20, above.

51. Ibid., ms. no. 676a, fol. 1^r. And three days later Wirsing recorded: "Ist fast bey 6 meze affter worden, das habern wir [Wirsing and Bartel] mit dem fuchsen auf zweimal auf des Thomae Sihdechern [*sic*] schlitten heile gefürt. Und auf den untern boden gesetzt" (fol. 2^r).

52. "Nach mi[t]tags haben wir die 3 pferd[en] das erstmal unter den hirten[?] geschlagen." Ibid., fol. 39^v.

53. Ibid., fol. 47^r.

54. LKA Stuttgart A12, no. 41, 1580 Kompetenzen, fols 262^r–320^v.

55. Vogler, *Le clergé*, p. 158.

56. Ibid., p. 5.

57. "Uber solche Competenz so die Widumb und garther woll erbauwen, mag uber den bawkosten nitt vill uber bleiben." LKA Stuttgart A12, no. 41, 1559 Kompetenzen, fol. 790ᵛ.

58. Clasen, *Die Weidertäufer*, p. 209.

59. Vogler, *Le clergé*, pp. 185–86.

60. "Vom gelt ist mir nie kein guldt in Seckel kommen oder uber ein Nacht drin blieben, dan ich mus ein gantz Jar drauf borgen." Quoted in ibid., p. 185 n. 93.

61. See Ch. 3, where Andreae's old pastor is out measuring hay fields in order to forestall cheating.

62. Abel, *Agrarkrisen und Agrarkonjunktur*, p. 147, fig. 33.

63. Dirlmeier, *Untersuchungen*, p. 419, table 15.

64. For an analysis of the nonlinear development of the state in Württemberg, see Vann, *Making of a State*, p. 86.

65. Hasselhorn, *Der altwürttembergische Pfarrstand*, pp. 6–16, and Sabean, *Power in the Blood*, pp. 8, 216 n. 21, describe the role of pastors as rent gatherers. Apparently relying on Hasselhorn, Fulbrook emphasizes the high social status of the Württemberg clergy in comparison with that of the clergy in England and Prussia. Fulbrook, *Piety and Politics*, pp. 98, 175.

Chapter 4

1. See Scribner, "Social History," for an analysis of the issues involved in doing social history of the Reformation. See also Van Engen, "Christian Middle Ages"; and Peters, "Religion and Culture." Some scholars have questioned whether the evangelical movement had any deep and lasting effect on the life of ordinary people during the sixteenth century, pointing to such evidence as the popular recourse to magic and witchcraft and widespread absenteeism from church services. Kittelson, forcefully refutes the notion that a vital, autochthonous folk religion persisted in the face of attempts by church and secular officials to reform and subdue it. In his investigation of the Strasbourg archives, he presents the Reformation as a success in the environs of the Alsatian city by concluding that evidence that "a few people engaged in exorcism and the casting of sign" is insufficient to prove that such practices were widespread. Kittelson, "Successes and Failures"; and his "Confessional Age," pp. 371–73.

2. Kittelson, "Successes and Failure," pp. 161–62.

3. "Diser Aberglaub unnd rhatsachen bey den Zauberern vil Im Stainacher thal gar gemein werden, weyl niemand darumb strafft würdt." LKA Stuttgart A12, 1587I fol. 7ᵛ.

4. This pattern would appear to correspond to Chaunu's finding. Chaunu, "Sorciers," p. 903. Vogler states: "Magic affects the highland and peripheral regions." Vogler, "Vie religieuse," vol. 2, pp. 833–34. Tübingen district was often considered two separate districts, Tübingen

and Bebenhausen, but administered as one. Some of the districts in Württemberg were very small, especially on the periphery of the duchy. Often they consisted only of the central administrative town (*Amtstadt*) and two or three outlying parishes. Württemberg was the largest political unit in southwestern Germany during the Reformation, consisting in 1545 of 50 districts (Ämter) and 4 cloister districts (*Klosterämter*) with a total of 648 village or town communities (*Amtgemeinden*). For a discussion of Württemberg's political administration, see Vann, *Making of a State*, pp. 38–40, 103–7; and Deetjen *Studien zur Württembergischen Kirchenordnung*, p. 29.

5. There appears to be no correlation between the pattern of magic complaints and other problems concerning Protestant-Catholic relations. In fact, it is of note that no complaints concerning magic, witchcraft, or healing occurred in the two parishes in Tübingen district that were surrounded by Catholics: Bodelshausen and Talheim. In these parishes there were repeated complaints about hiring out evangelical children as servants to Catholics.

6. According to Midelfort, at least 415 people were accused of witchcraft in Württemberg during the seventeenth century. Of these, only four cases were from Tuttlingen and Tübingen districts during our period (1581–1621), none of which led to capital punishment or appear to be duplicated in the visitation protocols. One of the accusations involving physical harm was a complaint against a conjurer who attempted a counterspell. LKA Stuttgart A1 1583 II fol. 42^v. For the correlations between gender and witchcraft, see Midelfort, *Witch Hunting*, pp. 179, 183–85; Monter, *Witchcraft*, pp. 119–20; Larner, *Enemies of God*, p. 91; Demos, *Entertaining Satan*, p. 61; and Bever, "Witchcraft," pp. 224–25. In a recent survey of early modern European witchcraft, Klaits repeats the feminist interpretation, that the gender bias was caused by male misogyny. Klaits, *Servants of Satan*, pp. 48–59. Cf. Larner, "Was Witch-hunting Woman-hunting?," pp. 84–88. In contrast to Larner, Weisner has recently argued that sixteenth-century humanist theory and practice contributed to the diminished legal status of women. Weisner "Frail, Weak and Helpless."

7. Vogler found that shepherds were the occupational group most often associated with magical healing. Vogler, "Vie religieuse," vol. 2, p. 820.

8. HStA Bü. 1329 (1603).

9. E.g., Ehralt Volzecher, who was also supposedly unable to say any prayers. HStA Bü. 1327 (1601).

10. "Sich erlich halte, auch inn die kirchen gehe, psalmen mitt sing." Some of Jelin's fellow parishioners did not think so well of him. They considered him a gossip and a fool: "werd aber von vilen für ein schwatzman unnd alberen menschen gehalten." LKA Stuttgart A1 1582 fol. 7^r.

11. Strauss, *Luther's House*, ibid., pp. 302–6. Findings for England have indicated that the practice of witchcraft usually involved no formal

break with Christianity. Thomas reports: "English witchcraft . . . was neither a religion nor an organization. Of course, there were many pagan survivals—magic wells, calendar customs, fertility rites—just as there were many types of magical activity. But these practices did not usually involve any formal breach with Christianity, and were, as often as not, followed by men and women who would have indignantly repudiated any aspersions upon their religious faith." Thomas, *Religion*, p. 616.

12. Jean-Pierre Goubert's summary of the art of French medicine at the end of the eighteenth century also applies to German healing at the end of the sixteenth century: "For the most part, . . . the French population practiced self-medication; it also consulted quacks, bone-setters, and matrons, listened to ambulant charlatans, and followed the course of treatment prescribed by the sorcerer-healer of the village." Goubert, "Art of Healing," p. 1. For England, see Thomas, *Religion*, pp. 10–11, 210. For Germany, see Vogler, "Vie religieuse," vol. 2, p. 818. There was good reason to doubt the efficacy of contemporary academic medicine, given its predilection for purges, emetics, and bleedings. A forthcoming work by Carolynn Lougee on the school of Saint Cyr, near Paris, will provide quantitative evidence that treatment by a medical doctor actually increased one's chances of dying.

13. The authorities allowed a woman whose life was threatened to have recourse to shepherds when the midwife was certain that the child was already dead and needed to be removed. *Cynosura Oeconomicae Ecclesiasticae*, pp. 122–23.

14. "Sich artzneyens understanden." LKA Stuttgart A1 1587I fol. 3ᵛ.

15. Vogler, "Vie religieuse," vol. 2, p. 821.

16. "Seindt alle gesegnet und wider gesund worden." LKA Stuttgart A1 1587I fol. 7ʳ.

17. "Ein Scherer leichtlich hailen kinden." HStA Bü. 1329 (1603).

18. Ibid.

19. HStA Bü. 1327 (1601), 1330 (1605), 1329 (1603); LKA Stuttgart A1 1589 fol. 42ᵛ.

20. HStA Bü. 1325 (1605).

21. "Ob er reichte naturliche Mittel oder neben demselben Zauberey brauch." LKA Stuttgart A1 1582 fol. 7ʳ.

22. "Natturlich und recht guete Cur und artzney zu Vertreibung." Ibid.

23. LKA Stuttgart A1 1587I fol. 68ʳ.

24. See Vogler, "Vie religieuse," vol. 2, pp. 827–29; Thomas, *Religion*, pp. 252–91.

25. LKA Stuttgart A1 1586II fol. 5ᵛ.

26. "Zum Zauberer geloffen." HStA Bü. 1285 (1605).

27. "Jedoch weyl er den leuten kreutter gibt, lassen Ihne auch hohe lewt passieren." LKA Stuttgart A1 1590, fol. 48ʳ.

28. "Sie drey schläf In einer Munchskutten thun lassen, so werde es besser mit Ihr werden." Ibid.

29. "Er nit mit ordenlichen mitteln umbgeht." Ibid.

30. Ibid.

31. LKA Stuttgart A1 1588II fol. 43ʳ.

32. Ibid.

33. See Vogler, "Vie religieuse," vol. 2, pp. 834–39; Thomas, *Religion*, pp. 537–38, 540–43, 547–51, 594–98, 670–74, 694–98; and Le Roy Ladurie, *Peasants of Languedoc*, pp. 203, 207–10.

34. "Vil weiber in bösem Verdacht unnd argwohn." HStA Bü. 1329 (1603).

35. LKA Stuttgart A1 1583II fol. 42ᵛ.

36. Ibid.

37. "Hatt solches Ime daruon abgemahnet, hatt solches zu underlassen, versprochen." LKA Stuttgart A1 1589 fol. 42ᵛ.

38. "Dieweil sie besserung versprochen und Ir Unrecht erkhennen, were also hierbey bleiben zulassen." Ibid., fol. 41ʳ.

39. HStA Bü. 1327 (1601), 1330 (1605).

40. Herrup has shown that seventeenth-century English legal practice was not simply a reflection of elite values but involved a complex interplay between the written law and the values of various social stata within the community. Herrup, "Law and Morality," pp. 107–8; and her *Common Peace*.

41. See Thomas, *Religion*, pp. 659–78, 694–98. For the Rhinelands, see Vogler, "Vie religieuse," vol. 2, pp. 838–39.

42. "Sonderlichen aber auch das Weib ihme zucohabitiren und hausshaltung geburender massen [Abzuwartten] Abzuwesen sein möchte." LKA Stuttgart A26 1586, 341 Kirchenzucht I, lf, /5. While Göppingen lies outside the defined geographic limits of this study, this case is the only "witchcraft" case in the extant special *Kirchenzucht* (church discipline) acts of the consistory preserved in the Archive of the Evangelical Church in Württemberg, Stuttgart.

43. Midelfort, *Witch Hunting*, pp. 50, 54, 83–84, 185. In general, Württembergers were less inclined to find witchcraft dangerous because of the providential view of nature taught by Tübingen theologians. Ibid., pp. 38–39. Mandrou and Thomas believe that the slow ascendancy of rationalist attitudes among the elites contributed to the decline of witchcraft as a crime. See Mandrou, *Magistrats*, pp. 554–56; and Thomas, *Religion*, pp. 773–85.

44. Although Kittelson does not specifically discuss attendance at the various services, he does conclude that in the environs of Strasbourg worship services were well attended and the established church was not opposed. Kittelson, "Successes and Failures," pp. 161–63. In contrast, Strauss

concludes that visitation after visitation in Germany shows both "an indisputable public aloofness" toward preachers and the gospel and "widespread absenteeism." Strauss, *Luther's House of Learning*, pp. 272–74. Vogler distinguishes among types of services; see his "Vie religieuse," vol. 2, pp. 650–57, 682–93. In addition, Vogler found that different parishes and districts demonstrated varying degrees of assiduousness in religious practice (p. 661). Although widely recognized in the French historical literature, Kittelson overlooks this phenomenon and Strauss effectually ignores it. For a summary of the French literature, see Delumeau, *Catholicism*, pp. 146–51.

45. *KO 1559*, fols. lxxxix^v–xc^r.

46. According to the 1559 church ordinance, the catechism could also be held in the villages in the evening, but a midday service seems to have been the normal practice. Ibid.

47. "Die Burger zu Tuttlingen besuchen die Morgenpredigen an Sonn- und feiertagen fleissig. . . . Die Oberamtleut tragen dem gemeinen man ein gut exempel fur mitt dem Kirchgang, dann sie alle predigen besuchen." LKA Stuttgart A1 1581 fol. 41^v.

48. HStA Bü. 1330 (1605).

49. "Aber inn den andern zwoen [Sunday] predigten erscheint grosse fahrlessigkeit, desgleichen auch in der wuchen predig, bey dem gemeinen gebett ist solcher unfleiss." LKA Stuttgart A1 1581 fol. 41^v. See also LKA A1 1583I fol. 35^v.

50. "Catechismus-Predigten sollen nit allein von den Jungen sondern auch von den alten. . . . mit allem fleiss besucht werden." (Catechism sermons shall be attended with all diligence not only by the young but also by older people.) *Cynosura Oeconomicae Ecclesiasticae*, p. 56. The *Cynosura* is a handbook and summary of several decades of decrees and ordinances concerning church life and discipline compiled by Johann Valentin Andreae in 1639.

51. "Als bald sie desselben [the catechism] ires Alters und Verstands halben vähig sein mögen." *KO 1559*, fol. ix^r. Vogler suggests these ages as the time of the beginning of catechism instruction in the Rhinelands. Vogler, "Vie religieuse," vol. 2, p. 775.

52. Vogler, "Vie religieuse," vol. 2, p. 775.

53. Compare early modern France, where village boys married in their early or mid twenties. Davis, *Society and Culture*, p. 104.

54. "Das sie nicht von dem Catechismo abgeschreckt sonder darzu lustig werden. *KO 1559*, fol. lxiii^r.

55. LKA Stuttgart A1 1584II fol. 1^v.

56. "Müssen sie bey den rossen sein, damit sie nit In die fruchten laufen." LKA Stuttgart A1 1590 fol. 47^v.

57. "Sovil den Kyrchgang dises ortts betrifft, klagt pfarrer nichts ussgenommen das fruelings zeytten die Rossbuben under den Morgenpredigen

ausfahren." Ibid., fol. 13ᵛ. "Es wurdt an disem ort besser vleiss inn zuhörung des Catechismi dann zuuor gespuret." LKA Stuttgart A1 1583I fol. 35ᵛ.

58. "[Die Jugendt] sommers zeiten fahrlessig zur predig des Catechismi khummen, lauffen den erdtbeeren nach, item spilen umb auss in den heüssern." LKA Stuttgart A1 1586II fol. 35ᵛ.

59. LKA Stuttgart A1 1587II fol. 3ᵛ. To adapt a hypothesis advanced by Davis, this adolescent indifference and resistance to the catechism service might possibly have been an indirect result of the Reformation's abolition of adolescent confraternities and the supression of traditional festivals, such as the Christmastide Feast of Fools, which decreased the religious resources, both formal and informal, available for adolescents to create a distinctive religious identity or organization. See Davis, "Tasks and Themes," p. 326.

60. *Cynosura Oeconomicae Ecclesiasticae*, p. 58. The catechumens, that is, children and young people from 6 or 8 to the mid-20's, made up a substantial proportion of the population. (See also Appendix C.) In the city of Tuttlingen, in 1605 they constituted 39 percent (497) of the total population excluding infants (1,283). HStA Bü. 1325 (1605). In 1621, they constituted 36 percent (400) of the total population (1,102). LKA Stuttgart A1 1621 fol. 30ʳ. Cf. Davis's observation for France: "The period of *jeunesse* lasted a long time and the total number of bachelors relative to the total number of men in the villages was quite high." Davis, *Society and Culture*, p. 104.

61. Sabean, "Kinship and Property," pp. 102–3; and Robisheaux, "Origins of Rural Wealth," pp. iv, 101–14, 172–77.

62. "Welche predig bissanher von dem gemeinen man mit fleiss besucht werden." LKA Stuttgart A1 1588II fol. 3ᵛ.

63. "Umb 4 uhr bin ich anhaims kommen. Noch in die vesper gangen. Hat sich aber niemandt angezaiget." Wirsing, Tagebuch, ms. no. 676a, fol. 1ʳ. See also Vogler, "Vie religieuse," vol. 2, pp. 690–93.

64. "Zu der Vesper predig am Suntag khummen Ihrer wenig." LKA Stuttgart A1 1590 fols. 7ʳ–7ᵛ.

65. "Under Ihnen ettliche handelsleut, welche offtermals an suntag an anderen orten seyen, unnd daselbsten die predigen besuchen." Ibid.

66. "Man sehe darauff zu." Ibid.

67. On the Rhinelands, see Vogler, "Vie religieuse," vol. 2, pp. 650–69, 682–90. On seventeenth-century Wiltshire, see Spaeth "Parsons and Parishioners." Spaeth concludes that although the parishioners neglected to attend church on the less important holy days, "most villagers went faithfully to divine service once on most Sundays and abstained from most labor" (pp. 80, 82).

68. "Even where people wish to visit church on Sundays and holidays, and had the leisure to act on this impulse, they evidently kept to their own side of the threshold of religious saturation planned for them." Strauss, *Lu-*

ther's House, p. 284. See Delumeau, *Catholicism*, pp. 134, 213–14, 226–27, for a discussion of the problems of using outward conformity as an indication of inward piety.

69. See Davis's provocative suggestions for studying Protestant liturgy in "Popular Religion," pp. 325–26.

70. *Die Bekenntnisschriften*, pp. 63–65:246–48.

71. Schlink, *Theology*, p. 185. Bossy has suggested that Luther's reformation of the communion liturgy resulted in an abandonment of the social and corporate emphases of the medieval mass in favor of an almost exclusive concentration on the individual's relationship to God. Bossy, "Sociographie de la Messe," p. 62.

72. See Sabean, "Communion and Community," p 98.

73. "Seyen zwar etlich personen verklagt worden, dz sie aus feindschafft nit communicieren." HStA Bü. 1282 (1601) fol. 21ʳ.

74. "Des alten Sixten Weyb hat vor Irem endt der Nachtmal empfangen." LKA Stuttgart A1 1586II fol. 5ʳ.

75. For infomation on Riepp, see Seigel, *Gericht und Rat*, p. 151. The visitor reports: "Gibt für weyl sie Ihre Stieffkynder In das gefengnus gebracht, wisse sie dasselbig nit zuemfangen." LKA Stuttgart A1 1590 fol. 8ʳ. Spaeth found that in early modern England infrequent communion reflected not irreligion but lay definitions of the rite of communion and religious faith that differed from those of the clergy. Spaeth, "Parsons and Parishioners," p. 72.

76. "Die weyl er den Weisenrichtern beygestanden, als sie Ihme Schulren solch sein verkauffen, vertauschen, kauffen mit seiner Schwester Kinder güter verwisen haben." HStA Bü. 1384 (1603).

77. HStA Bü. 1285 (1605).

78. "Haben ettliche vom Gericht solches auff Ihme aussgezogen, . . . Also dz alle schuld mehr auff denen vom Gericht als dem Pfarrer beruhet." Ibid.

79. "Ob er den Irgend einen Mangel an Unser Religion habe." Ibid.

80. Ibid.

81. The Religious Peace of Augsburg (1555) recognized the existence of both Catholicism and Lutheranism within the Empire. In each land subjects should follow the religion of their ruler. Those not content with this settlement were permitted, after selling their property, to migrate to other lands, hence the consistory's emphasis on property.

82. "Hans Conrad Männ so burger zu Weyl (und seine gutter alda hette) aber jetziger zeyt sein haushaltung zu Reytlingen hatt dann er daselbsten geheurat) wil weder zu Reytlingen noch zu Weyl das h. Abendtmal empfangen, Ist die gantz Charwochen zu weyl gewesen, aber In khein predig khummen, disputiert auch, wo er zu lewten kumpt, wider unser religion. [Margin:] Weyl er zu Weyl ain Burger ist und seine gutter alda hat, were dem Abbt Und

Vogt zu Bebenhausen zu schreiben ine wann er alhin kombt zuerfordern, der Religion halb mit ihme zu handeln, im zuerinnern, und aus Gottes Wort zuunderweisen, und wie er sich erklärt, schrifftlichen bericht zuthon." LKA Stuttgart A1 1587l fols. 14ʳ–14ᵛ.

83. Marggraf was identified in the protocols simply as an unmarried journeyman. Early-modern printers often had some university education. Marggraf was most likely a journeyman printer, for his father was a Tübingen bookseller and he himself had matriculated at Tübingen in 1554. Seigel, *Gericht und Rat*, p. 245. Hermelink, *Die Matrikeln*, vol. 1, p. 377.

84. "Dieweil er weder unnder der universitet noch der burgerschaft seye auch sich des abentmals halb nitt Christenlich erzeige. . . . " LKA Stuttgart A1 1582 fol. 2ʳ.

85. "Wann sie Gott aus disem iamerthal erfordere." Ibid.

86. "Bittet mit ihm gedult zutragen, biss sein mutter sterbe welle er alssdann wegziehen." LKA Stuttgart A1 1583l fol. 1ᵛ.

87. "Wann er beharren und nit unsers glaubens sein weltte, möchte er sein gelegenheit anderstwo suchen. July 15 Anno 83." Ibid.

88. "Verhoffentlich, er wird sich furthin Christenlich erzeigen unnd sunst gepurlich halten." LKA Stuttgart A1 1583II fol. 1ᵛ.

89. Seigel, *Gericht und Rat*, p. 245; Crusius, *Diarium*, p. 225.

90. In the Michaelmas 1583 visitation, in a rare exception to normal practice, Erhard Schnepf identifies himself in the text as the visitor. LKA Stuttgart A1 1583II fol. 41ʳ. The spring 1584 visitor is identified simply as the superintendant of Balingen. LKA Stuttgart A1 1584l fol. 43ʳ. At the same time, the report notes negligent attendance at the catechism service. "Es sein die wenig die ausserhalb Oesterlichen Zeit zu des hern nachtmal gehn." LKA Stuttgart A1 1583II fol. 42ᵛ. Also, once again, attendance was poor at the catechism service and the weekday sermon, as it was in nearly all the places visited. Ibid., fol. 41ᵛ.

91. "Es wurd an disem ort klagt, das ausserhalb der österlichen zeit, wenig der pfarkinder zu des herren nachtmal gehn." LKA Stuttgart A1 1584II fol. 39ᵛ. "Pfarrer klagt, das ausserhalb Oesterlicher zeit wenig seiner pfarkinder zu des herren Nachtmal gehn." Ibid., fol. 39ʳ.

92. "Sonst an zuhörung gottes worts wurd nitt klag fürgebracht oder mangel gespüret." LKA Stuttgart A1 1584II 39ʳ.

93. "Der Pfarrer explicire inen *usum Coenae Dominicae* fleissig und hallte bey inen an." Ibid.

94. LKA Stuttgart A1 1590 fol. 11ᵛ.

95. HStA Bü. 1284 (1603).

96. E.g., in Häslach in Tübingen district, a filial administered by Walddorf. LKA Stuttgart A1 1590 fol. 16ʳ.

97. "Wann ains In disem filial sterb, würdt Ihme khain leichtpredig gethan, sunder der pfarher gedenckt dessen in nechster predig zu weyl. [The

consistory orders:] Pfarrer soll inen in irem Kirchlin auch ein Leuch predig than." Ibid., fol. 17ᵛ.

98. "Machten die Einwoner wol leyden." Ibid., fol. 19ᵛ.

99. Ibid.

100. In 1583, the visitor records that the Reusten parishioners "begeren noch alle zeit, eines eignen Pfarrers." LKA Stuttgart A1 1583II fol. 13ʳ. This request was repeated frequently: LKA Stuttgart A1 1584I fol. 13ᵛ, 1584II fol. 11ᵛ, 1588II fol. 14ᵛ, and 1590 fols. 19ᵛ–20ʳ.

101. LKA Stuttgart A1 1590 fol. 18ʳ.

102. "Den altten und schwagern Weibern zu gutem." Ibid.

103. "Die einwoner dis filials sunthausen kommen zur predig, aber ire Weyber nitt." LKA Stuttgart A1 1586I fol. 34ʳ. See also LKA Stuttgart A1 1584I fol. 46ᵛ for an earlier report.

104. LKA Stuttgart A1 1586I fol. 33ʳ, 1586II fols. 37ʳ–37ᵛ.

105. HStA Bü. 1330 (1605).

106. "Es klagen die von Biesingen, es seye ihnen beschwerlich, die weil es unwegsam gehn Efingen zugehn, sunderlich diweil vil iungs volck an disen orten ist, bitten underthänig E.F.G. wollen gnädigen beuelch dem pfarrer zukommen lassen, das er zu 14 tagen ein Catechismi predig bey ihnen thue." LKA Stuttgart A1 1582 fol. 32ʳ.

107. LKA Stuttgart A1 1584I fol. 13ᵛ–14ʳ.

108. LKA Stuttgart A1 1590 fol. 21ᵛ.

109. Ibid.

110. Schnabel-Schüle, "Die Ämter"; Vogler, *Le clergé*, p. 34.

111. LKA Stuttgart A1 1582 fol. 32ʳ.

112. LKA Stuttgart A1 1590 fol. 19ᵛ.

113. "Es mochte ein feine Christliche Jugendt bey Ihnen gezogen werden." Ibid., fols. 19ᵛ, 20ʳ.

114. Vovelle, *Piété baroque*.

Chapter 5

1. See Vogler, "Vie religieuse," vol. 2, p. 897.

2. Burke has argued that between the fifteenth and eighteenth centuries Europe experienced a large-scale cultural transformation that can be summed up in the phrase "the reform of popular culture." Many games, calendar rituals, marriage festivities, and other popular customs and beliefs were increasingly condemned by the ecclesiastical and secular authorities. At the same time, there appeared a divergence between the culture of elite groups—nobles, gentlemen, clergy, and some townspeople—and that of the mass of common people. The elites withdrew and to an extent became hostile toward activities, such as carnival and church ales, which they had formerly patronized. Burke, *Popular Culture*, pp. 207–43, 270–81. Cf. the essays by Ingram that challenge the thesis of an exclusive cleavage between

popular and elite cultures portrayed by Burke and others. Ingram, "Ridings"; and his "Religion."

3. E.g., *Erste Polizei-Ordnung*, June 30, 1549, reprinted in Reyscher, *Sammlung*, vol. 12: *Regierungsgesetze* pt. 1, pp. 149–67 (1841). The general ordinances were periodically supplemented by specific laws, such as the *Verbot der Fastnacht-Mummerei und Maskeraden, auch überflüssigen Zu- und Volltrinkens*, January 21, 1600, reprinted in ibid., p. 538.

4. Brecht, *Kirchenordnung und Kirchenzucht*, pp. 19–20.

5. The extant Tübingen city court records begin in 1629. City Archive (Stadtarchiv) Tübingen s201 Tübingen Gerichtsprotokolle 1629–35.

6. See Althaus, *Theology*, pp. 251–73. Cf. Elert, *Morphologie*, vol. 1, pp. 31–38, and vol. 2, pp. 23–36.

7. For Luther's detailed treatment of the second table of the Decalogue, see WA vol. 8, pp. 482–563.

8. *Die Bekenntnisschriften*, pp. 112:13, 118:54–55, 119:61, 309:59, 379:9, 385:24, 389:39, 610:197.

9. WA 11, pp. 248–49.

10. Ibid., p. 249.

11. *Die Bekenntnisschriften*, p. 644:330.

12. *Die Bekenntnisschriften*, p. 644:330–31.

13. "Primo, ut externa quaedam disciplina conservetur et feri atque intractabiles homines quasi repagulis quibusdam coerceantur, secundo, ut per legem homines ad agnitionem, suorum peccatorum adducantur, tertio, ut homines iam renati, quibus tamen omnibus multum adhuc carnis adhaeret, eam ipsam ob causum certam aliquam regulam habeant, ad quam totam suam vitam formare possint et debeant." *Die Bekenntnisschriften*, p. 793:1.

14. See Laslett, *Family Life*, pp. 102–59 passim.

15. Research has illuminated the difficulty of attempting to verify this phenomenon empirically. In an examination of Constance marriage courts, Safley investigated the geographic distribution of cases brought before the marriage court (*Ehegericht*). He found, surprisingly, that not only the most distant but also the nearest jurisdictions were underrepresented, that is, those over 85 kilometers away from Constance and those within 15 kilometers. Safley, "Marital Litigation," p. 74; and his *Let No Man Put Asunder*. Proximity to the centers of ecclesiastical and political power cannot be discounted as an important factor in the ability of a territorial or city church to bring about religious uniformity among its populace. In Württemberg, the practice of local visitations mitigated somewhat the possible weakening of administrative and disciplinary control over distance because periodically the visitor would arrive in the village as a representative of the power of the central government. In Württemberg, both the church and the political visitations were apparently conducted by the district superintendent.

16. From its very origins, the Württemberg Reformation considered the

sanctioning of sexual offenses as simply one aspect of godly discipline. In the first ordinance, in 1536 [?], Ambrosius Blarer called for the duke to institute a discipline ordinance (*Zuchtordnung*), an examination and punishment intended to abolish several unchristian vices, such as blasphemy, adultery, drunkenness, and usury. Nothing in the sources indicates that evangelical sexual discipline was analogous to a puritanical regime, wherein sexual sins are viewed as the most heinous. Cited in Köhler, *Zürcher Ehegericht*, vol. 2, p. 234.

17. In Tübingen district seven cases of illegitimate births, and in Tuttlingen district five cases, are recorded.

18. Flandrin, "A Case of Naïveté," p. 313.

19. Laslett, *World We Have Lost*, p. 139. Flandrin, "Repression and Change," p. 203. See Goubert, who observed in the province of Beauvais a respect for the religious law that prohibited extramarital conception. *Cent mille provinciaux*, p. 54.

20. The Basel marriage court records reveal 32 cases of fornication in 42 years. No cases of illegitimate births were contained in the Basel records for 1550–92. Safley, "Marital State," p. 171. See also his *Let No Man Put Asunder*, pp. 160–61.

21. As Steven Ozment puts it, "The exercise of paternal duty at a distance was the burden of bastardy in Reformation Europe." Ozment, *When Fathers Ruled*, p. 158. In the case described, the unwed mother, Greitgen, later married. Apparently there was no stigma attached to her for having given birth to a bastard (pp. 159–60).

22. "Der aber mit gelt sie ningericht, das sie das Kindt behalte." HStA Bü. 1330 (1605).

23. Ibid.

24. Since Robisheaux has pointed out that couples in Hohenlohe could apparently start living together as soon as their families approved the marriage contract and before the church wedding, it is possible that these cases of sleeping together too soon are not all the consequence of clandestine engagements that occurred without parental consent. Robisheaux, "Origins of Rural Wealth," p. 175.

25. In Switzerland even after the Reformation, the public religious rite was secondary to the actual exchange of marriage vows administered at the town hall or a private home. See Köhler, *Zürcher Ehegericht*, vol. 2, pp. 268, 268 n. 160.

26. Quaife, *Wanton Wenches*, p. 89.

27. Robisheaux, "Origins of Rural Wealth," pp. 128–34, 164.

28. "Bartlin Schreinen Hausfraw soll ein halb Jahr zu bald nach Gehaltner Hochzeit des Kinds niderkommen sein. Im Vogtzeddel." HStA Bü. 1284 (1603).

29. Thirteen cases are recorded in the visitations during 1601–5. Of

them, seven (54 percent) name only the wife, three (23 percent) name husband and wife, and another three (23 percent) cite unnamed couples. In Tuttlingen the proportion is almost inverse. Only two out of twelve accusations (17 percent) name the wife alone.

30. "Anna Jerg Ulrichs Weib zu frü beygeschlaffen habe." HStA Bü. 1285 (1605).

31. Robisheaux, "Origins of Rural Wealth," p. 175.

32. See Safley, "Marital State," pp. 162–64.

33. "Hatt sich bemellter ledig gesell Hanns Jeylin zu bemeltts Webers weib . . . mit Ir gezecht, Volgenndt beede nächt, bey Ir Inn Irem beth gelegen, unnd alss den Ehebruch mit ainander begangen. . . . Alss bald er aber dess andern tag verlossener ohnzucht bericht worden, wie dann dass geschrei bei selbiger Nachpurschafft hieuon gar grob gewesen, hatt er sich von ir abgesondert." LKA Stuttgart A26, 341 Kirchenzucht I, 1c Stuttgart 1587. Sattler was, of course, at great pains to show that he was ignorant of the alleged adultery, since to continue sharing his bed with his wife after the fact weakened his case for the desired divorce.

34. "Zu Neera unnd umligend flecken, deshalb ein grosses unnd gemein geschrey ist." The daughter reportedly had asked: "Warumb kauffest du der huren (mitt undertheniger reuerentia zuuermelden) ein sölchen beltz)?" LKA Stuttgart A1 1584l fol. 3ᵛ.

35. "Hatt das töchterlin, so im bett gelegen, darauff ein gereusch auff dem letterbettlin gehoret." Ibid.

36. "Solchs hab ich darum vermelden sollen, dieweil zu Neera und umligenden flecken, deshalb ein grosses und gemein geschrey ist wie Specialis berichtet hatt." Ibid.

37. If upon investigation the report proved false, then the rumormongers might suffer punishment. See Sabean, *Power in the Blood*, p. 149.

38. The structure and genesis of this reformation of manners and sensibility have been either assumed or described only partially by such historians of culture as Elias, Ariès, and Burke, but the actual factors lying behind the rise of this new mentality, particularly the respective roles of northern humanism, Protestantism, and counterreformation Catholicism, still need investigation. Both Burke and Elias seem to recognize the crucial influence of Erasmus's pedagogical and moral ideals, but they do not analyze the possible connections between his concerns for correct demeanor and godly morals, expressed in his treatises and colloquies, and the subsequent change in civilized manners. Elias, *Prozess der Zivilization*, vol. 1: *Wandlungen des Verhaltens in den weltlichen Oberschichten des Abendlandes*. pp. 230–63; Ariès, *Centuries of Childhood*, pp. 100–128; and Burke, *Popular Culture*, pp. 223–43.

39. HStA Bü. 1282 (1601).   40. Ibid.

41. HStA Bü. 1284 (1603).   42. HStA Bü. 1328 (1602).

43. Thomas, *Religion*, p. 629.   44. HStA Bü. 1284 (1603).

45. The steps of admonition are described in the section of *Kirchen-Censur, KO 1559*, fol. ccl^v. The morals court jurisdiction over adultery is outlined on fol. ccxxx^r.

46. For a detailed analysis based on Italian sources, see Ruggiero, *Violence*, pp. 156–70; and Ruggiero, *Boundaries of Eros*. Flandrin discusses rape briefly and is always careful to identify alleged pretexts for such assaults. Flandrin, *Families*, pp. 99–101. In Le Roy Ladurie's account of life in a remote Pyrenees village, the women are often depicted as willing victims. Le Roy Ladurie, *Montaillou*, pp. 154–68. Cf. Quaife, *Wanton Wenches*, pp. 65, 172–73. Ozment's book on marriage and family life makes one brief reference to rape. Ozment, *When Fathers Ruled*, p. 197.

47. "Wann jemand ein Weibs-Person, mit Gewalt entführt, der mag sie mit Recht zur Ehe nicht behalten, wann er sie gleich auch geschwächet hat, da sie ihne zu haben niemalen bewilliget und noch nicht bey ihme wohnen will." *Cynosura Oeconomicae Ecclesiasticae*, p. 203.

48. "Mit Lust, Trug und anderer Hinderführung, selbsten oder durch andere Kuppler verführet." Ibid.

49. "Der Hinderführer wird ernstlich gestrafft." Ibid.

50. "Da sich auch begeben wurde, das ein Jungfraw oder fraw von einem, mit listen, trug, oder ander hinderfürungen, persuasionibus & inductionibus, one oder mit gewalt, per raptum, heimlicher oder truglicher weiss, weggefürt, und solchs vor unsern E[h]erichtern und Räthen beygebracht wurde, Alssdann soll nit allein zwischen solchen Personen, kein Ee erkennt, sonder auch der, so gehörter massen raptum begangen, in gemeiner Recht unnd unser ernstliche Straff gefallen sein, wölche wir auch an solchem übelthäter, nach gestalt und gelegenheit der übertrettung, an leib oder leben, mit rechtlicher erkanntnuss, volstrecken lassen wöllen." *Eheordnung von 1559, KO 1559*, fol. cxvi^v.

51. "Manchmal Falsch und Betrug heirmit spihlen." *Cynosura Oeconomicae Ecclesiasticae*, pp. 176–77. In England, conception seems to have been proof of the woman's consent to the intercourse and thus precluded the possibility of rape. Quaife quotes the legist Michael Dalton, "If the woman at the time of the supposed rape, do conceive with child, by the ravisher, this is no rape, for a woman cannot conceive with child except she do consent." Quaife, *Wanton Wenches*, p. 172.

52. "[Er] noch nicht nachlassen will." "Er [wölle] sein tochter mit Gewalt haben." HStA Bü. 1284 (1603).

53. HStA Bü. 1328 (1602).

54. HStA Bü. 1285 (1605).

55. HStA Bü. 1282 (1601).The baby is described graphically and gruesomely as an "Unformlich und ungestalter abscheuliches Kind." Ibid.

56. "Welches dan leider wa[h]r gewesen [ist]." HStA Bü. 1285 (1605).

57. HStA Bü. 1328 (1602) "One zweifel, sie, die mutter und das Kind hinzurichten." Ibid. Since calamities of the era such as war and famine were commonly seen as the direct result of criminal and ungodly living, the enforcement of public discipline and the institution of days of repentance (*Busstagen*) were seen as ways of warding off God's punishment. "Ausschreiben wegen der Verbrechen und Laster, 11 June 1629," in Reyscher, *Sammlung*, vol. 12: *Regierungsgesetze*, pt. 1, p. 1006 (1841).

58. HStA Bü. 1329 (1603).

59. This is the only example of apparent short-term concubinage evidenced in the protocols under investigation. HStA Bü. 1284 (1603).

60. HStA Bü. 1285 (1605).

61. See Le Roy Ladurie, *Montaillou*, p. 200.

62. Although some of the records of the marriage court are extant in HStA A211 and A238a, they do not appear to have stimulated much scholarly interest apart from Köhler's work. Irwin refers to an unpublished study of possible interest: De Marce, "Württemberg Marriage Court." Irwin, "Society and the Sexes," pp. 352, 357.

63. Kingdon, "Morals," pp. 95–106; Monter, "Consistory of Geneva," pp. 68–69.

64. HStA Bü. 1282 (1601).   65. HStA Bü. 1285 (1605).

66. HStA Bü. 1328 (1602).   67. HStA Bü. 1329 (1603).

68. The legal historian Martin Heckel has observed that this formula is not in the language of treaty itself but was coined afterward by apologists. Nonetheless, it cogently paraphrases the sections concerning the princely authority. Heckel, *Deutschland*, pp. 46–47.

69. According to Württemberg church law, Catholics could stand as godparents for children of evangelicals, provided they promised to bring the child to the evangelical catechism and the sacraments. Monks, nuns, priests, and priests' housekeepers were excluded. *Cynosura Oeconomicae Ecclesiasticae*, pp. 67–68. This was most likely a de jure concession to a prevalent de facto condition. HStA Bü. 1330 (1605).

70. "Nur umb dess schandtlichen guts wüllen, hette sie sonst gar wol verheuraten kinden." Ibid.

71. "Man habe nie keinen den kopf abgehauwen." "Darmit also seinen einigen Sohn der hoff gewerb unnd lehen allein bleibe." HStA Bü. 1328 (1602).

72. Ibid.

73. HStA Bü. 1325 (1605).

74. In contrast, Vogler has been able to document the rise of a strong confessional consciousness by the early seventeenth century in areas of the Rhinelands. Although even Vogler notes that in areas adjacent to Catholic

territories, Protestants continued to choose spouses and godparents from among members of the other confession. Vogler, "Vie religieuse," vol. 2, pp. 1106–11.

75. The emphasis on the moral content of the term "poor householder" in the discussion differs from the emphasis in Sabean's interpretation. Sabean has argued that the categories good and bad householder were code words for the village power structure: "The positive value [which the state] put on the aggressive characteristics necessary for maintaining or increasing an estate was apt to mask the fact that they were most likely to go along with wealth." Sabean, *Power in the Blood*, p. 150. The fact that there are affinities between the fiscal interest of the state in the farming household as a viable source of revenue, the economic interest of the peasant family itself in social and temperate ways of life, and the spiritual interest of the church in godly living does not entail any causal relationship among the three kinds of interest. Although it might seem self-evident that substantial peasant farmers would have a high regard for law, order, strict religion, and morality, different communities seem to have developed different characters. Quaife failed to find any correlation between social status and the moral rigorism of Puritan belief. Quaife, *Wanton Wenches*, p. 13. In contrast, Wrightson and Levine found the emergence of firmly committed Puritans among the early-modern yeomen of the parish of Terling who were instrumental in the attempts to impose social discipline on the community. Wrightson and Levine, *Poverty and Piety*, pp. 173–77. In Württemberg, we see the village Schultheissen both supporting and resisting various aspects of the visitation discipline.

76. "[Er] ist ein faulentzer, verlasst er alles auff den knecht." HStA Bü. 1327 (1601).

77. HStA Bü. 1328 (1602).

78. HStA Bü. 1329 (1603).

79. Balthass Bentzinger "ligt täglich im luder." Ibid.

80. The three parishes involved were Schwenningen, Trossingen, and Aldingen.

81. Robisheaux, "Origins of Rural Wealth," pp. 45–49, 164–78.

82. "Ist gar zerhafft, schwert Vbel." HStA Bü. 1329 (1603).

83. HStA Bü. 1330 (1605).

84. "Zert auch vil, halt nit gar wol hauss." HStA Bü. 1327 (1601).

85. In the city of Tübingen, during the 1581 visitation the visitor records that "ettliche böse haushalter gerichtlich beklagt und furgestellet, das sie mundthod erkandt werden." LKA Stuttgart A1 1581 fol. 2ᵛ. Again in 1584, the visitor reports: "Es sind ettlich böse haushalter, unnd prodigi fürkommen, die sind für gericht gestellet, rechtlich beklaget, unnd begert, das sie vermög f. Landesordnung, als prodigi, unnd unnutze haushalter erkennet,

unnd offentlich ausgerufft unnd mund todt sollen gemacht werden." LKA Stuttgart A1 1584I fol. 1ʳ.

86. HStA Bü. 1329 (1603).

87. HStA Bü. 1330 (1605).

88. "Dem gemainen flecken wirtt Vbel hauss gehalten." HStA Bü. 1328 (1602). "Sie khommen nach gelegenheit der zeitt fein in die predigen." Ibid.

89. HStA Bü. 1327 (1601).

90. HStA Bü. 1328 (1602), 1329 (1603).

91. "Wo einer im Wirtshauss seid, wüll er der ander der [dar] sein." HStA Bü. 1328 (1602).

92. Clark has argued that the alehouses in England did not serve as a focal point for values alternative to those in the mainstream culture. Clark, "Alehouse." Cf. Medick's study of the spinning bees (*Spinnstuben* or *Licht-karzen*), where he argues that gossip and facetious and even slanderous stories, which were shared among the unmarried women on winter nights, indicate some kind of consistently critical nexus of shared values (*jugendliche Sexualkultur*) vis-à-vis the rest of the village. Medick, "Spinnstuben," pp. 19–30.

93. HStA Bü. 1327 (1601).

94. HStA Bü. 1284 (1603).

95. HStA Bü. 1330 (1605).

96. "Die hebamm Conradt Göttins Wittib, ist gar zerhafft, vil zu Villin-gen, macht da Schulden, schlupff allenthalben in die heuser wan sie dan zue nott beruffen wirt, ist sie tru[n]cken." HStA Bü. 1328 (1602).

97. "Ganz Unbescheidenlichen Wortten, ein hessliches zugemuttet." HStA Bü. 1284 (1603).

98. Ibid.

99. HStA Bü. 1285 (1605).

100. "Jerg Winterlin sey ein Epicurer, Verschwender und gottloser Mensch, Welcher offt ermahnet aber nichts fruchtbarliches ausgereicht wor-den. Vogtzedel." HStA Bü. 1284 (1603).

101. One of the justices, Heinruch Haw, was described as "a lewd, evil-speaking man and a blasphemy" (ein liederlichen Ubelredender und Gotts-lästerer). HStA Bü. 1285 (1605). Buck's case is found in ibid.

102. "Das Gottslestern wüll alda schier einwurtzelt." HStA Bü. 1328 (1602). The wives and daughters were apparently attending Catholic wed-dings and staying on to attend the Roman mass. Ibid.

103. In Tübingen district between 1601 and 1695, all but one of the dances were allowed by the magistrates. In the one exception, the justice re-fused to discipline the merrymakers. HStA Bü. 1282 (1601).

104. "Daran sich die benachparen flecken umb errens geergert, Welche bey disen schweren laüffen solches abgeschafft." HStA Bü. 1284 (1603).

105. "Da man zusammen schlieffe." Ibid.
106. See Heiland in Appendix B.
107. HStA Bü. 1282 (1601). See Medick, "Spinnstuben," pp. 25–29.
108. "Weil es aber pars disciplinae, ob und wan man dz tantz zulassen soll, ist es Ihnen angezeigt worden dz sie künftig Ihne zuuor anreden sollen." HStA Bü. 1285 (1605).
109. HStA Bü. 1327 (1601).
110. Bossy, *Christianity in the West*, p. 34.
111. See ibid., pp. 14–34; and his "Blood and Baptism." For particulars about the situation in southwestern Germany, see Robisheaux, "Origins of Rural Wealth," pp. 100–151, 168–77; Sabean, "Kinship and Property." See also Sabean's book on Neckarhausen: *Property, Production and Family*.
112. LKA Stuttgart A1 1621. In 1624, Tuttlingen district records once again evidence more complaints. LKA Stuttgart A1 1641.
113. "Zunacht vff der gassen sich mit einander haben gebalget und [darnebn vbel] gefluchet." HStA Bü. 1283 (1602).
114. HStA Bü. 1325 (1605).
115. For example, in Derendingen the innkeepers' practice of keeping serving hours outside the legal limit caused "great mischief" (*ein grossen Mutwillen*). HStA Bü. 1285 (1605).
116. HStA Bü. 1284 (1603).
117. Ibid.
118. "Wölches sie doch gegen unns an iren feyrtagen nit leiden." HStA Bü. 1329 (1603).
119. HStA Bü. 1328 (1602). See also Bü. 1327 (1601).
120. HStA Bü. 1329 (1603).
121. "Lauffen alleut halben vor, unnd under der predig Uberveldt." Ibid.
122. Ibid.
123. "Redet der gemein Man schimpflich dauon." HStA Bü. 1284 (1603).
124. HStA Bü. 1282 (1601).
125. HStA Bü. 1285 (1605).
126. "Als da einer dem andern Gelt leihet, uund der Entlehner ein mehrere Summa, dann die entlehnet gewesen, verschreiben muss." *KO 1559*, fol. ccxxx^v.
127. HStA Bü. 1282 (1601).
128. In 1648, Keil encountered an angel in his vineyard in the Württemberg district of Leonberg. The angel gave him a prophetic message that included a condemnation of usury. The local pastor supported Keil's protest. In contrast, while the consistory agreed that "Jewish usury" was a plague, they admonished Keil for forgetting the justice of the authorities and overstating the case about usury. Sabean, *Power in the Blood*, pp. 71–72.

129. MacDonald has stressed the importance of both hegemony and mediation as aspects of the social dynamic between elite and popular culture in English villages. MacDonald, "Secularization," p. 97. Wrightson and Levine underline the importance of conflict in their important work *Poverty and Piety*, pp. 17–18, 139, 173–75. In a similar manner, studies of German society have characterized the social role of the evangelical clergy as principally coercive. See Strauss, *Luther's House of Learning*; and Sabean, *Power in the Blood*. Several articles have emphasized the role of mediation and compromise in the dynamics of social change in early modern England. For example, see Herrup, "Law and Morality," and Ingram, "Ridings."

Conclusion

1. We still await a reliable treatment of Luther's teachings on society, social groups, and social duties. See Brady, "Social History," p. 176. Though we have a fine analysis of the Johann Brenz's activities as a reformer in Württemberg and his fundamental views on church polity, we still need a full-length study of his social teachings. Estes, *Christian Magistrate*. For a review of Lutheran political thought, see Skinner, *Foundations*, pp. 65–108, 189–224.

2. The Württemberg protocols contain such terms as passable (*ziemlich*), negligent (*fahrlessig*), and good (*gut*).

3. Vovelle describes the work of the LeBras school in *Piété baroque*, pp. 285ff.

4. The records of these local church consistories are extant for many parishes and still lie in the manse libraries. See Brecht, *Kirchenordnung und Kirchenzucht*, pp. 83–104. Andreae also faced local opposition; see Hermelink, *Geschichte*, pp. 144–47.

5. Fulbrook, *Piety and Politics*, pp. 41–42, 131–37.

6. During the fourth century under the reign of the emperor Julian the Apostate, Cappadocia in Asia Minor was one of the most backward provinces in the Roman Empire, whose non-Greek-speaking residents had lived for centuries outside the pale of Hellenism and were considered intractable barbarians by the cultured pagan elites of Asia Minor. "The Christian bishops of the Cappadocian cities, however, . . . resolutely preached at them in Greek, recruited them into Greek-speaking monasteries, and sent Greek-speaking priests out to them in the countryside. As a result, Cappadocia became a Greek-speaking province up to the fourteenth century." In such a manner, one of the greatest cultural and linguistic transformations of the late Antique world was accomplished. Brown, *World of Late Antiquity*, p. 94.

7. WA, vol. 19, pp. 72–75.

8. While Luther termed the princes emergency bishops (*Notbischofe*), the mainstream Lutherans held that the Christian magistrate had a rather

more permanent role in the church. Melanchthon's position, represented in the "Treatise on the Power and Primacy of the Pope" (1537), described the princes and kings as first members of the church. *Die Bekenntnisschriften*, p. 488:54. As is well known, the Religious Peace of Augsburg (1555) confirmed the effectual right to reform (*jus reformandi*) and the episcopacy of the evangelical princes in their own lands. Heckel, *Deutschland*, p. 47.

Glossary

Amt	district (pl. Ämter)
Bürgermeister	chief financial officer of a village
corpus	salary contribution from the parish patron
Ehegericht	marriage court
Ehrbarkeit	territorial elite of officeholders
Gemeinde	village, village corporation
Gemeingebet	service of common prayer
Gericht	town or village court
Gerichtsverwandter	justice or court member (pl. Gerichtsverwandten)
Geschrei	scandal, rumor, clamor, stir
Geschwätz	gossip
Gesell	journeyman
Grollen	enmity
Haushalter	householder, head of a house
Haustafel	table of duties
Hofgericht	territorial court
Kirchenordnung	church ordinance (pl. Kirchenordnungen)
Kirchenrat	church council
Kompetenz	income record, salary (pl. Kompetenzen)
Konsistorium	consistory
Konventschule	cloister school (pl. Konventschulen)
Landesordnung	territorial ordinance
Landhofmeister	leading ducal councillor
Landtag	territorial parliament

Leichtkarze	spinning bee, candle room (pl. Leicht-karzen)
Magister	possessor of a master of arts degree
maleficium	harmful magic
Particularschule	Latin elementary school (pl. Particularschulen)
Rat	town or village council
Repetent	Magister pursuing a doctorate in theology; teaching assistant
Richter	justice, member of the Gericht
Rügegericht, Ruggericht	morals court
Schultheiss	village mayor or chief administrative officer (pl. Schultheissen)
Segensprechen	charming, folk healing, wizardry
Spezial, Special;	
Spezial Superintendent	church district superintendent; the chief church officer in a district who was usually responsible for conducting visitations
Spinnstube	spinning bee (pl. Spinnstuben)
Stift	a religious foundation. The Tübingen Stift is a seminary for theological instruction
Stipendiat	scholarship holder, generally "student" (pl. Stipendiaten)
Superattendent, Superattendant	Stift teaching staff or instructor
Superintendenz	district
Synodus	consistory
Vogt	ducal bailiff (pl. Vögte)
Vogtgericht	district court
Vogtzettel	list of complaints confirmed by a visitor
Wahrsagen	soothsaying
Widumb, Wittem, Widem	glebe lands
Wiese	pastureland (pl. Wiesen)
Wochenpredigt	weekly preaching service
Zauberei, Zaubern	magic

References Cited

The following abbreviations are used in the tables, appendixes, Notes, and References Cited:

ARG   *Archiv für Reformationsgeschichte*
BWKG   *Blätter für württembergische Kirchengeschichte*
HStA   Hauptstaatsarchiv, Stuttgart, A281 Visitationsberichte
KO 1559   *Württembergische Grosse Kirchenordnung 1559*
LKA   Landeskirchliches Archiv, Stuttgart
WA   Weimar Ausgabe: Luther, *D. Martin Luthers Werke*

Primary Sources

Manuscript Sources

Hauptstaatsarchiv, Stuttgart (HStA)

A281 Visitationsberichte Büschel 1282 (1601), 1283 (1602), 1284 (1603), 1285 (1605), 1325 (1601, 1602, 1603, 1605), 1327 (1601), 1328 (1602), 1329 (1603), 1330 (1605), 1384 (1603)

Landeskirchliches Archiv, Stuttgart (LKA)

A1 Synodus (Konsistorium) Protokolle 1581, 1582, 1583I, 1583II, 1584I, 1584II, 1585I, 1585II, 1586I, 1586II, 1587I, 1587II, 1588I, 1588II, 1589, 1590, 1621, 1641, 1653

A3, 7 (1651–58) Konsistorial-Protokolle

A12, no. 41, 1559 Kompetenzen "Ob der Steig"

A12, no. 41, 1580 Kompetenzen "Ob der Steig"

A13 Zeugnisbücher, no. 1 (1614–79)

A26, 341 Kirchenzucht I

Stadtarchiv Tübingen, S201 Tübingen Gerichtsprotokolle, 1629–35

Wirsing, Thomas. Tagebuch des Pfarrers Thomas Wirsing (1528–1601).

Band A (1573). Fürstlich Fürstenbergische Hofbibliothek, Donaueschingen. Ms. nos. 676a, 676b.

Printed Sources

Andreae (Andreä), Johann Valentin. *Alte Reime von der praktische Theologie.* Ed. Professor Baum. Strasbourg: G. Fischbach, 1873. Originally published as *Das Gute Leben eines rechtschaffenen Dieners Gottes* (1619).

Die Bekenntnisschriften der evangelisch-lutherischen Kirche. 7th ed. Göttingen: Vandenhoeck and Reprecht, 1976.

Binder, Christian, ed. *Wirtembergs Kirchen- und Lehrämter oder Vollständige Geschichte von Besetzung des Herzoglich-Wirtembergischen Konsistoriums und Kirchenrats.* . . . 2 vols. Tübingen, 1798.

Brenz, Johann. *Anecdota Brentiana: Ungedruckte Briefe und Bedenken.* Ed. Theodor Pressel. Tübingen: J. J. Heckelhauer, 1868.

Crusius, Martin. *Diarium Martinin Crusii.* Ed. Wilhelm Göz and Ernst Conrad. Vol. 1. Tübingen: Laupp'sche Buchhandlung, 1927.

———. *Schwäbische Chronik.* Trans. J. J. Moser. 2 vols. Frankfurt, 1733.

Cynosura Oeconomicae Ecclesiasticae. Ed. Johann Valentin Andreae. Stuttgart, 1658.

Hermelink, Heinrich, ed. *Die Matrikeln der Universität Tübingen.* Im Auftrag der Württembergischen Kommission für Landesgeschichte. Vol. 1 in two pts. Stuttgart: Kohlhammer, 1906, 1931. Vol. 2 in two pts., ed. Albert Bürk and Wilhelm Wille. Tübingen: Universitäts-Bibliothek, 1953, 1954.

Luther, Martin. *D. Martin Luthers Werke: Kritische Gesamtausgabe* (WA). Weimar: Hermann Böhlaus, 1914–67.

Rauscher, Julius, ed. *Württembergische Visitationsakten*, vol. 1: *(1534) 1536–1540.* Württembergische Geschichtsquellen, vol. 22, ed. Württembergische Kommission für Landesgeschichte. Stuttgart: Kohlhammer, 1932.

Reyscher, A. L., ed. *Vollständige, historisch und kritisch bearbeitete Sammlung der württembergischen Gesetze.* 19 vols. Stuttgart, 1828–51.

Roth, Rudolph von, ed. *Urkunden zur Geschichte der Universität Tübingen aus den Jahren 1476 bis 1550.* Rpt. ed. Aalen: Scientia Verlag, 1973. Originally published Tübingen, 1877.

Sehling, Emil, ed. *Die evangelischen Kirchenordnungen des 16. Jahrhunderts*, vol. 1: *Sachsen und Thüringen.* Leipzig: Institut für evangelisches Kirchenrecht, 1902–4.

Sigel, Christian, comp. and ed. "Das evangelische Württemberg. II. Hauptteil. Generalmagisterbuch. Mitteilungen aus dem Leben der evangelichen Geistlichen von der Reformation an bis auf die Gegenwart." Typescript, LKA Stuttgart, vols. 1–14, 1910–32.

Stoll, Johann Nicolas, ed. *Sammlung aller Magister-Promotionen, welche zu Tübingen von Anno 1477–1755 geschehen. . . .* Rpt. ed. Amsterdam: B. R. Grüner, 1972. Originally published Stuttgart, 1756.

Württembergische Grosse Kirchenordnung 1559. Facsimile of 1st ed., Stuttgart: In Kommission bei der Schriftenniederlage des evangelischen Jugendwerke, 1968. Originally published Stuttgart, 1559.

Secondary Sources

Abel, Wilhelm. *Agrarkrisen und Agrarkonjunktur: Eine Geschichte der Land- und Ernährungswirtschaft Mitteleuropas.* Hamburg: Paul Pary, 1978.

Althaus, Paul. *The Theology of Martin Luther.* Trans. Robert C. Schultz. Philaldelphia: Fortress Press, 1966.

Die Archivpflege, in der Kreisen und Gemeinden: Lehrgangbericht für die Archivpfleger in Württemberg und in Hohenzollern. Ed. Württembergische Archivdirektion. Veröffentlichungen der Württembergischen Archivverwaltung, vol. 5. Stuttgart: Württembergische Archivdirektion, 1955.

Ariès, Philippe. *Centuries of Childhood: A Social History of Family Life.* Trans. Robert Baldick. New York: Vintage Books, 1962.

Bader, Karl Siegfried. *Das Dorf,* vol. 2: *Dorfgenossenschaft und Dorfgemeinde.* Studien zur Rechtsgeschichte des mittelalterlichen Dorfes, pt. 2. Weimar: Hermann Böhlaus Nachfolger, 1962.

Bernhardt, Walter. *Die Zentralbehörden des Herzogtums Württemberg und ihre Beamten, 1520–1629.* Veröffentlichungen der Kommission für geschichtliche Landeskunde in Baden-Württemberg, Reihe B, Forschungen, vol. 70. Stuttgart: Kohlhammer, 1972.

Bever, Edward Watts Morton. "Witchcraft in Early Modern Württemberg." Ph.D. diss., Princeton University, 1983.

Boles, Susan C. "The Economic Position of the Lutheran Pastors in Ernestine Thuringia, 1521–1555." *ARG,* 63 (1972): 94–125.

Bossy, John. "Blood and Baptism: Kinship, Community and Christianity in Western Europe from the Fourteenth to the Seventeenth Centuries," in Derek Baker, ed., *Sanctity and Secularity: The Church and the World,* pp. 129–44. Studies in Church History, vol. 10. Oxford: Basil Blackwell, 1973.

———. *Christianity in the West, 1400–1700.* Oxford: Oxford University Press, 1985.

———. "The Counter-Reformation and the People of Catholic Europe," *Past and Present,* 47 (1970): 51–70.

———. "Essai de Sociographie de la Messe, 1200–1700." *Annales: Economies, Sociétés, Civilisations,* 36 (1981): 44–70.

Brady, Thomas. "Social History," in Steven Ozment, ed., *Reformation Europe: A Guide to Research*, pp. 161–82. St. Louis, Mo.: Center for Reformation Research, 1982.

———. *Turning Swiss: Cities and Empire, 1450–1550*. Cambridge: Cambridge University Press, 1985.

Brecht, Martin. "Die Entwicklung der alten Bibliothek des Tübinger Stifts in ihrem theologie- und geistesgeschichtlichen Zusammenhang: Eine Untersuchung zur württ. Theologie." *BWKG*, 63 (1963): 3–103.

———. "Herkunft und Ausbildung der protestantischen Geistlichen des Herzogtums Württemberg im 16. Jahrhundert." *Zeitschrift für Kirchengeschichte*, 80 (1969): 163–75.

———. *Kirchenordnung und Kirchenzucht in Württemberg vom 16. bis zum 18. Jahrhundert*. Quellen und Forschungen zur Württembergischen Kirchengeschichte, vol. 1. Stuttgart: Calwer Verlag, 1967.

———. "Les visites pastorales en Württemberg," in Société Savante d'Alsace, *Sensibilité religieuse*, pp. 19–26.

Brown, Peter. *The World of Late Antiquity: From Marcus Aurelius to Mohammed*. London: Thames and Hudson, 1971.

Burke, Peter. "From Pioneers to Settlers: Recent Studies of the History of Popular Culture. A Review Article." *Comparative Studies in Society and History*, 25 (1983): 181–87.

———. *Popular Culture in Early Modern Europe*. London: Temple Smith, 1978.

Chaunu, Pierre. "Sur la fin des sorciers au XVIIe siècle." *Annales: Economies, Sociétés, Civilisations*, 24 (1969): 895–911.

Clark, Peter. "The Alehouse and the Alternative Society," in Donald Pennington and Keith Thomas, eds., *Puritans and Revolutionaries*, pp. 47–71. Oxford: Clarendon Press, 1978.

Clasen, Claus-Peter. *Die Wiedertäufer im Herzogtum Württemberg und in benachbarten Herrschaften: Ausbreitung, Geisteswelt und Soziologie*. Veröffentlichungen der Kommission für geschichtliche Landeskunde in Baden-Württemberg, Reihe B, Forschungen, vol. 32. Stuttgart: Kohlhammer, 1965.

Davis, Natalie Z. "From 'Popular Religion' to Religious Cultures," in Steven Ozment, ed., *Reformation Europe: A Guide to Research*, pp. 321–41. St. Louis, Mo.: Center for Reformation Research, 1982.

———. *Society and Culture in Early Modern France: Eight Essays*. Stanford, Calif.: Stanford University Press, 1975.

———. "Some Tasks and Themes in the Study of Popular Religion," in Charles Trinkaus, ed., with Heiko Oberman, *The Pursuit of Holiness in Late Medieval and Renaissance Religion*, pp. 307–36. Studies in Medieval and Reformation Thought, vol. 10. Leiden: E. J. Brill, 1974.

Decker-Hauff, Hansmartin. "Die geistige Führungsschicht Württembergs," in Günther Franz, ed., *Beamtentum und Pfarrstand, 1400–1800: Büdinger Vorträge, 1967*, pp. 51–80. Deutsche Führungsschichten in der Neuzeit, vol. 5. Limburg: C. A. Starke, 1972.

Deetjen, Werner-Ulrich. *Studien zur Württembergischen Kirchenordnung Herzog Ulrichs, 1534–1550. Das Herzogtum Württemberg im Zeitalter Herzog Ulrichs (1498–1550): Die Neuordnung des Kirchenguts und der Klöster (1534–1547).* Quellen und Forschungen zur Württembergischen Kirchengeschichte, vol. 7. Stuttgart: Calwer Verlag, 1981.

Delumeau, Jean. *Catholicism Between Luther and Voltaire: A New View of the Counter-Reformation.* Trans. Jeremy Moiser. London: Burns and Oates, 1977.

Demandt, Dieter, and Hans-Christoph Rublack, eds., *Stadt und Kirche in Kitzingen: Darstellungen und Quellen zu Spätmittelalter und Reformation.* Spätmittelalter und Frühe Neuzeit, vol. 10. Stuttgart: Klett-Cotta, 1978.

Demos, John Putnam. *Entertaining Satan: Witchcraft and the Culture of Early New England.* Oxford: Oxford University Press, 1982.

Dirlmeier, Ulf. *Untersuchungen zu Einkommensverhältnissen und Lebenshaltungskosten in oberdeutschen Städten des Spätmittelalters.* Abhandlungen der Heidelberger Akademie der Wissenschaften, vol. 1. Heidelberg: Carl Winter Universitätsverlag, 1978.

Drews, Paul. *Der evangelische Geistliche in der deutschen Vergangenheit.* Monographien zur deutschen Kulturgeschichte, vol. 12, ed. Georg Steinhausen. Jena: Eugen Diederichs, 1905.

Duncker, Christoph. *Verzeichnis der Württembergischen Kirchenbücher,* 2d ed. Stuttgart, 1938.

Ehmer, Hermann. "Bildungsideale des 16. Jahrhunderts und die Bildungspolitik von Herzog Christoph in Württemberg." *BWKG,* 77 (1977): 5–24.

———. *Valentin Vannius und die Reformation in Württemberg.* Veröffentlichungen der Kommission für geschichtliche Landeskunde in Baden-Württemberg, Reihe B, Forschungen, vol. 81 Stuttgart: Kohlhammer, 1976.

Elert, Werner. *Morphologie des Luthertums.* 2 vols. Rev. 1st ed. Munich: C. H. Beck'sche Verlagsbuchhandlung, 1952–53.

Elias, Norbert. *Über den Prozess der Zivilization: Sociogenetische und psychogenetische Untersuchungen.* 2 vols. Suhrkamp-Taschenbuch Wissenschaft, vols. 157–58. Frankfurt am Main: Suhrkamp, 1981. Originally published 1969.

Elze, Theodor. *Die Universität Tübingen und die Studenten aus Krain.* Rpt. Geschichte, Kultur, und Geisteswelt der Slowenen, vol. 14. Munich: Rudolf Trofenik, 1977. Originally published Tübingen, 1877.

Estes, James Martin. *Christian Magistrate and State Church: The Reform-*

ing Career of Johannes Brenz, Toronto: University of Toronto Press, 1982.

Evans, R. J. W. "Culture and Anarchy in the Empire, 1540–1680." *Central European History,* vol. 18, no. 1 (1985): 14–30.

Flandrin, Jean-Louis, "A Case of Naïveté in the Use of Statistics" *Journal of Interdisciplinary History,* vol. 9, no. 2 (1978): 309–15.

——. *Families in Former Times: Kinship, Household and Sexuality.* Trans. Richard Southern. Cambridge: Cambridge University Press, 1979.

——. "Repression and Change." *Journal of Family History,* 2 (1977): 196–210.

Franz, Günther. *Geschichte des deutschen Bauernstandes.* 2d ed. Deutsche Agrargeschichte, vol. 4. Stuttgart: Eugen Ulmer, 1976.

Frijoff, Willem, and Dominique Julia. *Ecole et société dans la France d'ancien régime. Quatre exemples: Auch, Avallon, Condom et Gisors.* Paris: Armand Colin, 1975.

Fritz, Fritz. "Der württembergische Pfarrer im Zeitalter des dreissigjährigen Krieges." *BWKG* n.s., 33 (1929): 191–296.

Fulbrook, Mary. *Piety and Politics: Religion and the Rise of Absolutism in England, Württemberg and Prussia.* Cambridge: Cambridge University Press, 1983.

Furet, François, and Jacques Ozouf. *Reading and Writing: Literacy in France from Calvin to Jules Ferry.* Cambridge Studies in Oral and Literate Culture, vol. 5. Cambridge: Cambridge University Press, 1982.

Goubert, Jean-Pierre. "The Art of Healing: Learned Medicine and Popular Medicine in the France of 1790," in Robert Forster and Orest Ranum, eds., *Medicine and Society in France: Selections from the Annales: Economies, Sociétés, Civilisations,* trans. Elborg Forster and Patricia M. Ranum. Baltimore: Johns Hopkins University Press, 1980.

Goubert, Pierre. *Cent mille provinciaux au XVIIe siècle: Beauvais et le Beauvaisis de 1600 à 1730.* Paris: Flammarion, 1968.

——. *The French Peasantry in the Seventeenth Century.* Trans. Ian Patterson. Cambridge: Cambridge University Press, 1986.

Grafton, Anthony. "The World of the Polyhistors: Humanism and Encyclopedism." *Central European History,* 18, no. 1 (1985): 31–47.

Greyerz, Kasper von. "Stadt und Reformation: Stand und Aufgaben der Forschung." *ARG,* 76 (1985): 6–63.

Grundherren, Gerichte, und Pfarreien im Tübinger Raum zu Beginn der Neuzeit. Ed. Kommission für geschichtliche Landeskunde in Baden-Württemberg. Arbeiten zum historischen Atlas von Südwestdeutschland, vol. 1. Stuttgart: Kohlhammer, 1954.

Hahn, Friedrich. *Die evangelische Unterweisung in den Schulen des 16. Jahrhunderts.* Pädagogische Forschungen, Veröffentlichungen des Comenius-Instituts. Heidelberg: Quelle and Meyr, 1957.

Hasselhorn, Martin. *Der altwürttembergische Pfarrstand im 18. Jahrhundert*. Veröffentlichungen der Kommission für geschichtliche Landeskunde in Baden-Württemberg, Reihe B, Forschungen, vol. 6. Stuttgart: Kohlhammer, 1958.

Heckel, Martin. *Deutschland im konfessionellen Zeitalter*. Deutsche Geschichte, vol. 5. Göttingen: Vandenhoeck and Ruprecht, 1983.

Hermelink, Heinrich. *Geschichte der evangelische Kirche in Württemberg, von der Reformation bis zur Gegenwart: Das Reich Gottes in Wirtemberg* [*sic*]. Stuttgart: Rainer Wunderlich Verlag, 1949.

Herrup, Cynthia P. *The Common Peace: Participation and the Criminal Law in Seventeenth-Century England*. Cambridge Studies in Early Modern British History. Cambridge: Cambridge University Press, 1987.

———. "Law and Morality in Seventeenth-Century England." *Past and Present*, no. 106 (1985): 102–23.

Hoffman, Philip. *Church and Community in the Diocese of Lyon, 1500–1789*. New Haven, Conn.: Yale University Press, 1984.

Holl, Karl. "Luther und das landesherrliche Kirchenregiment," in his *Gesammelte Aufsätze*, vol. 1, pp. 326–80. 7th ed. Tübingen: J. C. B. Mohr (Paul Siebeck), 1948.

Hsia, R. Po-Chia. *Society and Religion in Münster, 1535–1618*. New Haven, Conn.: Yale University Press, 1984.

Ingram, Martin. "Religion, Communities and Moral Discipline in Late-Sixteenth- and Early-Seventeenth-Century England: Case Studies," in Kasper von Greyerz, ed., *Religion and Society in Early Modern Europe, 1500–1800*, pp. 177–93. London: Allen and Unwin, 1984.

———. "Ridings, Rough Music, and the 'Reform of Popular Culture' in Early Modern England." *Past and Present*, no. 105 (1984): 79–113.

Irwin, Joyce. "Society and the Sexes," in Steven Ozment, ed., *Reformation Europe: A Guide to Research*, pp. 343–59. St. Louis, Mo.: Center for Reformation Research, 1982.

Jens, Walter. *Eine Deutsche Universität: 500 Jahre Tübinger Gelehrtenrepublik*. 2d ed. Munich: Kindler, 1977.

Karant-Nunn, Susan C. *Luther's Pastors: The Reformation in the Ernestine Countryside*. Transactions of the American Philosophical Society, vol. 69, pt. 8, 1979. Philadelphia, 1980.

Keck. Rudolph. *Geschichte der Mittleren Schule in Württemberg*. Veröffentlichungen der Kommission für geschichtliche Landeskunde in Baden-Württemberg, Reihe B, Forschungen, vol. 47. Stuttgart: Kohlhammer, 1968.

Kingdon, Robert. "The Control of Morals by the Earliest Calvinists," in Peter DeKlerk, ed., "Renaissance, Reformation, Resurgence: Papers and Responses Presented at the Colloquium on Calvin and Calvin Studies

Held at Calvin Theological Seminary, Grand Rapids, Michigan, April 22 and 23, 1976," pp. 95–106. Photocopied typescript.

Kittelson, James M. "The Confessional Age: The Late Reformation in Germany," in Steven Ozment, ed., *Reformation Europe: A Guide to Research*, pp. 361–81. St. Louis, Mo.: Center for Reformation Research, 1982.

———. "Successes and Failures in the German Reformation: The Report from Strasbourg." *ARG*, 73 (1982): 153–74.

Klaits, Joseph. *Servants of Satan: The Age of the Witch Hunts*. Bloomington: Indiana University Press, 1985.

Klaus, Bernhard. "Soziale Herkunft und theologische Bildung lutherischer Pfarrer der reformatorischen Frühzeit." *Zeitschrift für Kirchengeschichte*, 80 (1969): 22–49.

Köhler, Walther. *Zürcher Ehegericht und Genfer Consistorium*. 2 vols. Quellen und Abhandlungen zur Schweizerischen Reformationsgeschichte (2. Serie der Quellen zur Schweizerischen Reformationsgeschichte), vols. 9–10. Ed. Zurich Zwingli Verein. Leipzig: M. Heinsius, 1932, 1942.

Kolb, Christoph. *Die Bibel in der evangelischen Kirche Altwürttembergs*. Stuttgart: C. Belser, 1917.

———. "Luthertum und Calvinismus in Württemberg." *BWKG*, n.s. 32 (1928): 132–204.

———. "Zur Geschichte des Pfarrstandes in Altwürttemberg." *BWKG*, 57 (1957): 69–190.

Das Königreich Württemberg: Eine Beschreibung nach Kreisen, Oberämten und Gemeinden. Ed. Das Königliche Statistisch-Topographische Bureau. 4 vols. Stuttgart: Kohlhammer, 1904–7.

Kriedte, Peter. *Peasants, Landlords and Merchant Capitalists: Europe and the World Economy, 1500–1800*. Trans. V. R. Berghahn. Cambridge: Cambridge University Press, 1983.

Larner, Christina. *Enemies of God: The Witch-hunt in Scotland*. Baltimore: Johns Hopkins University Press, 1981.

———. "Was Witch-hunting Woman-hunting?" in her *Witchcraft and Religion: The Politics of Popular Belief*. Oxford: Basil Blackwell, 1984.

Laslett, Peter. *Family Life and Illicit Love in Earlier Generations: Essays in Historical Sociology*. Cambridge: Cambridge University Press, 1977.

———. *The World We Have Lost: England Before the Industrial Revolution*. 2d ed. New York: Scribner, 1971.

Lau, Franz, and Ernst Bizer. *Reformationsgeschichte im Deutschland*. 2d ed. Die Kirche in Ihrer Geschichte, vol. K. Göttingen: Vandenhoeck and Ruprecht, 1969.

Lemp, Wilhelm. *Der Württembergische Synodus (1553–1924): Ein Beitrag zur Geschichte der Württembergischen evangelischen Landeskirche*. *BWKG*, Sonderheft 12. Stuttgart: Chr. Scheufele, 1959.

Léonard, Emile. *A History of Protestantism*, vol. 2: *The Establishment*. Ed. H. H. Rowley, trans. R. M. Bethell. London: Thomas Nelson and Sons, 1967.

Le Roy Ladurie, Emmanuel. *Montaillou: The Promised Land of Error*. Trans. Barbara Bray. New York: Vintage Books, 1979.

———. *Peasants of Languedoc*. Trans. John Day. Urbana: University of Illinois Press, 1976.

Leube, Martin. "Bursa und Stift in Tübingen." *BWKG*, n.s., 32 (1928): 1–10.

———. *Geschichte des Tübinger Stifts*, vol. 1. *BWKG*, Sonderheft 1. Stuttgart: Chr. Scheufele, 1921.

———. "Die Zweckbestimmung des Tübinger Stifts." *BWKG*, 49 (1949): 154–76.

Liebel, Helen P. "The Bourgeoisie in Southwestern Germany, 1500–1789: A Rising Class?" *International Review of Social History*, vol. 10, no. 2 (1965): 283–307.

MacDonald, Michael. "Secularization of Suicide in England, 1660–1800." *Past and Present*, no. 111 (1986): 50–97.

Mandrou, Robert. *Magistrats et sorciers en France au XVIIe siècle: Une analyse de psychologie historique*. Paris: Plon, 1968.

Medick, Hans. "Spinnstuben auf dem Dorf: Jugendliche Sexualkultur und Feierabendbrauch in der ländlichen Gesellschaft der frühen Neuzeit," in Gerhard Huck, ed., *Sozialgeschichte der Freizeit: Untersuchungen zum Wandel der Alltagskultur in Deutschland*, pp. 19–30. Wuppertal: Hammer, 1980.

Midelfort, H. C. Erik. *Witch Hunting in Southwestern Germany, 1562–1684: The Social and Intellectual Foundations*. Stanford, Calif.: Stanford University Press, 1972.

Mitterauer, Michael, and Reinhard Seider. *The European Family: Patriarchy to Partnership from the Middle Ages to the Present*. Trans. Karla Oosterveen and Manfred Hörzinger. Chicago: University of Chicago Press, 1983.

Molitor, Hansgeorg. "Frömmigkeit in Spätmittelalter und früher Neuzeit als historisch-methodisches Problem," Horst Rabe, Hansgeorg Molitor, and Hans-Christoph Rublack, eds., in *Festgabe für Ernst Walter Zeeden*, pp. 1–20. Reformationsgeschichtliche Studien und Texte. Supplementband 2. Münster: Aschendorf, 1976.

Monter, E. William. "The Consistory of Geneva, 1559–1569," in Peter DeKlerk, ed., "Renaissance, Reformation, Resurgence: Papers and Responses Presented at the Colloquium on Calvin and Calvin Studies Held at Calvin Theological Seminary, Grand Rapids, Michigan, April 22 and 23, 1976," pp. 63–84. Photocopied typescript. Grand Rapids, Mich.: Calvin Theological Seminary, 1976.

————. *Witchcraft in France and Switzerland*. Ithaca, N.Y.: Cornell University Press, 1976.

Müller, Karl. "Kirchliches Prüfungs- und Anstellungswesen in Württemberg im Zeitalter der Orthodoxie. Aus der Zeugnisbüchern des herzoglichen Konsistorium." *Württembergische Vierteljahresheft für Landesgeschichte* n.s., 25 (1916): 431–88.

Nau, Elizabeth. *Die Münzen und Medaillen der Oberschwäbischen Städte*. Freiburg: Kricheldorf Verlag, 1964.

Oberman, Heiko. "Martin Luther: Vorläufer der Reformation," in Eberhard Jüngel, Johannes Wallmann, and Wilfred Werbeck, eds. *Verifikationen: Festschrift für Gerhard Ebeling*, pp. 91–119. Tübingen: J. C. B. Mohr (Paul Siebeck), 1982.

Oestreich, Gerhard. *Verfassungsgeschichte vom Ende des Mittelalters bis zum Ende des alten Reiches*, in *Gebhardt: Handbuch der deutschen Geschichte*, 9th ed., ed. Herbert Grundmann. Taschenbuchausgabe, vol. 11, 3d ed. Stuttgart: Klett, 1970.

Ozment, Steven. *When Fathers Ruled: Family Life in Reformation Europe*. Studies in Cultural History. Cambridge, Mass.: Harvard University Press, 1983.

Peters, Edward M. "Religion and Culture: Popular and Unpopular, 1500–1800." *Journal of Modern History*, 59 (1987): 317–30.

Pfarrbuch. Württembergisch-Franken, pt. 2. *Die Kirchen und Schuldiener*. Ed. Otto Haug, with Max-Adolf Cramer and Marlene Holtzman. Stuttgart: Chr. Scheufele, 1981.

Quaife, G. R. *Wanton Wenches and Wayward Wives: Peasants and Illicit Sex in Early-Seventeenth-Century England*. New Brunswick, N.J.: Rutgers University Press, 1979.

Robisheaux, Thomas Willard. "The Origins of Rural Wealth and Poverty in Hohenlohe, 1470–1680." Ph.D. diss., University of Virginia, 1981.

Rublack, Hans-Christoph. *Eine bürgerliche Reformation: Nördlingen*. Quellen und Forschungen zur Reformationsgeschichte, vol. 51. Gütersloh: Gerd Mohn, 1983.

Ruggiero, Guido. *The Boundaries of Eros: Sex Crime and Sexuality in Renaissance Venice*. Studies in the History of Sexuality. Oxford: Oxford University Press, 1985.

————. *Violence in Early Renaissance Venice*. New Brunswick, N.J.: Rutgers University Press, 1980.

Sabean, David Warren. "Aspects of Kinship Behavior and Property in Rural Western Europe Before 1800," in Jack Goody, Joan Thirsk, and E. P. Thompson, eds., *Family and Inheritance: Rural Society in Western Europe, 1200–1800*, pp. 96–111. Cambridge: Cambridge University Press, 1976.

————. *Power in the Blood: Popular Culture and Village Discourse in Early Modern Germany*. Cambridge: Cambridge University Press, 1984.

————. *Property, Production, and Family in Neckarhausen, 1700–1870*. Cambridge: Cambridge University Press, 1990.

Safley, Thomas Max. *Let No Man Put Asunder: The Control of Marriage in the German Southwest: A Comparative Study, 1550–1600*. Kirksville, Mo.: Sixteenth Century Journal Publishers, 1984.

————. "Marital Litigation in the Diocese of Constance." *Sixteenth Century Journal*, 12 (1981): 61–78.

————. "To Preserve the Marital State: The Basler Ehegericht, 1550–1592." *Journal of Family History*, 7 (1982): 162–79.

Schlink, Edmund. *Theology of the Lutheran Confessions*. Trans. Paul F. Koehnecke and Herbert J. A. Boumann. Philadelphia: Fortress Press, 1961.

Schmid, Eugen. *Geschichte des Volkschulwesens in Altwürttemberg*. Veröffentlichungen der Württembergischen Kommission für Landesgeschichte. Stuttgart: Kohlhammer, 1927.

Schnabel-Schüle, Helga. "Die Ämter Tübingen und Stuttgart des Herzogtums Württemberg um die Wende des 16. Jhrts. im Spiegel der Visitationsberichte." Typescript, n.d.

Schröeder-Lembke, Gertrude. "Protestantische Pastoren als Landwirtschaftsreformer." *Zeitschrift für Agrargeschichte und Agrarsoziologie* 27 (1979): 94–104.

Scribner, Robert. *For the Sake of Simple Folk: Popular Propaganda for the German Reformation*. Cambridge Studies in Oral and Literate Culture, vol. 2. Cambridge: Cambridge University Press, 1981.

————. "Is There a Social History of the Reformation?" *Social History*, 4 (1977): 483–505.

Seigel, Rudolf. *Gericht und Rat in Tübingen von den Anfängen bis zur Einführung der Verfassung 1819/22*. Veröffentlichungen der Kommission für geschichtliche Landeskunde in Baden-Württemberg, Reihe B, Forschungen, vol. 13. Stuttgart: Kohlhammer, 1960.

Skinner, Quentin. *The Foundations of Modern Political Thought*, vol. 2: *The Age of Reformation*. Cambridge: Cambridge University Press, 1978.

Société Savante d'Alsace. *Sensibilité religieuse et discipline ecclésiastique: Les visites pastorales en territoires protestants (Pays rhénan, comté de Montbeliard, pays de Vaud) XVIe–XVIIIe siècles*. Publications de la Société savante d'Alsace et des Régions de l'Est. Collection "Recherches et Documents," vol. 21. Strasbourg: Istra, 1975.

Sohm, W. *Die Schule Joh. Sturms und die Kirche Strassburgs, 1530–1581*. Strasbourg, 1912.

Spaeth, Donald Arragon. "Parsons and Parishioners: Lay-Clerical Conflict and Popular Piety in Wiltshire Villages, 1660–1740." Ph.D. diss., Brown University, 1985.

Spitz, Lewis. *The Protestant Reformation, 1517–1559*. New York: Harper and Row, 1985.

Stahlecker, Reinhold. *Geschichte der Lateinschule in Altwürttemberg*, in Württembergische Kommission für Landesgeschichte, ed., *Geschichte des humanistischen Schulwesens in Württemberg*, vol. 3, pt. 1, pp. 1–290. Stuttgart: Kohlhammer, 1927.

Stone, Lawrence. "Social Mobility in England, 1500–1700." *Past and Present*, 33 (1966): 16–55.

Strauss, Gerald. *Luther's House of Learning: Indoctrination of the Young in the German Reformation*. Baltimore: Johns Hopkins University Press, 1978.

Theiss, Maria. "Pfarrer und Gemeinden in der zweiten Hälfte des 16. Jahrhunderts in den Stiften Magdeburg und Merseberg: Studien zur Sozial- und Bildungsgeschichte des Pfarrstandes nach der Reformation." Ph.D. diss., University of Freiburg, 1960.

Thomas, Keith. *Religion and the Decline of Magic*. Harmondsworth, Eng.: Penguin Books, 1973.

Tietz, Gunter. "Das Erscheinungsbild von Pfarrstand und Pfarrgemeinde des sächsischen Kurkreises im Spiegel der Visitationsberichte des 16. Jahrhunderts." Ph.D. diss., University of Tübingen, 1971.

Van Engen, John. "The Christian Middle Ages as an Historiographical Problem." *American Historical Review*, 91 (1986): 519–52.

Vann, James Allen. *The Making of a State: Württemberg, 1593–1793*. Ithaca, N.Y.: Cornell University Press, 1984.

Vogler, Bernard. *Le clergé protestant rhénan au siècle de la réforme, 1555–1619*. Association des publications près les universités de Strasbourg. Paris: Editions Ophrys, 1976.

———. "Vie religieuse en pays rhénan dans la seconde moitié du XVIe siècle, 1556–1619." 3 vols. Thèse, University of Paris, 1972. Lille: Service de reproduction des thèses, Université de Lille III, 1974.

Vovelle, Michel. *Piété baroque et déchristianisation en Provence au XVIIIe siècle: Les attitudes devant la mort d'après les clauses des testaments*. Civilisations et mentalités. Paris: Plon, 1973.

Weisner, Merry. "Frail, Weak and Helpless: Women's Legal Position in Theory and Practice," in Jerome Friedman, ed., *Regnum, Religio et Ratio: Essays Presented to Robert M. Kingdon*, pp. 161–69. Sixteenth Century Essays and Studies, vol. 8. Kirksville, Mo.: Sixteenth Century Journal Publishers, 1987.

Wrightson, Keith, and David Levine. *Poverty and Piety in an English Village: Terling, 1525–1700*. Studies in Social Discontinuity. New York: Academic Press, 1979.

Zeeden, Ernst Walter. "Grundlagen und Wege der Konfessionsbildung in Deutschland im Zeitalter der Glaubenskämpfe," in his *Konfessionsbil-*

dung: Studien zur Reformation, Gegenreformation und katholischen Reform, pp. 67–112. Tübinger Beiträge zur Geschichtsforschung Spätmittelalter und Frühe Neuzeit, vol. 15. Stuttgart: Klett-Cotta, 1985.

Zeeden, Ernst Walter, and Hansgeorg Molitor. *Die Visitation im Dienste der kirchlichen Reform.* Katholisches Leben und Kirchenreform im Zeitalter der Glaubensspaltung, Heft 25/26. 2d ed. Münster: Aschendorf, 1977.

Zeeden, Ernst Walter, ed., with Peter T. Lang, Christa Reinhardt, Helga Schnabel-Schüle. *Repertorium der Kirchenvisitation aus dem 16. und 17. Jahrhundert in Archiven der Bundesrepublik Deutschland*, vol. 1: *Hesse.* Tübinger Beiträge zur Geschichtsforschung Spätmittelalter und Frühe Neuzeit. Stuttgart: Klett-Cotta, 1982.

Zieger, Andreas. *Das religiöse und kirchliche Leben in Preussen und Kurland im Spiegel der evangelischen Kirchenordnungen des 16. Jahrhunderts.* Forschungen und Quellen zur Kirchen- und Kulturgeschichte Ostdeutschlands, vol. 5. Cologne: Böhlau, 1967.

Index

In this index an "f" after a number indicates a separate reference on the next page, and an "ff" indicates separate references on the next two pages. A continuous discussion over two or more pages is indicated by a span of page numbers, e.g., "57–59." *Passim* is used for a cluster of references in close but not consecutive sequence.

Library of Congress Cataloging-in-Publication Data

Tolley, Bruce.
    Pastors and parishioners in Württemberg during the late
Reformation, 1581–1621 / Bruce Tolley.
        p.   cm.
    Includes bibliographical references and index.
    ISBN 0-8047-1681-1
    1. Reformation—Germany—Württemberg. 2. Württemberg (Germany)—
Church history—16th century. 3. Germany—Church history—16th
century. 4. Clergy—Germany—Württemberg—History—16th century.
5. Clergy—Germany—History—16th century. I. Title.
BR358.W8T65   1995
284.1′4347′09031—dc20   93-40636
                                                            CIP

⊗ This book is printed on acid-free paper.